The Role of Imagination in Culture and Society:
Owen Barfield's Early Work

The Role of Imagination in Culture and Society: Owen Barfield's Early Work

Astrid Diener

LEIPZIG EXPLORATIONS IN LITERATURE AND CULTURE 6

WIPF & STOCK · Eugene, Oregon

Wipf and Stock Publishers
199 W 8th Ave, Suite 3
Eugene, OR 97401

The Role of Imagination in Culture and Society: Owen Barfield's Early Work
By Diener, Astrid and Hipolito, Jane
Copyright©2002 by Diener, Astrid
ISBN 13: 978-1-62564-130-4
Publication date 6/15/2013
Previously published by Galda + Wilch Verlag, 2002

Foreword to the 2013 Edition

IN WHAT WAY IS *the imagination true?* As Astrid Diener lucidly and engagingly demonstrates, this question was crucial for Owen Barfield – and in Barfield's view, it is crucial for the world as well.

Throughout his entire adult life, Barfield experienced imagination as a powerful agent of change in his own consciousness. In his Introduction to *Romanticism Comes of Age* (1944), he recalled the moment, some 25 years earlier, when imagination's transformative effects became apparent to him: "The first serious thing that happened to my mind was (at about the age of twenty-one) a sudden and rapid increase in the intensity with which I experienced lyric poetry. This was a fact. It was not something I could convict myself of believing because I wanted to believe it....Thus, without any particular exertion or theorising on my part I had two things strongly impressed on me, firstly that the poetic or imaginative use of words enhances their meanings and secondly that those enhanced meanings may reveal hitherto unapprehended parts of reality."

With characteristic resolve, energy, and resourcefulness, Barfield immediately set out to clarify, deepen, extend, and solidify his understanding of what the imagination truly involves. One aspect of his exploration was scholarly. As an undergraduate student at Oxford University, he chose to major in what was then the very new subject area of English Language and Literature, and followed this by earning a B.Litt. degree for developing a theory of poetry as a form of knowledge. During these same years, he published numerous essays and reviews about language, literature, and the imagination, as well as two substantial books, *History in English Words* (1926) and *Poetic Diction: A Study in Meaning* (1928).

Barfield was not only a scholar of the imagination, however; he was also an impressively eloquent and versatile creative writer. His first published work was a poem, "Air-Castles" (1917), and he wrote poems all his life. Several of them are included in *A Barfield Sampler* (1993), the anthology of his poetry and fiction which is, like *The Role of Imagination in Culture and Society*, an essential resource for students of Barfield's life and work. In the 1920s, Barfield was widely known and respected as a poet; one measure of this is that two of the many poems he published then were selected for re-publication in "best of" volumes. He also published several short stories and a book-length fairytale for children of all ages, *The Silver Trumpet* (1925). The most ambitious project that Barfield undertook in the '20s was his novel *English People*, in which he imaginatively portrays and critiques modern English culture and society; regrettably, only a portion of the novel has been published to date, its brilliant epilogue, *The Rose on the Ash-Heap* (2009).

Barfield, who knew that "Imagination is really thinking with a bit of will in it," emphatically "not the fenced preserve of poetry, or even of the fine arts in general" (*History, Guilt and Habit*, 1979), recognized in the 1920s that the imagination is essential for creating healthy human communities and for developing balanced, responsible ecological awareness. In addition to exploring cultural and societal questions in his imaginative writings, he wrote a great many nonfiction essays about these matters, and participated actively in progressive social and arts movements; and in the early 1930s he studied economics at the University of London while at the same time earning his law degree.

Beginning in 1923, he also took up serious study of anthroposophy, the "science of the spirit" inaugurated by the Austrian philosopher and reformer Rudolf Steiner. "Steiner's method of knowledge is, in its essence, *systematic imagination*," Barfield appreciatively noted in his 1930 essay "An Introduction to Anthroposophy." Steiner's

Christ-centric worldview affirmed, focused, and enlarged Barfield's dawning awareness of the significance of the Logos throughout world history and in the ongoing evolution of human consciousness. Steiner's insights into human psychology helped Barfield to understand how and why it is that the imagination makes possible "the most important thing in a meeting of two human beings – that it should be not merely a relation between two phenomena, but a relation between two spirits" (Barfield, "Matter, Imagination, and Spirit," 1974). And anthroposophically-informed initiatives in education, medicine, agriculture, economics, the arts, and other fields tremendously impressed Barfield, who thought them encouraging evidence that the danger, ugliness and waste he found endemic in modern life could be remedied by Steiner's method of systematic imagination – truly "Romanticism come of age."

Cultural and societal issues continued to engage Barfield all through his life. He addressed them both in nonfiction writings and in imaginative works such as his dystopian novella *Night Operation* (1983-84) and *Eager Spring* (published posthumously in 2008), the ecological novel which was his last full-length book. Astrid Diener is the first to have recognized this core aspect of Barfield's life and work. Clear-sighted and solidly researched, *The Role of Imagination in Culture and Society* is a genuinely foundational contribution to Barfield studies.

Jane Hipolito
Placentia, California
May 2013

Contents

List of Plates IX

Acknowledgements XI

Foreword – A.D. Nuttall 13

Introduction 15

I. The Intellectual Context: Owen Barfield, C. S. Lewis and
   Contemporary Philosophy 25

   1. Contemporary Philosophy 26

   2. Barfield's and Lewis's Response 30

   3. The Argument of *Poetic Diction* 36

   4. Conclusions 52

II. The Anthroposophical Background 61

   1. Steiner and Anthroposophy 62

   2. A Critical Evaluation of Steiner's Work 77

   3. A Historical Evaluation of Steiner's Work 79

   4. Conclusions: Barfield and Anthroposophy 90

III. Barfield as Cultural and Social Critic 101

   1. Dualism and the Intellectual Roots of the Crisis: 106

   2. Dualism, Individual and Culture 114

   3. Dualism and Politics 129

    4. Conclusions 134

IV. Barfield as Reformer 135

    1. Barfield, Arnold and Eliot 136

    2. The Turning Point: Towards Reform 152

    3. The Function of Industry 161

    4. Social and Economic Reform 164

    5. Conclusions 170

General Conclusions 173

Afterword: Owen Barfield Today – Elmar Schenkel 175

Appendix: An Interview with Owen Barfield 181

    1. Introduction 181

    2. The Interview 182

Notes 197

Bibliography 207

List of Plates

Plate 1:
C.S. Lewis, Letters to Owen Barfield, "The Great War", fol. 76........56

Plate 2:
C.S. Lewis, Letters to Owen Barfield, "The Great War", fol. 77........57

Plate 3:
C.S. Lewis, Letters to Owen Barfield, "The Great War", fol. 78........58

Three drawings by C.S. Lewis, from Letters to Owen Barfield, "The Great War", c. 1927-1930s, with two letters from Barfield to Lewis, 1927, n.d., 156 leaves (The Marion E. Wade Center, Wheaton College, Illinois, U.S.A.; also available as photocopies at the Bodleian Library, Oxford, Ms. Facs. c. 54). Extracts reprinted by permission of C.S. Lewis Pte. Ltd. UK and The Marion E. Wade Center, Wheaton College, Illinois, U.S.A., © C.S. Lewis Pte. Ltd. UK.

Acknowledgements

I am most deeply indebted to my former supervisor at Oxford, Professor Tony Nuttall (New College), who throughout my research on this book offered his time and help so generously. I profited enormously from the expertise which he readily brought to bear on all aspects of my work. Whatever the matter, he always responded swiftly, patiently and effectively. I couldn't have hoped for a more reliable and conscientious supervisor.

Warm thanks are also due to Professor Dr. Elmar Schenkel (now Leipzig, formerly Freiburg University). He introduced me to Barfield while I was an undergraduate in English and History at Freiburg and thereby inspired a lasting interest in this and related authors. I have profited from many conversations with him and from his readiness to share his ideas. He has encouraged me in all my academic efforts and has offered his help generously whenever needed.

I am grateful to the late Owen Barfield who took a kind interest in my work. He read and commented on parts of the text and responded swiftly to my queries. I profited, above all, from the interview he gave me. The insights I gained from this conversation are the basis on which my book builds. Moreover, I owe a debt to Dr. Andrew Welburn (New College, Oxford) for advising me on anthroposophy and romanticism, to Stephen Medcalf (Sussex University) for reading parts of the text and for advising me on C.S. Lewis, the philosophical context and the interview, and to all those who in conversations have helped me to clarify my ideas.

I am grateful to C.S. Lewis Pte. Ltd. UK and The Marion E. Wade Center, Wheaton College, Illinois, U.S.A. for the permission to reproduce three drawings and extracts from letters by C.S. Lewis. I would like to thank Elizabeth Stevens of Curtis Brown for handling the difficult and protracted matter of obtaining the permission, and Professor Christopher Mitchell and Alicia Van Dyke of the Marion E. Wade Center for photocopying the drawings and for sending them over quickly so that I was able to include them in my book.

For their financial support, I would like to express my gratitude to the following institutions: Deutscher Akademischer Austauschdienst

(Bonn), The Michael Wills Trust (Oxford) and Exeter College (Oxford). Moreover, I owe special thanks to the tutors and staff of Exeter College, particularly to Dr Helen Spencer and Anne Macdonald, for handling my affairs so kindly and effectively.

A big thank you to all my friends who actively helped to bring this book to its conclusion. Warm thanks are especially to Katty Bjurstedt, whose encouragement, advice, conversations, humour and friendship helped me through the last phase of my work, and to my proof-readers, Claire Fitzpatrick, Phil Lucas, Angus Stevenson, Anthony Binnington, and Terry and Antonia Davies.

Last but not least, I would like to thank my family to whom I owe my greatest debt. I owe very many thanks to Dieter Rodrian and Anne Janousch who have supported me intellectually and financially. I'd like to thank them for their interest, their care and simply for being such good friends. My warmest thanks are to my parents Ernst and Sieglinde Diener and my brother Frank. It is to them that I dedicate my book. They have participated in my activities with more interest, love and patience than anyone else I know. I would like to thank them for uncountable enlightening conversations, for their clear-headed advice and their practical help (financial and otherwise). Without their help I would never have been able to bring this enterprise to its conclusion.

Foreword –
A.D. Nuttall

This remarkable book began as a D.Phil. thesis for Barfield's university – the University of Oxford. I was in on it from the beginning, because I had the (wholly delightful) job of acting as the formal supervisor of Astrid Diener's work. I vividly remember her first coming to explain her plans to me. She had chosen, she explained, to work on Owen Barfield, a philosopher, historian of thought and theoretician of literature whose life very nearly filled the twentieth century. I was at once attracted by the proposal because I felt before we began, that the sheer quality and complexity of Barfield's ideas had not received the attention it deserves. My only worry was: could this young German woman, whose native language and culture is not English, really take on an author who is alertly responsive to innumerable movements and counter-movements in his own intellectual context? How, for example, could she possibly deal with what C.S. Lewis called 'the Great War with Barfield' – a huge, protracted argument fought out, mostly in letters, from the mid-1920s to the early 1930s , between two almost pathologically well-read Englishmen? I could see at once that Ms Diener (as she then was) was unusually well-equipped to deal with German influences on Barfield, such as Rudolf Steiner, but I still kept asking myself, 'How can she possibly be expected to know when Barfield is tacitly responding, say, to Bertrand Russell, or Matthew Arnold, or H.G. Wells, or Coleridge? As it turned out I had no need to worry. Ms Diener moved through the minefield of English/British thought over the last three hundred years or so in an extraordinarily sure-footed manner. She knew from the beginning that Barfield's thought was important, and in this she was, simply, right. She was never the uncritical panegyrist of her author but was always open to counter-argument and indeed initiated certain counter-arguments of her own. She has understood better than anyone else the way in which Barfield, stimulated by the 'objectivist' criticisms of C.S. Lewis, developed, from a basis in Romanticism to a position which in certain respects transcends earlier Romantic thought. She brings out admirably a side of Barfield virtually forgotten now in England, his interest in social questions. Throughout, however, opposition to various forms of dualism and the quest for certain underlying organizing unities remains fundamental in his writings.

Astrid Diener has shown that indeed Owen Barfield has been undervalued. If we measure his mind against that of the generally revered T.S. Eliot, Barfield, carefully read, holds his own. Where Eliot can be seduced by what were in his day highly fashionable anti-Romantic austerities (poetry as the extinction of personality and so forth) Barfield's inner intellectual drive kept him on course; his work has a progressive, evolving coherence (which may have something to do with the fact that he was for years a professional lawyer) and became more powerful as it became more learned. Astrid Diener understands that neither Barfield nor Lewis would have thought very much of a book which inertly summarised – or vacuously canonised – its subject. She has instead brought intelligence to bear on intelligence; when she detects error or falsity, she is critical; when, as often, she finds strength of reasoning, she makes that strength clear to her reader. Her book has what I can only call a special quality of tender fair-mindedness. Barfield, who died just as this book was nearing completion, would have loved it.

A.D. Nuttall, New College, Oxford.

Introduction

In 1921 Owen Barfield began his research for the higher degree of B.Litt. at Oxford. The results were published seven years later as *Poetic Diction: A Study in Meaning*. This book contains in nucleus what became the central concern of his subsequent work: the evolution of human consciousness and the philosophy of unity and participation. The title *Poetic Diction*, then, is a little misleading. It suggests that the book is a guide for aspiring poets, while its real concern is with the way in which historical changes in the meanings of words reflect changes in human consciousness. In *Poetic Diction* as well as in the earlier book *History in English Words* (1926) Barfield, by examining historical developments in language, traced the roots of dualism and showed how it came to dominate modern thought. In both of these books, as well as a flood of smaller publications of the 1920s, Barfield then analyzed what he identified as the negative consequences of dualistic thought. At the same time, he was, beyond a merely negative criticism, also concerned with an alternative vision of the world: over against dualism he placed his own philosophy of unity and participation – a philosophy in which an important role is attributed to poetry and the imagination.

Barfield's theory of poetry and imagination is both a theory of cognition, and a philosophy of life. If one takes it really seriously, it soon emerges that it has far-reaching consequences. His key concept is that of unity, together with the associated idea of participation. He justifies this concept on an epistemological level, and then applies it to the practical sphere. In this book I shall explore both of these aspects of Barfield's work: the intellectual justification of his ideas on the one hand, and their application on the other. There are two central questions with which I shall be particularly concerned: First, what are the special circumstances (intellectual, social and political) that prompted Barfield to develop a sophisticated philosophy of unity and participation? And secondly, what are the implications and consequences of his philosophy – not only for the mental and spiritual sphere, but also for the practical (social, economic and political) sphere? A survey of secondary literature reveals that neither of these questions so far appear to have been answered satisfactorily. Let us have a look at what scholarship has actually offered to date.

The two most obvious books suggesting themselves as an introduction to Barfield are Humphrey Carpenter's *The Inklings, C.S. Lewis, J.R.R. Tolkien, Charles Williams and their Friends* (1978), and Gareth Knight's *The Magical World of the Inklings* (1990). Both of these books are studies of the Oxford-based literary circle called the *Inklings* with whom Barfield was associated through his acquaintance with C. S. Lewis. The two books are concerned with a set of ideas and values which all of the *Inklings* authors, however different they may have been otherwise, had in common. By placing Barfield in the context of these authors, we gain a first glimpse of his own central concerns. However, Carpenter's book, as is indicated in its subtitle, is mainly concerned with Lewis's life, especially, in relation to that of Tolkien and Williams. Only one page, out of about 250, has been devoted to "a summary" of Barfield's life. There are some twenty more pages relating to him, but they seem designed merely to furnish the background to Lewis's own development. Thus we learn hardly enough about Barfield to be able to form a proper judgement either about the value or the significance of his thought. The question arises why so little has been said about someone whom Lewis described as "the man of all my acquaintance whose character both moral and intellectual I should put highest, or very nearly so".[1] Carpenter himself claims – more than once – that, as a friend, Barfield had an immense influence on Lewis throughout his life. In the light of their long-standing friendship, it is a little surprising, then, that Carpenter has not allowed more space for a deeper exploration of their mutual influence. His book is at present the most popular book on the *Inklings* available. However, it seems to underestimate the real importance of Barfield as an intellectual presence in the *Inklings* group. One of the reasons for this may be the fact that in the 1930s Barfield became a solicitor, and the heavy demands of legal practice, in addition to those of a literary career, tied him down. This, no doubt, removed him somewhat from the centre of the Oxford circle. And a popular book, such as Carpenter's, which seems to take more account of physical presence than of intellectual, has perhaps helped Barfield to retreat further into the background.

---

[1] Barfield, undated letter in Wade Collection, cited in Adey 1978, 11.

A little more is to be found in Gareth Knight's book. Knight devotes a whole (though the last and smallest) chapter to Barfield. He offers a thoughtful analysis of Barfield's more important works and thus provides a useful introduction to his thought. He suggests, however, that Barfield's thought "appears to have been remarkably consistent over the years" and concludes that his "fundamental opinions changed little over the years, save in natural development and increasing cogency of expression" [Knight 210–1]. Indeed, this is how Barfield himself liked to present himself: as an absolutely consistent and straightforward thinker. This is evident, for example, in a letter he wrote in 1994 in which he commented on an earlier version of the introduction to the present book:

> There is a difference between development and *volte face*. People distinguish between "early Heidegger" and "late Heidegger", between "early Wittgenstein" and ["]late Wittgenstein" – and incidentally between ["]early Lewis["] (before his conversion) and "late Lewis" – but I myself have pointed out before now that there is no "late Barfield" and "early Barfield" and have even said or written once that I sometimes feel I go on writing the same book over and over again. So I feel that both Knight's "fundamental opinions change[d] little" and his "remarkably consistent over the years" are quite justified.[2]

Barfield was evidently careful to stress the unity, coherence and continuity of his thought. For a writer, of course, whose fundamental concern is with the philosophy of unity and wholeness this is of special importance. Any inconsistencies or gaps in his thought might be seen as a failure to live up to what he preaches. On the other hand, it is the gaps and inconsistencies which make an author interesting. So far, however, Barfield's self-image has been accepted too uncritically. It will therefore be one of the aims of this book to investigate whether he was indeed as consistent and as straightforward as he claimed.

In addition to Carpenter's and Knight's books, there is a number of highly specialized studies which analyze certain aspects of Barfield's

---

[2] Cf. Barfield 1994, the square brackets indicate my corrections.

work, such as his concept of imagination in comparison to Lewis's[3], the language of poetry [cf. e.g. Flieger and Nemerov], or his ideas in parallel to those of other thinkers [cf. e.g. Mood, Avens, Grant 1979, Potts, and Hocks]. What is usually missing in these studies is a perspective which would allow us to assess Barfield's achievement in the light of larger historical processes. A real break-through in this respect came only with the new study by Jason Randall Peters, "Owen Barfield and the Heritage of Coleridge", which places Barfield in the long line of thinkers who have their roots in Coleridge's thought. The special merit of this study is that it allows us to see that Barfield is not an isolated thinker. Instead we gain a sense that there is the weight of a strong intellectual tradition behind his ideas and his argument. Peters, however, appears to be more interested in the tradition than in the contemporary context of Barfield's thought. Therefore my study will take up the matter where that of Peters leaves off.

It cannot be overemphasized how essential it is to have a proper awareness of Barfield's contemporary context (intellectual, social and political). It is only when we investigate how he addresses the concrete issues and problems of his period that we are able to assess the significance and value of his thought both for that period and, by analogy, for our own. However, what is characteristic of Barfield scholarship, as I hope my survey has shown, is that it appears to be mainly concerned with the nature, or else with the historical roots of Barfield's thought. Thus it may happen that we learn much about his concept of the evolution of consciousness (and its roots), for example, but remain ignorant as to why and how he developed it. It seems, then, that there is little interest either in Barfield's development or his immediate context, with the result that the concrete relevance of his thought is lost from sight.

This, then, will be the task of the present book: to create a proper insight not only into the nature and the roots, but also into the context, the development and the relevance of Barfield's thought. There is as yet no study which has attempted to do so, and I hope to take a new step in this direction. I shall proceed as follows: The period with

---

[3] Cf. e.g. Colbert, Adey 1975 and 1984, Morris and Wendling, and Thorson 1990 and 1991.

which I shall be concerned is the 1920s. This is the period during which Barfield developed the principal ideas for what was to become the central concern of his mature work: the evolution of consciousness and the philosophy of wholeness and participation. First, (besides considering some of the sources which influenced him) I shall trace the process by which he arrived at his central ideas. Secondly, I shall place him in his contemporary context (intellectual, social and political) and investigate how he addressed the concrete problems and concerns of the time. I shall, thirdly, discuss the implications and consequences of his ideas – both for the mental and spiritual sphere and for the practical (social, economic and political) sphere. And, finally, I shall attempt an assessment of the value and the significance of his work. My approach is both biographical and expository, and contains elements of intellectual, social and political history. I cannot claim competence in all of these areas, but I felt it necessary to employ an approach which is broad enough to enable us to make a proper assessment of an author whose interests are as wide-ranging as Barfield's. My chapters will be organized as follows:

I. The Intellectual Context: Owen Barfield, C.S. Lewis, and Contemporary Philosophy[4]

This chapter will be concerned with the genesis of Barfield's thought. It was, as is well known, during the early 1920s that a controversy arose between Barfield and C.S. Lewis. I shall discuss the differences between the two authors and explore Lewis's part in shaping as well as sharpening and correcting Barfield's thought. Barfield's controversy with Lewis, moreover, will be placed in the context of contemporary philosophy. It will thus, I hope, become possible to see that Barfield's philosophical position emerged as a reaction against current dualistic thought. I shall, finally, offer a deliberately brief discussion of Barfield's roots in Coleridge's thought. What I hope to show is that Barfield was one in a line of thinkers – Coleridge among them – who also resisted dualism and on whom he could draw for a defence of his own position.

---

[4] This chapter was published in a shorter and slightly different version in Diener 1998.

II. The Anthroposophical Background

In this chapter I shall pay special attention to the second most important influence on Barfield after Coleridge: that of Rudolf Steiner. I shall give a general outline of Steiner's basic ideas, focussing on those aspects which are specially relevant for Barfield. Barfield's anthroposophical background is an area which has been almost completely neglected.[5] This is why I feel obliged to devote a whole chapter to it. Steiner is generally held to be a wilfully esoteric, intellectually dubious figure, which is why he has been mostly shunned by 'serious' scholars. As soon as we take a proper look at his essential writings, however, it rapidly emerges that anthroposophy has a sounder philosophical basis than is generally allowed and has, in fact, very practical aims. Steiner, as I hope to show, is part of the same intellectual tradition to which Barfield belongs: that of romantic cultural and social criticism. Like Barfield after him, he drew on the romantic ideals of wholeness and participation and sought to bring them to life. This, he believed, was necessary at a time which by many was felt to be a time of crisis. It was Steiner's great aim – this, I believe, is not generally realized – to go to the root of the crisis and to effect a reform: reform not only in culture (the world of mind and spirit), but also in society (the world of practical affairs at large). This, I argue, is why Steiner's work had a special appeal to Barfield. Indeed, as I hope to show, there are striking parallels in the two authors' work. It will be the aim of this chapter to draw out these parallels and thereby to shed some light on the reasons why anthroposophy became important for Barfield and continued to fascinate him throughout his life.

---

[5] There is, to my knowledge, only one serious study of Steiner and Barfield: Patrick Grant's "The Quality of Thinking".

III. Barfield as Cultural and Social Critic

Chapter II has, through the backdoor (via Steiner), introduced Barfield in a role for which he is not normally known: that of the practical critic. Usually we think of him as a philosopher and theorist of language and consciousness. It will therefore come as a surprise to discover that during the 1920s he released a flood of articles which are concerned with practical (social, economic and political) issues: e.g. unemployment, the world economic crisis and the rise of fascism. These articles appeared in current topical journals, such as *New Age*, *Criterion*, *G.K's Weekly* and others. They have, unfortunately, never been reprinted which may be one of the reasons why they have been ignored in scholarship. The result is that we have remained entirely unaware of the practical aspect of Barfield's thought. In this chapter, then, I shall introduce these articles for the first time and attempt a detailed interpretation. I shall pay special attention to his criticism of modern dualism and its in his view detrimental effect both on the sphere of mind and spirit and the sphere of practical affairs. My purpose is to revise our present misconception that Barfield was merely a theorist who had no interest whatsoever in the world of action. What I hope to show is that, on the contrary, he, like Steiner and his romantic predecessors, was the kind of critic who wishes to effect reform.

IV. Barfield as Reformer

While the previous chapter was mainly concerned with Barfield the critic, this fourth and last chapter will be concerned with Barfield the reformer. His ideals, once more, were unity and participation. What I hope to show is that he based on these ideals the vision of a complete transformation of culture and society. My final task, then, will be to investigate how convincing and how successful he was in this for us completely new and unexpected role of the cultural and social reformer.

Appendix: An Interview With Owen Barfield

There is as yet no biography of Barfield. Apart from a few scanty remarks about himself in some of the prefaces of his books and in a short autobiographical piece we actually know surprisingly little about this thinker. In March 1994 I therefore took the opportunity to visit Owen Barfield and to interview him about details of his work, his context and his development specifically during the 1920s. The information which he kindly gave me became the basis on which the present book builds. The interview has in the meantime been published [cf. Diener 1995]. However, as an integral part of my research I felt that it ought to be immediately available to the reader, which is why I have included it in the form of an appendix.

A Note on the Text:

First, where I quote Greek terms or phrases from Barfield's or other authors' texts I have consistently transliterated the Greek. Secondly, where I quote longer passages in German or other foreign languages I have provided translations. The originals are in the Notes section toward the end of the book. Unless otherwise indicated, the translations are my own. Finally, where I quote from manuscripts or from texts of the early 1920s which have not been reprinted, I have preserved the original spellings which are sometimes slightly different from late twentieth-century spellings. Where in any of these texts I detected any spelling or printing mistakes I have indicated these with square brackets and in a footnote.

I.
The Intellectual Context: Owen Barfield, C. S. Lewis and Contemporary Philosophy

Owen Barfield and C.S. Lewis were both undergraduates at Oxford, where they met in 1919 and formed a close friendship that would last for the rest of their lives. Barfield read English at Wadham College, taking a First Class in 1921. Lewis studied at University College, taking a First in Classical Moderations (Latin and Greek Literature) in 1920, another First in Literae Humaniores, or 'Greats' (Ancient History and Philosophy) in 1922, and an additional First in English in 1923. During those formative undergraduate years, their friendship proved intellectually highly stimulating. Indeed, the influence they had on each other's work, as they later came to acknowledge so frequently, goes back to those early years.

Although their friendship was characterized by "a community of mind and a deep affection", it was not one of complete harmony and perfect agreement [Lewis 1977a, 161]. In fact, Lewis humorously describes his friend Barfield as

> the man who disagrees with you about everything. He is not so much the *alter ego* as the anti-self. Of course he shares your interests; otherwise he would not become your friend at all. But he has approached them all at a different angle. [...] When you set out to correct his heresies, you find that he forsooth has decided to correct yours! [ibid.].

Their common interest in poetry and literature in general was accompanied by a vivid exchange of differing opinions. And the question on which their argument soon centred is summed up by Barfield thus: "whether imagination is a vehicle for truth or whether it is simply a highly desirable and pleasurable experience of the human soul" [ibid.]. It is, in essence, the question out of which later Barfield's *Poetic Diction* would grow – a work which strongly influenced Lewis.

Barfield's and Lewis's discussion of the nature of imagination and the value of poetic experience in relation to the common-sense experience of the factual world is intensely philosophical in nature and has wider implications than might, at first glance, be recognizable. It is, as I hope to show, closely bound up with the current philosophical debates of the early twentieth century. Contemporary philosophy, as it partly mirrored and partly formed the general *Zeitgeist*, is the common background and the starting point of Barfield's and Lewis's debates. In order, therefore, to understand the nature and the actual significance of those debates, and eventually of *Poetic Diction*, it is essential first of all to shed some light on this philosophical background.

1. Contemporary Philosophy

In *Surprised by Joy* Lewis describes their common philosophical outlook as follows:

> We had been, in the technical sense of the term, "realists"; that is, we accepted as rock-bottom reality the universe revealed by the senses. But at the same time we continued to make for certain phenomena of consciousness all the claims that really went with a theistic or idealistic view. We maintained that abstract thought (if obedient to logical rules) gave indisputable truth, that our moral judgement was "valid", and our aesthetic experience not merely pleasing but "valuable". The view was, I think, common at the time; it runs through Bridges' *Testament of Beauty*, the work of Gilbert Murray, and Lord Russell's "Worship of a Free Man". [Lewis 1977a, 167]

The philosophical realism of the time is described by Lewis here as being somewhat mixed up with an "idealistic view" of the world. And a few passages later he says that the dominant philosophy at Oxford at that period was not actually realism but idealism. A brief preliminary survey of these two philosophical modes will therefore be needed to provide a context for Barfield's and Lewis's own views; a discussion of their specific reactions will follow in the next section. Idealism had been the prevailing philosophy at Oxford since the late nineteenth century. As it was represented by its most eminent exponent, Francis Herbert Bradley, in the early twentieth century, it had taken on the form of absolute idealism. Bradley's idealism owes much to Hegel's, which is why the form of philosophy he represents is sometimes referred to as Neo-Hegelianism. Hegel assumed an ultimate spiritual reality, the Absolute, which underlies and embraces all that exists. In his dialectic of thesis – antithesis – synthesis he endeavoured to show that all dualities are ultimately summed up in the totality of the Absolute. For Hegel, mind and matter, or subject and object, are ultimately no dualities at all, but are grounded in the synthesis of the Absolute. Man is capable of attaining an essential understanding of the nature of the Absolute, "both in itself and in its concrete manifestations in Nature and spirit" [Copleston, 188]. For all things are an expression of the Absolute, which equally expresses itself in and through the human mind. The earlier English idealism of the nineteenth-century (notably that of T. H. Green at Oxford) basically shared this outlook, but its emphasis lay on the subject-object relationship rather than the metaphysics of the Absolute – which is where it differs from Hegelian idealism. With the following generation of idealists, however, the emphasis on the metaphysics of the Absolute moved more and more into the foreground.

It has sometimes been pointed out that Hegel's enormous sense of an all-embracing Absolute, which sums up everything in its totality, shows the following tendency: things, as well as the human self, begin to lose their independence; they cease to exist in their own right and degenerate to a mere epiphenomenon of this overarching one-ness [cf. eg. Hirschberger, 435]. This is, in fact, how Bradley in his books, e.g. *Appearance and Reality* (1893) or *Essays on Truth and Reality* (1914), drew Hegel's philosophy to its logical conclusion. For Bradley, the finite, including the human mind, is nothing but the 'unreal' appearance of the Absolute, which is the ultimate and actual reality. He therefore did not share Hegel's trust in the capacity of human thought to attain an essential understanding of this ultimate reality, for he believed that human discursive thought distorts reality, rather than representing it adequately, because it inevitably reveals contradictions of which the Absolute is entirely free. Bradley's idealism has sometimes been said to be "a peculiar combination of scepticism and fideism" [Copleston, 188]: Bradley intensely distrusted the human capacity to grasp reality in its ultimate unity while at the same time he believed that there *is* such an ultimate unifying reality. Thus his philosophy created a vast, and utterly unbridgeable, gulf between the two. In spite of its sense of an ultimate reality, the all-embracing Absolute, Bradley's idealism was deeply dualistic in its outlook.

Such was the idealism which Lewis describes as the dominant philosophy at the time. It is true, as James Patrick has observed, that the outlook of the 'Greats' curriculum at Oxford, for instance, was coloured by Hegelianism until the 1930s.[6] But when Barfield and Lewis entered Oxford the particular kind of Bradleian idealism was, though still influential, already in decline [cf. Bell, 176]. In the shade of idealism a counter-movement, philosphical realism, had been growing up. Reinforced by the Cambridge realists, it actually came to rival idealism at Oxford.

As early as the late nineteenth century, philosophers came to criticise the idealists' attempt to regard mind and matter, subject and object under one unifying spiritual principle. Thomas Case's book *Physical Realism* (1888) probably gave realism its name. Case regarded himself as "restoring the realism of Francis Bacon and of scientists as for instance Newton and as an opponent of the then fashionable idealist movement" [Copleston, 380]. He and subsequent realists (such as John Cook Wilson and H. A. Prichard) reacted against the idealist sense of a unity of subject and object by declaring the object as existing independently from the perceiving subject. With the restoration of the independence of fact came the reassertion of its reality. That, of course, stood in marked contrast to Bradley's definition of reality as the Absolute. Reality for the realists was now reality as revealed by the sciences.

In the early twentieth century, the realists had already gained a foothold at Oxford. Moreover, they were reaffirmed by the influence of the Cambridge realists, among them Bertrand Russell. In *Surprised by Joy*, Lewis mentions especially Russell's "A Free Man's Worship" (1917) as an example of the kind of realism which had begun to make a deep impression at Oxford. Here Russell declared that the views of reality as presented by the sciences "are so nearly certain, that no

---

[6] Patrick, 3; G. R. G. Mure, Warden of Merton College in the 1950s, and author of *Retreat from Truth*, was a surviving Hegelian.

philosophy which rejects them can hope to stand."[7] Accordingly, in Russell's scientific outlook, the world is governed by cause and effect; it is purposeless and without any higher meaning. Man is the helpless product of these causes; his life is controlled by the forces of a Nature which is "omnipotent but blind". In Russell's realism the factual world is reality; but side by side with this factual reality there is also a world of ideals. Man is free because he is conscious of "unconscious" matter; and in spite of a world which reveals itself only in disconnected fragments he can perceive something of such ideals as beauty and perfection. Those ideals, however, being the outcome of creative imagination, "are not realized in the realm of matter" [ibid., 11, 15, 13]. There is no link between ideal and reality. Ideals are assertions purely of the mind, and are thus exclusively subjective. As we can see, the philosophy of realism strictly divorces subject and object, mind and matter, fact and ideal. It is therefore essentially dualistic in its outlook.

The positive achievement of realism, as expounded by e.g. Russell, was to have resurrected fact from the un-reality to which Bradley had condemned it. And while for Bradley ideal was reality and fact appearance, for Russell it was almost exactly the other way round: fact was restored to reality and ideal began to look more like appearance. Although Bradley's idealism and Russell's realism stand in stark contrast to each other they are surprisingly similar in one important respect: both philosophies are entirely dualistic in their outlook. Therefore, in spite of their essential difference, they can somehow be seen as representing two sides of the same coin.

Such was, in outline, the philosophical climate when Barfield and Lewis came up to Oxford. Current philosophy, as we have seen, was largely dualistic in its outlook. Both Barfield and Lewis were deeply affected by this dualism. But their reactions to it, as I hope to show, were to differ in some very important respects.

---

[7] Russell, 10. All subsequent quotations will be taken from this essay.

2. Barfield's and Lewis's Response

Since Barfield's own intellectual development is very much intertwined with Lewis's it is necessary to give a rather more detailed preliminary account of Lewis's reaction to contemporary philosophy. This will help us to see Barfield's achievement in clear focus, both as a reaction to Lewis in particular and as a reaction to the general intellectual climate of the time.

Lewis describes the attitude he assumed when he came up to Oxford as follows:

> During my first two years at Oxford I was busily engaged [...] in assuming what we may call an intellectual "New Look". There was to be no more self-pity, no flirtations with any idea of the supernatural, no romantic delusions. In a word, like the heroine of *Northanger Abbey*, I formed the resolution "of always judging and acting in future with the greatest good sense". And good sense meant, for me at the moment, a retreat, almost a panic-stricken flight, from all that sort of romanticism which had hitherto been the chief concern of my life. [Lewis 1977a, 162]

What he describes himself here as reacting against is his earlier experience of what he calls "joy". In his autobiography, he compares his experience of "joy" with Traherne's sense of "felicity": the experience of a transformation of the world in a moment of beatific vision. But for Lewis, in contrast to Traherne, this experience of "joy" was not so much a concrete and lasting experience as "an unsatisfied desire which is itself more desirable than any other satisfaction" – a sense of longing rather than fulfilment [ibid., 20]. "All Joy reminds. It is never a possession, always a desire for something longer ago or further away or still 'about to be'" [ibid., 66]. Joy is inspired by nature but does not manifest itself in her; it is present in imagination (through literature and poetry) but absent from any concrete experience in everyday life. That sense of division runs through Lewis's autobiography like two almost exactly parallel red threads: it is a strict division of outer and inner, of ordinary experience and beatific vision, of reason and imagination. While he was still at school, he reports, this dichotomy was felt by him as being so absolute that it began to determine his whole outlook. As he himself puts it: "my secret, imaginative life began to be so important and so distinct from my outer life that I almost have to tell two separate stories. The two lives do not seem to influence each other at all" [ibid.]. Stephen Medcalf, who tries to find a cause for Lewis's enormous sense of dichotomy, explains: "the important cause is the extraordinary contrast in him of clear, aggressive intellect both with an immense receptiveness to literature and friendship and an enormously active involuntary imagination" [Medcalf, 115]. Medcalf's proposed explanation is dangerously close to tautology. Lewis, it is of course true, was endowed with an extraordinary range of gifts. It does, however, not necessarily follow from this that he *had* to separate these gifts as strictly as he did. One must look deeper for an explanation. But instead of delving into a hasty search for 'deeper causes' (such speculations should be reserved for psychoanalysts, biographers and film-makers), I shall confine myself, for the present purposes, to an investigation of likely influences. And these influences are to be looked for partly in the general intellectual climate and partly in Lewis's own education.

Lewis, as we have already seen, felt a strong sense of duality even before he went to university. That he did not for a long time attempt to bring together his different experiences clearly has something to do with the fact that he grew up in an age that did not exactly inspire anyone to do so. When he came to Oxford he encountered a spirit at the university which matched the experience he brought to it: the spirit of dualism as it characterized mainstream philosophy.

With all that has been said above, it is not difficult to see how philosophy, as it was taught at Oxford, helped Lewis to strengthen and to fortify his own sense of dualism. Through his tutor, E.F. Carritt (himself a pupil of H.A. Prichard's, one of the Oxford realists) he underwent a thorough training in philosophical realism [cf. Patrick, 13 and 109]. It is therefore hardly surprising that his own outlook soon began to resemble that of Russell, for example, in whose philosophy, as we have seen, ideals are "not realized in the realm of matter", and reality is the reality of the sciences. However powerful the imagination (with all its revelations), it had, as Lewis then felt, no point of intersection with factual reality; it was not 'real' in the same sense as fact was.[8] It was views like these which formed the essential ingredients of his "intellectual 'New Look'". Soon he was even prepared to think of "joy", and all that went with it, as "romantic delusions", for he came to associate it with the spiritualism and occultism which he vaguely believed had driven a friend of his into insanity.[9] During that period, philosophical realism provided Lewis with a matter-of-fact reality which he could set firmly against a vague experience of "joy" – an experience which, he was then inclined to believe, might just be "wishful thinking" [ibid., 164], leading to delusion or eventually to insanity.[10] With all that, Lewis was perfectly ready to deepen the gulf between imaginative experience and factual reality along the lines of philosophical realism.

Thus Lewis had no difficulties in accepting the pervasive dualism in the form of philosophical realism. In the passage quoted above, he describes it as the "common" view of the time – something that was simply taken for granted. Keeping this in mind, we shall now turn to Barfield's development to see how his came to differ not only from Lewis's but from the whole intellectual outlook of the time.

---

[8] It is not difficult to follow Barfield when he diagnoses this divided outlook of Lewis's both as materialistic and as idealistic: "He didn't like the idea of having any concrete relation between imagination and knowledge: Knowledge was a job for science. He was, philosophically, really a materialist – in the kind of deepened form where it was called Subjective Idealism." Cf. Appendix, 183.

[9] This was in March 1923. Lewis spent two weeks with his friend, Dr Askins, witnessing his severe mental disturbance leading to insanity and ending in death. Cf. Lewis 1977a, 163.

[10] With this, of course, Lewis went a step further than Russell ever did. While, to begin with, he greatly admired Russell and shared his outlook, he later became highly sceptical of any kind of metaphysical insight. Cf. e.g. the entry in his journal dated 1 January 1924: "In his [Russell's] 'Worship of a Free Man' I found a very clear and noble statement of what I myself believed a few years ago. But he does not face the real difficulty – that *our ideals are after all a natural product*, facts with a relation to all other facts, and cannot survive the condemnation of the fact as a whole. The Promethean attitude would be tenable only if we were really members of some other whole outside the real whole: wh. we're not". Lewis 1993a, 281 (my italics). For further discussion of this point, cf. Wilson, 85–7.

Unfortunately, we do not know as much about Barfield's early development as we know about Lewis's. We have very little evidence as to whether he had already experienced as deep a sense of dualism as Lewis before he went to university. However, according to Lewis, as we saw earlier, he was very ready to share with Lewis the dualistic outlook that goes with philosophical realism. It should be noted though that Barfield did not study philosophy. But, as we have already seen with Lewis, an ingrained sense of dualism was not necessarily a matter of specialized training. One might say, philosophy helped to shape and systematize something more generally inherent in the intellectual climate of the time. We get a glimpse of that in a short passage by Barfield about the way of perceiving the world in which he was brought up:

> The world in which the subject was growing up was the world of Wells and Shaw. The old Victorian confidence in unlimited progress was still going strong. It was a few years before Wells published his *Outline of History*. There was a new world in front of us; mankind had begun to move on and on and up and up, and to control the outer world with an ever-increasing multitude of gadgets, and everything was going to be wonderful. What was not mentioned so often, although it was regarded as equally certain, was that, at the end of the whole process the entire universe would crumble or freeze into a mere conglomeration of inanimate matter. It was – for anybody who really took a long view – you could say a pretty hopeless perspective.[11]

It was, however, the perspective of the age in which Barfield and Lewis had grown up: the perspective of a universe as "inanimate

---

[11] Barfield 1976, 3. This short autobiographical piece was delivered by Barfield to the Anthroposophical Society at Rudolf Steiner House, London, in 1976; he talks there about himself in the third person and as "the Subject". Cf. Barfield's observations here with the 'entropic' conclusion of H. G. Wells' *The Time Machine* (1895) – a work which strongly influenced C. S. Lewis. There is a passage in *Surprised by Joy* which expresses an outlook that is very similar to that in the above passage from Barfield: "my early reading – not only Wells but Sir Robert Ball – had lodged very firmly in my imagination the vastness and cold of space, the littleness of Man. It is not strange that I should feel the universe to be a menacing and unfriendly place." Lewis 1977a, 57.

matter", and of the world as an object for the scientists, but in itself devoid of any higher meaning. To begin with, Barfield took this essentially Russellian view for granted as much as Lewis did. Before long, however, Barfield came to question and then to reject this view. As we shall see, it was his love of literature which eventually led him in a completely different direction.

Barfield, like Lewis, had a great love for literature. He gives us a picture of himself as a schoolboy who immensely enjoyed languages, and who was strongly impressed by common expressions from Latin which came to him as enlightening metaphors [Barfield 1976, 2]. At the same time he began to develop a particular love for lyric poetry. The impact lyric poetry made on him, he describes as follows:

> Well the subject was somewhere between the ages of 17 and 20, I think, when he definitely concluded that lyric poetry was perhaps one of the best things in life, and certainly the most hopeful thing, in the prevailing materialistic climate of opinion in which he was being brought up; and furthermore that the *metaphors* in lyric poetry were what constituted the principle substance of it. It was not just a matter moreover of enjoying lyric poetry, the world became a profounder and a more meaningful place when seen through the eyes that had been reading poetry. That was perhaps the most important thing of all. Poetry had the power to change one's consciousness a little. [ibid., 3]

As we can see, the experience of reading poetry was for Barfield something like Lewis's experience of "joy". It was a profound and enlightening experience, changing in one moment his entire outlook onto the world. But, in spite of the fact that he felt it to be a deep and most real experience, he was "conditioned by the whole intellectual climate in which he was brought up, to suspect that somehow it might all be a subjective illusion" [ibid., 6]. How deeply ingrained this "suspicion" was in Barfield is very well depicted in a remark he made to Lewis, which Lewis noted down in his journal:

> I [Lewis] walked back to Wadham with him [Barfield] in the moonlight. He said that when one had accepted the materialist's universe one went on and on to a point and suddenly exclaimed "Why should *my* facts be the only facts that don't count?": then came the revulsion and you took a

more spiritual view till that too worked itself to its reaction and flung you back to materialism: and so to and fro all the days of your life ... .[12]

This remark resembles the realization of a prisoner who, after checking the two only routes of escape, discovers that they do not actually lead anywhere, but cannot accept the fact. It reflects very well the intellectual deadlock in which Barfield found himself: there were only two ways of thinking, and both were equally unsatisfactory. As we have seen, Lewis was (at that particular time of his life) perfectly ready to accept the views offered to him in the form of philosophical realism. But, in the long run, Barfield was not. From this radical discrepancy sprang the debate between Barfield and Lewis on the nature of poetic experience in relation to the world of fact, which lasted almost for a whole decade.

For Barfield, the experience of reading poetry was strong enough to prompt the impulse, "not merely to go on enjoying the experience, but to examine it" [Barfield 1976, 6]. In contrast, Lewis went on "enjoying" it (his journal, written between 1922 and 1927, is full of flashes of poetic insight), but refused to examine it, pushing it aside and thus supplanting it by the common views which declared it to be delusory. Barfield, meanwhile, on the basis of his poetic experience, began to develop a completely new outlook. The outcome was *Poetic Diction*. This book was to have a profound effect on Lewis's mind, helping him, in the long run, to recover his poetic experience from his sense of delusion, convincing him that it was not a subjective, but an objective and real experience. Let us consider the argument, which brought about this change of heart, in some detail.

---

[12] Lewis 1993a, 186. The entry is dated 26 January 1923.

3. The Argument of *Poetic Diction*

In 1921, Barfield completed his active and highly successful undergraduate career at Wadham with the distinction of a First Class Honours degree in English.[13] Clearly his academic abilities were highly appreciated by the college authorities, and he was obviously regarded as a most promising candidate for the higher degree of B.Litt. In the following academic year (1921–2) he set out to work on his project "Poetic Diction". His starting-point was, as has already been observed above, his own experience of reading poetry. He records in the introduction to *Romanticism Comes of Age*:

> [W]ithout any particular exertion or theorising on my part, I had two things strongly impressed on me, firstly, that the poetic or imaginative use of words enhances their meanings and secondly that those meanings may reveal hitherto unapprehended parts or aspects of reality. All this seemed to promise a way out of the vacuum and I began to pursue my investigations more systematically. [Barfield 1986e, 10]

Unfortunately, none of the records of Wadham College survive to tell us who Barfield's tutors were, and whether he received any immediate intellectual support for his new ideas. What we do know, as this passage clearly shows, is that the prevailing philosophical climate left him in what he himself describes as an intellectual "vacuum" from which he wanted to escape. We saw earlier that the commonly

---

[13] Cf. the brief note in *Wadham College Gazette* 5 (1916–22), 328, for the Summer Term 1921: "We congratulate Mr. A. O. Barfield on his First Class, a distinction all the more to be valued as this year the examiners disappointed a good many candidates, who had hoped to win that distinction. Mr. Barfield will be in residence next year, writing for the B.Litt. degree; his subject is the difficult one of 'Poetic Diction', his articles on which in the *Saturday Review* have already attracted the favourable attention of good critics." In the same volume he is variously mentioned as having acted, over several terms, as an "officer" of the "Diagnostic Society" (debating society) and as "president" of the literary society at Wadham. Moreover he was a member of the "Oxford University Folk Dance Society", of which various other Wadham men were also members, and which held weekly practices at Wadham. Cf. e.g., *Wadham College Gazette* 5, 288, 337, 358, 369.

accepted view of the period was the dualistic view that denied a link between ideal and reality. And out of a dissatisfaction with contemporary dualism – which favoured views such as Russell's that nature is "omnipotent but blind" and the ideal "not realized in the realm of matter" – sprang a deeply felt need to develop an alternative vision of the world: a vision as it occurred to him naturally when he read poetry. "The world became a profounder and more meaningful place when seen through the eyes that had been reading poetry" [Barfield 1976, 3]. Reading poetry was for that very reason for Barfield not a simple form of escapism from an otherwise hostile and meaningless reality. It suggested to him that reality could be seen as something completely different from what he was conditioned to believe. In poetry lay the clue, which is why Barfield was not content merely to "enjoy poetry", but wanted to "penetrate" the experience of poetic revelation in order "to reach what, if anything, lay behind it" [Barfield 1986e, 10]. His aim was to formulate and to justify an alternative vision inspired by the reading of poetry.

Having no model for what he intended to do, he had to take a particular route of his own. But we must not imagine this route to be a very clear one for it was easily obliterated by the doubts which affected him as much as they affected everyone else; after all, he was conditioned by his time to consider his experience of poetic revelation as being merely a subjective illusion. The first steps he took were to read extensively in philosophy. It is obvious enough that it was not from contemporary philosophy that he took his inspiration. He had already developed a strong taste for the "imaginative treatment of language and life" of the English Romantic poets; now it was in the philosophy of romanticism that he found a "natural starting point" for his enquiries [ibid.]. In particular, it was Coleridge's philosophy which proved to be a major stimulus to his own approach.

What Barfield perceived as immediately congenial to his own ideas was Coleridge's concept of polarity and his concept of imagination. In order to understand their special significance for Barfield it will be essential to consider these two concepts in the light of the intellectual context in which Coleridge developed them. M. H. Abrams gives the following account:

> In the several decades beginning with the 1780s [...] a number of the keenest and most sensitive minds found radically inadequate, both to immediate human experience and to basic human needs, the intellectual ambiance of the Enlightenment, with (as they saw it) its mechanistic world view, its analytic divisiveness (which undertook to explain all physical and mental phenomena by breaking them down into irreducible parts, and regarded all wholes as a collocation of such elementary parts), and its conception of the human mind as totally diverse and alien from its nonmental environment. [Abrams 1971, 170–1]

Coleridge was among those writers and thinkers who profoundly disagreed with what Abrams describes as the divisive, mechanistic outlook of the Enlightenment. These writers made it their aim to develop an alternative to the current analytic philosophy which they regarded as unsatisfactory and even destructive. Consider, for example, the following passage from a letter by Coleridge to Wordsworth. The passage, while discussing the intended outline of one of Wordsworth's poems, also reflects some fundamental views which Coleridge held himself and which he shared not only with Wordsworth, but with many of his like-minded contemporaries:

> I supposed you first [...] to have laid a solid and immovable foundation for the Edifice by removing the sandy Sophisms of Locke, and the Mechanic Dogmatists. [...] Next, I understood that you would take the Human Race in the concrete [...] to have affirmed a Fall in some sense, as a fact, the possibility of which cannot be understood from the nature of the Will, but the reality of which is attested by Experience & Conscience [...] to point out however a manifest Scheme of Redemption from this Slavery, of Reconciliation from this Enmity with Nature [...] in short, the necessity of a general revolution in the modes of developing & disciplining the human mind by the substitution of Life and Intelligence [...] for the philosophy of mechanism which in every thing that is most worthy of the human Intellect strikes *Death* [...]. [Coleridge 1956–71, vol. iv, 574–5]

According to Coleridge, then, the intended theme of Wordsworth's poem[14] is the history of mankind interpreted (in terms of the biblical fall) as a falling away from an original state of unity into a state of "Enmity" between man and nature. This fall is closely associated with the influence of a certain way of thinking, attributed to Locke and the "Mechanic Dogmatists". However, division and conflict is not considered to be man's final predicament. On the contrary, man can look forward to a "Redemption from this Slavery". And redemption is to be effected by a special "Scheme" which involves "a general revolution in the modes of developing & disciplining the human mind".

This view of history – interpreted in terms of unity, fall into division and future recovery of unity – pretty much sums up not only Coleridge's own view but that of many of his contemporaries. For him, as for them, it was the beginning of human rationality that was seen as one of the principal causes of the Fall:[15]

> The rational instinct, therefore, taken abstractedly and unbalanced, did *in itself*, ("ye shall be as gods!", Gen.iii.5) and in its consequences, [...] form the original temptation, through which man fell: and in all ages has continued to originate, even from Adam, in whom we all fell [...]. [Coleridge 1972, Appendix C, 61]

The disastrous consequence of the predominance of reason, "taken abstractedly and unbalanced", is that it causes us to "think of ourselves as separated beings, and place nature in antithesis to the mind, as object to subject, thing to thought, death to life", instead of leading us to feel "one with the whole" [Coleridge 1969b, vol. i, 520]. In other words, according to Coleridge, the result of the false separation of reason is that it isolates the individual from others, and

---

[14] The tone of the letter suggests that the two authors were agreed on the original plan (as well as the fundamental ideas) for the poem, but that Coleridge did not actually think the poem itself was very successful at carrying out this plan. For a discussion of this, cf. e.g. Leask, 115–6.

[15] For a detailed study of the centrality of this idea in romantic thought (including that of Schiller, Goethe, Schelling, Hegel, Coleridge, Wordsworth and others), cf. Abrams 1971, chapters iv and v.

places mind in absolute opposition to an alien external world. The individual thus feels a division within himself, with others and with his environment. This view of things, as we shall see, was utterly unacceptable for Coleridge. For him the experience of unity is man's original and his highest state:

> 'Tis the sublime of man,
> Our noontide Majesty, to know ourselves
> Parts and proportions of one wondrous whole!
> This fraternises man. This constitutes
> Our charities and bearings. But 'tis God
> Diffused through all, that doth make all one whole [...].
>
> [Coleridge 1912, vol. i, 113–4]

Throughout his life Coleridge was, as Abrams puts it, a "compulsive monist" [Abrams 1971, 267]. "My mind", as the poet himself writes in a letter to John Thelwall (14 October 1797), "feels as if it ached to behold & know something *great* – something *one & indivisible*" [Coleridge 1956–71, vol. i, 349]. This, as he mentions in the same letter, had been a strong urge in him since his childhood and youth. It was Coleridge's fundamental belief that man's true and original condition was not one of division and fragmentation, but one of unity and participation in a greater whole. He therefore made it his cardinal aim to help restore man's original wholeness. Earlier, when I discussed his letter to Wordsworth, we saw that both authors were agreed upon a special "Scheme of Redemption" from man's disunity and conflict. In this "Scheme" it was art in general and the imagination in particular which were conceived as playing a key role. In this context another Coleridgian concept is of great relevance: that of polarity. A proper grasp of the concept is essential for our understanding of the function of art and the imagination.[16]

---

[16] Owen Barfield, with his book *What Coleridge Thought* (1971) is among the pioneers of Coleridge studies to have recognized the centrality of this concept to all of Coleridge's thought. He writes: "polarity is at the root of what Coleridge thought" [Barfield 1983, 145]. This view is shared by Abrams, who also identifies polarity as the "root principle in Coleridge's thought" [Abrams 1971, 268], and by McFarland, who, with special reference to Barfield, acknowledges the concept as "the Archimedes lever

Coleridge believed, as Mary Warnock points out, that "ideas are *in*, or are *constitutive of*, nature" [Warnock, 94]. He therefore reacted very strongly, as we have seen, against a philosophy which divided mind and nature into two independent, irreconcilable entities which absolutely excluded one another. "But if', as Abrams explains, "irredeemable division is the essential evil, what Coleridge calls 'distinction' is not only redeemable but the necessary condition for progressive development" [Abrams 1971, 267]. In the philosopher's own words:

> In all subjects of deep and lasting Interest you will detect a struggle between two opposites, two polar Forces, both of which are alike necessary to our human Well-being, & necessary each to the continued existence of the other [...]. [Coleridge 1956–71, vol. v, 35]

As we can see, according to Coleridge, our whole existence depends on the co-existence as well as interaction of two polar forces. We are reminded of the interdependence of the opposing forces in a magnet or an electric current. Indeed, it has been argued that Coleridge, like many of his contemporaries, was alert to such a connection and that his metaphysic of the polar structure of our existence was to some degree fired by current scientific investigations of magnetic and electrical phenomena.[17] Like the positive and negative forces of a magnet or electric current, then, polar opposites were for Coleridge a "productive *unity*" in which "the two opposite poles constitute each other, and are the constituent acts of *one and the same power*" (my italics) [Coleridge 1848, 50]. In his view, it was possible and

---

not merely of Coleridge's criticism but of the entirety of his mental activity" McFarland, 289. Complementary to Barfield's exclusive concern with Coleridge, McFarland, moreover, provides a wider view by showing the centrality of polarity not only to Coleridge but to all major European romantic thinkers. Cf. ibid., 289–341.

[17] Cf. McFarland, 298–315. There is an interesting parallel in Barfield's intellectual development. Barfield relates that when (in 1917) he began his military training as a "wireless officer" for the Signals unit of the Royal Engineers he had to study the theory of electricity. This, he says, prepared him for a thorough grasp of the concept of polarity and its "decisive epistemological function" in Coleridge. Cf. Barfield 1993, 174–5.

necessary to *distinguish* between these opposites but wrong to *divorce* them and place them in the dead and unproductive juxtaposition of mutually exclusive entities. Barfield comments:

> Polar opposites exist by virtue of each other *as well as* at the expense of each other; "each is that which it is called, relatively, by predominance of the one character or quality, not by the absolute exclusion of the other," Coleridge wrote in *Church and State*. Moreover, each quality is present *in* the other. We can and must distinguish, but there is no possibility of *dividing* them. [Barfield 1989b, 49]

For Coleridge, the faculty that can grasp the difference of the polar opposites without dividing them is the imagination. While logic (or falsely separated reason), in his view, divides opposites into *contraries*, the imagination, in contrast, is able to perceive *unity* in their difference. In Coleridge's own words:

> The poet, described in *ideal* perfection, brings the whole soul of man into activity, with the subordination of its faculties to each other, according to their relative worth and dignity. He diffuses a tone, and spirit of unity, that blends and (as it were) *fuses*, each into each, by that synthetic and magical power, to which we have exclusively appropriated the name of imagination. This power [...] reveals itself in the balance or reconciliation of opposite or discordant qualities: of sameness, with difference; of the general, with the concrete; the idea, with the image; the individual, with the representative; the sense of novelty and freshness, with old and familiar objects; a more than usual state of emotion, with more than usual order; judgement ever awake and steady self-possession, with enthusiasm and feeling profound or vehement; and while it blends and harmonizes the natural and the artificial, still subordinates art to nature; the manner to the matter; and our admiration for the poet to our sympathy with the poetry. [Coleridge 1983, vol. ii, 15–7]

We may sum up the essential quality of the imagination as follows: it is a "synthetic" power, whose special function it is to create "balance", "sympathy" and "reconciliation". Coleridge attributed a similar function to art which he defined as "the mediatress between, and reconciler of, nature and man" [ibid., 253]. As we have seen, he believed that man had fallen into division from nature as a result of the false predominance of divisive reason. Division, however, he was convinced, was not man's true and therefore not his ultimate condition. On the contrary, division was only a temporary experience in man's development which Coleridge envisaged both as starting and ending in unity:

> The dim Intellect *sees* an absolute Oneness, the perfectly clear Intellect *knowingly perceives* it. Distinction & Plurality lie in the Betwixt. [Coleridge 1957 ff., vol. i, 1725]

Man's development, then, as this passage clearly indicates, is from an *unconscious* experience of unity, through division, to a *conscious* recreation of that original experience. The mediating faculty in the process is the imagination. It is thus by a conscious and deliberate exercise of this faculty that man can once more experience the wholeness and integration which are his true condition.

From the interpretation just given, we might gain the impression that Coleridge's attitude is profoundly anti-rationalistic. But is this really the case? One argument that would seem to support this view is the fact that Coleridge associates man's experience of division with the beginning of human rationality, which he equates with the biblical account of the fall. Consequently, his stress on unity appears to reflect a nostalgia for a pre-rational condition of undifferentiated unity and simplicity. The stress on the need to recover unity therefore looks deceptively like a return to an earlier stage of a simple undifferentiated life before the arrival of reason. What the imagination seems to offer, then, is a retreat fom the diversity and complexity of modern life.

However, we would do injustice to Coleridge if we reduced him to this narrow position. It is true, of course, that he regarded the coming of rationality as a fall. Nevertheless, as we saw earlier he did not actually condemn the differentiations of reason as such. What he condemned was the degeneration of such differentiations into absolutely irreconcilable opposites. What he strove for was therefore not an abandonment of reason, but its redemption. The role of the imagination in this sense is not to effect a short cut back to simplicity. Imagination in this sense is a power of transformation, which helps to reintegrate all diversity created by reason into a new whole, which is, not the simple one of the beginning, but a "higher" unity. That

Coleridge held this view is obvious in his concept of polarity which I discussed above. Here is another example:

> In Life, much more in spirit, and in a living and spiritual philosophy, the two component counter-powers actually interpenetrate each other, and generate a *higher* third, *including* both the former, ita tamen ut sit alia et major. [Coleridge 1972, 89 (my italics)].

Abrams makes the following general comment on romantic thought, which is highly relevant to what I have just said about Coleridge:

> It is only by an extreme historical injustice that Romanticism has been identified with the cult of the noble savage and the cultural idea of a return to an early stage of simple and easeful 'nature' which lacks conflict because it lacks differentiation and complexity. On the contrary, all the major Romantic writers [...] set as the goal for mankind the reachievement of a unity which has been earned by unceasing effort and which is [...] an 'organized' unity, an equilibrium of opposing forces which preserves all the products and powers of intellection and culture.
>
> The typical Romantic ideal, far from being a mode of cultural primitivism, is an ideal of strenuous effort along the hard road of culture and civilization. [Abrams 1971, 260 and 185]

In this sense, it is right to say that Coleridge must be seen not merely as a philosophical monist, but as a "diversitarian monist for whom the intellectual, cultural, and moral aim of man is not to return to the undifferentiated unity at the beginning of development, but to strive toward the multeity-in-unity at its end" [ibid., 269]. From here it is now time to return to Barfield and to examine what significance the ideas, which I have just outlined, have for his own work.

The first thing that is very striking when we compare the two authors is that Barfield, like Coleridge, reacted very strongly against the prevailing dualism in contemporary thought. Like his predecessor, he made it his cardinal aim to develop a counter-metaphysic to a way of thinking which he felt was profoundly unsatisfactory if not destructive. In this respect, it seems that Barfield's development is exactly parallel to Coleridge's. It is therefore hardly surprising that in Coleridge he would immediately recognize a viable ally for his own cause. Indeed, if we examine Barfield's approach carefully, we shall see that he follows very closely in his predecessor's footsteps.

Barfield's starting point, as we know, was the experience of reading poetry. On examining this experience he developed an interest in the special function of metaphor. The kind of metaphor which, he tells us, attracted his special interest was the metaphor that combines "a *material* image with an *immaterial* content." He gives an example from Shelley: "When Shelley speaks of the West Wind making him its lyre, he is drawing a material picture of an immaterial relation, a mental or spiritual relation between himself and the world of nature, a relation of inspiration, as it were" [Barfield 1976, 4]. Metaphor, then, he concluded, arouses a "felt change of consciousness" [Barfield 1987, 48]. He expands on this in *Poetic Diction* and observes that metaphor not only changes but expands consciousness. The reader's consciousness is enlarged in such a way that his outlook is completely transformed: he experiences a knowledge of the world he did not have before. In the case of the example I have just quoted, it is the knowledge of the material and the immaterial, or of himself and the world, as something intimately intertwined. Barfield says further that a change of consciousness, with an increase of knowledge, is also experienced when one learns a new language, and, above all, when one contemplates language in its past stages. He agrees with Shelley that the further one traces language back into the past, the more poetic it becomes – or at least it seems so from the perspective of the modern beholder.

Barfield dived into this more deeply by studying carefully the history of the changing meanings of words. The outcome was published in 1926, as *History in English Words*. His findings here served directly as a background for *Poetic Diction* (1928). In both of these books he explores the connection between modern dualism and certain developments in the history of language. He observes that words which are now merely abstract had once a concrete basis: "one of these two things – a solid sensible object, or some animal (probably human) activity" [Barfield 1987, 64]. The word 'abstract' itself can be traced to verbs meaning 'draw' or 'drag'. 'Spirit', while now signifying something entirely intangible, once had the meaning of 'breath' or 'wind'. The rendering in English of the Latin 'spiritus' as 'spirit' *or* 'breath' fails to comprehend the two meanings incorporated in the originally single, undivided word. Barfield's findings reveal that, if one looks back into the history of words which are now exclusively abstract, one discovers that originally they had just such a fused meaning. Barfield calls it variously "undivided meaning", "original unity" or "living unity" [ibid., 80, 86, 87]. From such observations he concludes that the overall history of language is the history of a "splitting up of meanings" – from single meanings to divided meanings, "from homogeneity to dissociation and multiplicity".[18]

For Barfield, language mirrors consciousness. Consequently, he bases a whole theory of an evolution of consciousness on his observations about the historical development of language. It is very striking that the account he gives of this evolution is exactly analogous to Coleridge's account of man's fall into division and conflict. That is, Barfield, like Coleridge before him, interprets the history of mankind as an evolution from relative unself-consciousness to relative self-consciousness – from an original unity of self with nature to a consciousness of self as distinct from her. This view of human evolution suggested itself inevitably to Barfield who found evidence for this in the historical changes of words. Consider the following account of early metaphorical language and what, in Barfield's view, it tells us about the corresponding stage in human consciousness:

> We notice, we *relish* figurative quality in older language, and we experience this figurative element in the same way that we experience a metaphor before it has faded or before it has become fossilised. That is also the way in which we experience those new metaphors which poets make for us. But

---

[18] Ibid, 102 and 81. With the linguistic evidence of his research, Barfield expressly criticizes the Darwinian theory of language (as, for instance, expounded by the nineteenth-century philologist Max Müller), which assumes a development in language from simple, concrete meanings to more complex meanings. By showing that language divides up from complex meanings (at once material *and* immaterial) to more simple meanings (either material *or* immaterial), Barfield actually turns the whole Darwinian theory upside down; and he exposes the Darwinian approach to language as a projection of "post-logical thoughts back into a pre-logical age." ibid., 90. For further discussion of this, cf. Reilly, 40–4.

it does not follow from this (and this is where most of the philologists of the 19th century and the early Twenties have really made their mistake) [...] that that figurative element, that presence of living imagery, that we find in early language was *made*, invented, created by the individual genius of a poet. On the contrary, it couldn't have been. It was simply *there* in the language as such; it was a 'given' kind of meaning, a 'given' kind of imagery.

And further:

> If the figurative, or let's say the imaginal, meaning in the earliest words was really "given", and was not something added to them by an individual speaker (which is what happens when metaphor is invented), then there must have been going on, not only a different kind of thinking but a different kind of perceiving. The picture quality, the given meanings must have been present not only in the perceiver but also in what he perceived; it must have been present in fact in the world about him. There must have been a kind of participation between perceiver and perceived, between man and nature. That is something we no longer experience, only get an occasional glimpse of its quality through the creative imagination of a modern painter or poet. [Barfield 1976, 7 and 9]

The correlative developments in language and consciousness, then, are in Barfield's view as follows: Early metaphorical language with its two fused meanings reveals an original experience of unity and participation of man with nature. What man experienced then – (this is Barfield's basic premise, a premise on which he is in complete agreement with Coleridge) – is not just a subjective experience, but is something that is objectively "present" in the external world. That is, unity and participation are man's original and true condition. They are the fundamental principles of our existence, and indeed of reality as a whole. This is what, in Barfield's view, is conveyed in early unified, metaphorical language. Early language, Barfield comments, must be seen

> as originating in that participation, so that in the earliest stages of all it would have to be described as nature speaking through man, rather than man speaking about nature; and you see the

> subsequent development of language as evincing the gradual diminution of that participation as time went on. [ibid., 9]

In the subsequent development of language, as we saw earlier, Barfield observed a continuous splitting up of the original fused meanings. This development "from homogeneity to dissociation and multiplicity", he then concluded, is exactly parallel with a corresponding development in consciousness. The splitting up of meanings, that is, signifies man's fall into dissociation and conflict with nature. What Barfield identifies as the immediate cause of that fall – on this point he again entirely agrees with Coleridge – is the arrival of human rationality (or "the prosaic spirit", as Barfield also calls it):

> [I]t is only by means of this prosaic spirit that the separate perceptual groups ('phenomena'), which metaphor is to combine or relate, could ever have *become* separate. Moreover, it is only by means of the same principle that the individual consciousnesses, which are assumed to have done the creating, could ever have come into being. For the rational principle, the *to logizein*, is above all that which produces self-consciousness. It shuts off the human ego from the living meaning in the outer world, which it is for ever 'murdering to dissect', and encloses that same ego in the network of its own, now abstact, thoughts. [Barfield 1987, 142–3]

The history of thought, Barfield comments, reveals "some indication of the moment at which the ascending rational principle and the descending poetic principle [...] are passing one another" [ibid., 94]. In the course of history, that is, the rational outlook of discursive logic and science gradually superseded the imaginative or poetic outlook of earlier times. And where the former outlook has finally begun to dominate, man finds himself caught in the inevitable fall further down into separation. Separation, dissociation, isolation – these, Barfield concludes, have finally come to dominate modern consciousness:

> Such a separation, a separation of consciousness from the real world, is today only too conspicuous alike in philosophy, science, literature, and normal experience. Isolated thus, suspended, as it were, *in vacuo*, and hermetically sealed from truth and life, not only the proper name, but the very ego itself, of which that is but the symbol, pines and dwindles away before our eyes to a thin nothing – a mere inductive

abstraction from tabulated card-indexed behaviour, whose causes lie elsewhere. [ibid., 143]

Barfield's observations about a development both in language and in consciousness "from homogeneity to dissociation" have a memorable parallel in T.S. Eliot's famous concept of the "dissociation of sensibility" (formulated in 1921).[19] Moreover, in 1923 Eliot published Barfield's short story 'Dope', which in spirit strikingly resembles his *Waste Land* [cf. Barfield 1993b]. 'Dope' is about a young factory worker who experiences life as rushing past him like a film consisting solely of a rapid succession of disconnected scenes. Individuals exist side by side, isolated from each other and from the world around them. The story is pervaded by an overall sense of fragmentation and dividedness and is entirely in tune with the literary fashion of the period as represented by no less a figure than T.S. Eliot. Apparently, Eliot wrote to Barfield in praise of the short story and invited him to write more in the same vein. Barfield, however, boldly replied in a letter dated 30 April 1924: "I believe at present that it is a waste of energy to record an impression of that sort more than once. I am a little tired of literature which can do nothing but point out ironically that there is nothing much going on but disintegration and decay."[20] It seems obvious that here he parted company with Eliot, or rather, with the outlook Eliot represented.

Barfield was dissatisfied with the sense of division and fragmentation that pervaded philosophy, literature and the whole intellectual climate of the time. He was not content to accept it. Nor did he stop short at only observing its coming about historically, but in

---

[19] Cf. Eliot 1986b, 288 and 287: "In the seventeenth century a dissociation of sensibility set in, from which we have never recovered [...]." "It is something which had happened to the mind of England between the time of Donne or Lord Herbert of Cherbury and the time of Tennyson and Browning; it is the difference between the intellectual poet and the reflective poet. Tennyson and Browning are poets, and they think; but they do not feel their thought as immediately as the odour of a rose. A thought to Donne was an experience; it modified his sensibility."

[20] Barfield (1924-48), Letter to T.S. Eliot, dated 30 April 1924 (Bodleian Library, Oxford, MS.Eng.Lett. c.782), fol. 25. For a more detailed discussion, cf. Kranidas 1985, 23–33.

his conclusion of *Poetic Diction* he attempted to move a step beyond it. He had recently been introduced to the writings of Rudolf Steiner, who had developed a theory of an evolution of consciousness, which was very similar to Coleridge's and which Barfield recognized, in due course, as being congenial to his own approach, confirming and strengthening it.[21] As we saw earlier, Barfield agreed with Coleridge – this was a view which Steiner held too – that division and fragmentation were neither man's original nor his true condition. Barfield therefore looked for a remedy to restore man's original condition, and like both Coleridge and Steiner[22] he found it in the imagination and in art (especially in poetry and in the poetic language of the past). Consider, for example, the following passage from a relatively early publication of 1922:

> The world is not young, and the burden of the coils of memory hangs heavier and heavier on the race. Always the individual spirit increases, according to its knowledge, its dreadful consciousness of solitude. Language has done this; but language, which was born in order to permit social relationships between men, is striving still towards that end and consolation. As it grows subtler and subtler, burying in its vaults more and more associations, more and more mind, it becomes to those same spirits a more and more perfect medium of companionship. [Barfield 1923c, 170]

And in *Poetic Diction* he concludes in a similar vein:

> Men do not *invent* those mysterious relations between separate external objects, and between objects and feelings or ideas, which it is the function of poetry to reveal. [...] The language of primitive men reports them as direct perceptual experience.

---

[21] In an interview with Elmar Schenkel Barfield remarks: "The point about me as an anthroposophist is that I had stumbled (laughs) on the notion of the evolution of consciousness before I came across Steiner, in what is revealed by language used as a theory of knowledge. It's all in *Poetic Diction*." Schenkel 1993, 25. For a discussion of Barfield's independent approach, and how it was strengthened and confirmed by the discovery of Steiner's work, cf. Grant 1982.

[22] I shall discuss Steiner's work and its special significance for Barfield in more detail in the next chapter.

The speaker has observed a unity, and is not therefore himself conscious of *relation*. But we, in the development of consciousness, have lost the power to see this one as one [...]; and now it is the language of poets, in so far as they create true metaphors, which must *restore* this unity conceptually, after it has been lost from perception. Thus the 'before-unapprehended' relationships of which Shelley spoke, are in a sense 'forgotten' relationships. For though they were never yet apprehended, they were at one time seen. And imagination can see them again. [Barfield 1987, 86–7]

Barfield's observations about the evolution of consciousness in *Poetic Diction* and elsewhere, then, suggested to him that the rational outlook is only one stage in history – the imaginative outlook is another. The latter is therefore not less valid than the former. By failing to recognize this, modern man runs the risk of absolutizing a momentary outlook as the final truth about the world, while that very outlook is itself subject to change and may equally be surpassed in the course of time. The recognition that the dividedness of modern consciousness is the outcome of a historical evolution led Barfield to the conclusion that this dividedness did not have to be taken for granted. On the contrary, in his view, the experience of unity and wholeness, while it had vanished from modern consciousness, was not irrevocably lost, but could be restored, with the help of poetry and the imagination.

From this summary of Barfield's essential position it is now time to return to our starting point: our comparison of Barfield with Lewis. What remains, finally, to be discussed is Lewis's response to Barfield's conclusions in *Poetic Diction*. As we shall see, Lewis, very candidly, spotted both the strength and the essential weakness in Barfield's approach.

4. Conclusions

For Barfield the view of human nature and reality revealed by poetry was both richer and more truthful than that suggested by an exclusively rational, scientific world view. Poetry for him was therefore not just a pleasurable 'pastime'; it was an important challenge to modern reductionist assumptions about life. Lewis, who, as we know, had originally subscribed to a hard-nosed scientific rationalism, eventually came to acknowledge the importance of this challenge. As he tells us in his autobiography, Barfield alerted him to certain dangers inherent in the modern world view – dangers of which he had previously not been aware. Barfield warned him, he explains, that if

> one kept (as rock-bottom reality) the universe of the senses, aided by instruments and co-ordinated so as to form "science", then one would have to go much further – as many have since gone – and adopt a Behaviouristic theory of logic, ethics, and aesthetics. [Lewis 1977a, 167]

Lewis, it appears, was deeply impressed by Barfield's theory of the evolution of consciousness. As a result, he found that he could no longer maintain the exclusive claims to truth of the current scientific world view. He came to accept that previous, more imaginative or poetic, views of the world could not simply be dismissed as being less true. He comments:

> [Barfield] made short work of what I have called my "chronological snobbery", the uncritical acceptance of the intellectual climate common to our own age and the assumption that whatever has gone out of date is on that account discredited. You must find why it went out of date. Was it ever refuted (and if so by whom, where, and how conclusively) or did it merely die away as fashions do? If the latter, this tells us nothing about its truth or falsehood. From seeing this, one passes to the realisation that our own age is also "a period", and certainly has, like all periods, its own characteristic illusions. [ibid., 167]

Eventually, as a result of Barfield's observations about the 'evolution of consciousness', Lewis came to appreciate the poetic or imaginative outlook of earlier times as an important counterbalance to the modern scientific world view which, he now admitted, he had accepted too uncritically. This new sensibility is reflected, for example, in his sympathetic treatment of the medieval world picture in *The Discarded Image* (1964). *The Discarded Image* is only one example. Barfield's influence is evident, and has indeed frequently been acknowledged, in many of Lewis's other books: academic, religious and fictional. *The Allegory of Love* (1936), Lewis's first major scholarly work, for instance, is dedicated to Owen Barfield, "wisest and best of my unofficial teachers";[23] there is a reference to Barfield's position on consciousness in *Letters to Malcolm* (1964);[24] and another one in *Perelandra* (1943).[25] No doubt many more can be found.[26]

---

[23] In the preface he writes: "Above all, the friend to whom I have dedicated the book, has taught me not to patronize the past, and has trained me to see the present as itself a 'period'. I desire for myself no higher function than to be one of the instruments whereby his theory and practice in these matters may become more widely effective." Lewis 1935, viii.

[24] "You remember the two maxims Owen [Barfield] lays down in *Saving the Appearances*? On the one hand, the man who does not regard God as other than himself cannot be said to have a religion at all. On the other hand, if I think God other than myself in the same way in which my fellow-men, and objects in general, are other than myself, I am beginning to make Him an idol. I am daring to treat His existence as somehow *parallel* to my own. But He is the ground of our being. He is always both within us and over against us. Our reality is so much from His reality as He, moment by moment, projects into us. The deeper the level within ourselves from which our prayer, or any other act, wells up, the more it is His, but not at all the less ours." Lewis 1988, 71.

[25] Lewis 1989, 170. The whole book is an interesting attempt to portray a world which is characterized by an undivided consciousness in a Barfieldian sense: "Long since on Mars, and more strongly since he came to Perelandra, Ransom had been perceiving that the triple distinction of truth from myth and both from fact was purely terrestrial – was part and parcel of that unhappy division between soul and body which resulted from the Fall. Even on Earth the sacraments existed as a permanent reminder that the division was neither wholesome nor final." ibid, 273–4.

All of these examples illustrate a clear indebtedness to Barfield. From this, however, we should not jump to the hasty conclusion that Lewis simply accepted Barfield's doctrines without criticism. On the contrary, his criticism is evident, for example, in the so-called "Great War" correspondence – letters exchanged between Barfield and Lewis between the mid 1920s and the early 1930s. As we have seen, Barfield criticised Lewis's rational, scientific outlook because in his view it implied a leaning towards materialist reductionism. As the "Great War" letters reveal, in Lewis's view, the danger in Barfield's approach lay in the opposite direction: Barfield's poetic, or 'imaginative' outlook implied a leaning towards idealist reductionism. Lewis suspected that – with his stress on the unity of subject and object, idea and matter – Barfield did not so much elevate ideas to the status of reality, as reduce reality to the status of ideas. The effect of this, he warns Barfield, is solipsism (which restricts all possibility of knowledge to the level of what we find in our own minds):

> Now for your "snag".
>
> From the dismay (it is hardly too strong a word) with wh. you greeted my suggestion, made on our walking tour, that there might be no such thing as *Ego* in the ultimate sense (tho' of course there might be phenomena called "me" and "Barfield"), I confess I had concluded that for you, at any rate, the subject was an ultimate: and therefore that "here am I and over there is Reality" was a scheme you refused to go behind. As I was very uncertain about my own powers of continuing an argument behind it (whatever might happen in odd moments when the light of soul goes out), and not *perfectly* convinced of the truth of my extreme "un-egotistic" doctrine, I assumed subjects as the framework of our whole discussion. And if "we" exist, i.e. real, but individual and separate selves, I certainly think that you must either (a.) Assume a reality which is something other than our thinking and common to us all, *or* (b.) Relapse into extreme subjective idealism, *at least* more probably into solipsism. If the reality thought of is nothing more than the thinking, and if the thinking is *that of a real individual* Ego, then the world is the content of an individual, personal *psyche*, and I (there's only one of me)

---

[26] For a more detailed tracing of references to Barfield and of Barfieldian ideas in the work of Lewis, cf. e.g. Colbert.

may as well cut my throat to night. I know you can't mean that: and therefore [a]wait with interest what you will say next. You see my dilemma. *Either* there is such a thing as a self & and therefore such a thing as thinking over and above the Reality thought about *or* the reality is the whole thing: in which case there is no thinking and no selves or else everything is the thinking of this self. Which means solipsism.[27]

In one of his other letters,[28] Lewis illustrates his objections to Barfield, as well as his own contrasting position in a number of comic drawings [cf. plates 1-3, pp. 56–58]. In the first of these drawings (plate 1) we see a gentleman (i.e. Lewis) who is tied against a pole (i.e. "finite personality") and who stands in the middle of a vague cloud (i.e. reality as a whole). He is quite content to rely on common sense to grasp, not indeed total reality, but a picture of it. Next (plate 2) we see a gentleman (i.e. Barfield) who is also tied against a pole, but who is *not* content to rely on common sense. Instead, he takes up hammer and chisel (i.e. the imagination) to destroy the narrow picture given by common sense in order to penetrate the vague cloud and to gain a larger view of reality. Last (plate 3) we see the same gentleman who, by destroying that picture, has not actually grasped a fuller reality, but has instead conjured up a world of chimaeras and horrible creatures. What awaits this gentleman is not some wonderful insight, but the ambulance, the (mental) hospital and the grave. These drawings are highly amusing, but nevertheless imply a serious criticism.

Lewis depicts Barfield in these drawings as a person who is so exclusively preoccupied with the imagination that he loses touch with the world of our ordinary experience; his rejection of the common sense approach to reality in favour of a more imaginative approach meant, not a better understanding of the world, but a withdrawal into a world of one's own fashioning. In short, what Lewis was so critical of was the irrationalism which he felt was implied in Barfield's views.

---

[27] Undated Letter, in Lewis n.d., Letters to Owen Barfield, (The Bodleian Library holdings, from which I quote, are facsimiles. The originals are held at the Marion E. Wade Center, Wheaton College, Illinois, U.S.A.).

[28] Undated Letter, ibid., fols. 76–8.

The Clouds behind me are Τὸ ὄν. The post to which I am tied so that I can't turn round is finite personality. In front of me is a mirror, representing as much of the reality (and such disguises of it) as can be seen from my position. It includes, of course, "myself" as an empirical object. It is surrounded by a steel frame which represents the finitude and deadness of every mere object. I am studying the mirror with my eyes (equal 'explicit cognition') but reach back with my hands so as to get some touch (implicit "taste" or "faith") of the real.

Plate 1: C.S. Lewis, Letters to Owen Barfield, "The Great War", fol. 76.

OWEN BARFIELD, C.S. LEWIS AND CONTEMPORARY PHILOSOPHY 57

Here we see a gentleman (not identified) engaged on seeing whether a departure from dry academical methods and a newer, freer theory of knowledge may not get some new images out of the mirror. The mirror seems to be playing up well so far. Meanwhile the clouds have ebbed to his ankles. Something like despairing hands stretches to reach from behind but he doesn't notice them. Overhead I detect a curious figuration of cloud that fancy may interpret as a gigantic face in laughter. The hammer and chisel are occult science, yoga, "meditation" (in technical sense) etc.

Plate 2: C.S. Lewis, Letters to Owen Barfield, "The Great War", fol. 77.

An orful example. Study of a gentleman reaching vainly for the inner reality he has scorned, while he shrinks in horror from the phantom he has created on the black wall from which he has succeeded in chipping off all the looking-glass. (Only those who are not Lewis's get as far as this, of course) On a second mirror invisible to him but visible to his neighbours, ambulance, asylum, cemetery appear successively.

Plate 3: C.S. Lewis, Letters to Owen Barfield, "The Great War", fol. 78.

Barfield, he felt, exalted the imagination at the expense of reason and the sciences; he was preoccupied with a mythical, allegedly more participatory and holistic existence in the past and lost touch with the realities of modern life; his preoccupation with the imagination and with the past meant that he did not meet, but evaded the challenges of modern thought and life. In short, his approach was anti-rationalistic, backward-looking and escapist. This is how one might boldly sum up Lewis's criticism of Barfield – it must be admitted, though, that Lewis's criticism is far more subtle and complex than this.[29]

Although Barfield does not blatantly express any extreme anti-rationalistic or indeed reactionary views, there is a certain danger in his approach, to lend support to such views. This danger, we remember, is already inherent in Coleridge whose position, as I have pointed out, can easily be misunderstood as being profoundly anti-rationalistic and essentially escapist. Lewis alerted Barfield to this danger. Barfield therefore recognized and valued Lewis's criticism as an important and valid criticism. He admits: "I owe quite a lot to Lewis. He forced me to think my position out responsibly and fully, to defend it against his" [Diener 1995; Appendix, 249].

One of the results was that he did not abandon himself to merely abstract, or mystical speculations about an allegedly more holistic, participatory past; instead he concerned himself with the question of what wholeness and participation meant to modern man, and how it could be realized under the conditions of modern life.[30] From the mid

---

[29] For a more detailed interpretation of the "Great War" letters, cf. Adey 1978.

[30] In this we may locate the roots of the important distinction between "original" and "final participation" in *Saving the Appearances* (1957): "The systematic use of imagination, then, will be requisite in the future, not only for the increase of knowledge, but also for saving the appearances from chaos and inanity. Nor need it involve any relinquishment of the ability which we have won to love nature as objective and independent of ourselves. Indeed, it cannot involve that. For any relinquishment would mean that what was taking place was not an approach towards final participation (which is the proper goal of imagination) but an attempt to revert to original participation (which is the

1920s onwards we therefore find that he began to interest himself in this question also in a seriously practical manner.[31] All in all, we may conclude, Barfield's concern from the mid 1920s, not only with a *theoretical* justification of the value of the imagination, but also with questions of its *practical* application, owes much to Lewis's down-to-earth criticism.

It is evident that Barfield valued Lewis's criticism as much as Lewis valued Barfield's. Barfield acknowledges this by dedicating *Poetic Diction* to Lewis with the Blakean epigraph: "Opposition is true friendship" – a dedication which Lewis accepted, as he puts it, with a "mixture of hidden sentimentalism, genuine friendship, common vanity, and downright yankee love of advertisement".[32]

---

goal of pantheism, of mediumism and of much so-called occultism)." Barfield 1988, 146–7.

[31] Examples of how seriously and systematically he concerned himself with e.g. questions of social and economic reform include *Danger, Ugliness and Waste* (1925?), "Financial Inquiry", (December 1929), and "The Relation between the Economics of C.H. Douglas and those of Rudolf Steiner". For more examples, cf. Tennyson 1976, 227–39.

[32] Undated Letter, in Lewis n.d., Letters to Owen Barfield, fol. 42. Note that this warm response comes directly after the attack in which he accuses Barfield of solipsism!

II.
The Anthroposophical Background

In many of his books Barfield has acknowledged his debt to Rudolf Steiner (1861-1925), the founder of anthroposophy. He has also expressed his disappointment at the fact that sympathetic readers of his own books approach anthroposophy, if at all, only reluctantly or else with prejudice [Barfield 1986e, 17]. In spite of his repeated insistence on his debt to Steiner, Barfield scholars have given very little consideration to anthroposophy, or have ignored it altogether. This is, perhaps, not surprising, considering the sheer bulk of Steiner's work. The founder of anthroposophy has left us with a huge legacy. During his life-time he published more than twenty monographs and several volumes of collected essays. Since his death his autobiography, letters and hundreds of separate lectures have been published. And there is still more material being prepared for future publication. The list of topics he wrote and talked about is extraordinary in its variety. It spans philosophy, the sciences, religion, the occult and numerous other fields. A solid philosophical base underpins the vast edifice of his ideas, and a number of his initiatives have led to practical applications, for instance, in education, art, medicine and agriculture.

There are isolated attempts to compare and contrast various of Steiner's themes and ideas with those of Barfield [cf. eg. Grant 1982, and Adey 1978, 25–31]. There is, however, no satisfactory study of Barfield that would attempt an investigation into the philosophical base of anthroposophy. Students of Barfield seem generally reluctant to engage in a more detailed and systematic examination of the principles of anthroposophy. There is, moreover, a curious lack of interest in Steiner's own intellectual context and development, with a consequent lack of any real insight into the driving force, significance and impact of Steiner's approach. It is illuminating to learn something about Steiner as a source of Barfield. But in order to understand the real importance of Steiner for Barfield we cannot avoid asking other, perhaps, more urgent questions, such as: What are the principles of anthroposophy? What are its implications and consequences? What is its significance for (and impact on) the general intellectual development of the late nineteenth and early twentieth centuries? How and why did Barfield get interested in anthroposophy? And what exactly does it offer that was of more importance to him than any other system of ideas? No serious Barfield scholar can ignore these questions.

This chapter is an account of the philosophical premises and essential teachings of anthroposophy. It also discusses the role of anthroposophy in its wider intellectual context. My aim is, first, to determine the precise points and actual extent of Steiner's influence on Barfield. Secondly, the discussion of anthroposophy in a wider context is intended to shed some more light on the larger intellectual developments in which Barfield is involved. I hope to be able thus to create a better understanding of Barfield's own special contribution to, and his position within this development.

1. Steiner and Anthroposophy

From Steiner's earliest philosophical reflections to his esoteric writings and practical concerns there is one theme that runs persistently through the whole of his work. It is the theme of the relation between idea and reality, subject and object, mind and body, spirit and matter. In his childhood he had a mystical experience that confronted him with the extraordinary. Soon he began, in an as yet childlike manner, to distinguish between things "which 'are seen' and those which are 'not seen'" – a distinction that would gradually grow into the conviction that there must be a spiritual world that is as real as the physical world. As a schoolboy he was especially interested in geometry as a field where knowledge is gained purely through the mind's own operation. This experience of an independent life of the mind seemed to parallel his earlier spiritual experience and gave him some kind of a justification for it. In his autobiography he gives the following account of his ideas as they developed over a period of time up to the age of about twenty:

> I said to myself: 'The objects and occurrences which the senses perceive are in space. But, just as this space is outside man, so there exists within man a sort of soul-space which is

the scene of action of spiritual beings and occurrences'. I could not look upon thoughts as something like images which the human being forms of things; on the contrary, I saw in them revelations of a spiritual world on this field of action in the soul. Geometry seemed to me to be a knowledge which appears to be produced by man, but which, nevertheless, has a significance quite independent of him. Naturally, I did not as a child say this to myself distinctly, but I felt that one must carry knowledge of a spiritual world within oneself after the manner of geometry.

For the reality of the spiritual world was to me as certain as that of the physical. [...] With regard to geometry, I said to myself: 'Here one *is permitted* to know something which the mind alone through its own power experiences'. In this feeling I found the justification for speaking of the spiritual world that I experienced just as of the physical. [Steiner 1951, 11–2; cf. also Note 1, 197]

Notice the close relation that Steiner perceived between mind and spirit. It is interesting that he linked spiritual experience with mental operations such as those performed in geometry. Steiner was looking for a way of approaching the spiritual by making it accessible to the mind through thinking. This passage reveals an early desire to be able to speak of spiritual experience as a kind of knowledge. He was convinced that such knowledge was as real and as valuable as the knowledge of the physical and material, and he was eager to find a way of justifying this conviction.

We ought to consider this urge for a justification against the background of Steiner's education. Steiner, who enjoyed a predominantly scientific training, received secondary education at a period when scientific materialism was beginning to determine the general outlook of the nineteenth century. He encountered mechanistic and atomistic theories of nature, but realized that such theories did not account for either mind or spirit. For a clarification of the actual link between mind and spirit on the one hand and nature as the sciences presented it to him on the other he turned to Kant. That there might be a link between the two he was, however, not exactly encouraged to believe. For his precocious reading of Kant at the age of fifteen had appeared to suggest that Kant believed the exact opposite – that there was no link. With his concept of an inaccessible *Ding-an-sich* Kant divorced the mind from reality and thereby advocated a dualism that inspired, equally, subjective idealism and hard core materialism. In the sciences this dualism encouraged the development of a pure interest in the material at the expense of mind and spirit, and in all other fields it nourished the general sense of an unbridgeable gap between the two. In due course, Steiner would return to Kant with a full-blown refutation of his ideas, but at that early stage, he read him apparently quite uncritically, and without much profit. Kant simply didn't help Steiner, for Steiner's was a different direction, as he tells us in his autobiography:

> [...] I was constantly occupied with the question of the scope of the human capacity for thinking. It seemed to me that thinking can be developed to a faculty which actually lays hold upon the things and occurrences of the world. A 'substance' which remains outside thinking, which we can merely reflect about, was to me an unendurable conception. Whatever is in things, this must enter into human thought, I said to myself again and again. [Steiner 1951, 26; cf. also Note 2, 197]

As this passage reveals, Steiner was unconvinced by a view that reduced reality to the material, thereby relegating mental activity and spiritual experience to the realm of subjective abstractions. So he moved on from Kant in search of a different approach. He continued his scientific education at the Technical University of Vienna where he read mathematics, physics and the history of natural science (*Naturgeschichte*). Meanwhile he also carried on studying philosophy, notably German idealism (Schelling and Fichte), but real inspiration came for him only with his discovery of Goethe. His enthusiasm for Goethe eventually led to his appointment as the editor of Goethe's scientific writings at the Goethe-Schiller-Archive in Weimar. Steiner's encounter with Goethe proved seminal to his own subsequent creative career. In Goethe he found an author who does not exclude mind from reality and idea from nature, but includes them. He distinguishes between the two but does not separate them. For him the difference between the two is one of degree, not kind. His basic premise is founded on the Platonic concept of the idea as the underlying principle in nature. Ideas are, in his view, not something applied to, but inherent in nature, and it is in the human mind that nature reveals herself in her essence:

> She (Nature) has thought and she broods unceasingly, not as a man but as Nature ... She has neither language nor speech, but she creates tongues and hearts through which she speaks and feels. It was not I that spoke of her. Nay, it was she who spoke it all, true and false. [Steiner 1928, 34; cf. also Note 3, 197]

Steiner shared these views and emulated Goethe, as in that important passage where he compares thinking to a plant, vehemently contradicting the view that thinking is a subjective abstraction from reality.

> The naive consciousness [...] treats thinking as something which has nothing to do with things, but stands altogether aloof from them and contemplates them. The picture which the thinker makes of the phenomena of the world is regarded not as something belonging to the things but as existing only in the human head. The world is complete with all its substances and forces, and of this ready-made world man makes a picture. Whoever thinks thus need only be asked one question. What right have you to declare the world to be complete without thinking? Does not the world produce thinking in the heads of men with the same necessity as it produces the blossom on a plant? Plant a seed in the earth. It puts forth root and stem, it unfolds into leaves and blossoms. Set the plant before yourself. It connects itself, in your mind, with a definite concept. Why should this concept belong any less to the whole plant than leaf and blossom? [Steiner 1964, 65; cf. also Note 4, 197]

The ideal was a reality for Goethe, and thinking was something alive, not dead and abstract. And it was in Goethe, not Kant, that Steiner found the guidelines for his own approach. But unlike Goethe, who disliked theorizing, Steiner felt the need to give his convictions a theoretical basis. Thus, starting from Goethe's premises, he developed a theory of knowledge which became the intellectual foundation of anthroposophy. He developed his new theory in the introductions to Goethe's scientific writings (1883-1897) and three other books, *Grundlinien einer Erkenntnistheorie der Goetheschen Weltanschauung* (1886), *Wahrheit und Wissenschaft* (1892) and *Die Philosophie der Freiheit* (1894), which he considered to be his most important work. Steiner's explicit aim is to refute dualism and the subjectivism it inspires, and to argue the case for an "objective idealism".

> But we cherish the hope that we have laid the ground for an overcoming of the subjectivism that clings to the epistemologies connected with Kant. And we believe we have done this by showing that the subjective form in which the world picture arises for the act of knowledge – before science works upon this picture – is only a necessary transitional stage that is then overcome in the process of knowledge itself. [...] And in showing this, we establish *objective idealism* as the necessary consequence of an epistemology that understands itself. [Steiner 1993, 3; cf. also Note 5, 198]

Inspired by German idealism (especially Fichte), Steiner makes his starting point the individual ego and the role of thinking. He begins by pointing out the paradox that dualism divides thinking from the thing, but makes this division only by means of thinking itself. For Steiner it is consequently necessary, before making a statement about anything else, to explore, first of all, thinking itself. Our knowledge of things always involves, and depends on thinking, he says, and therefore it is important to understand the role of thinking in the process of acquiring knowledge. This process involves, according to Steiner, two elements, the percept (his term for the object of our observation) and the concept (his term for the result of our thinking). Steiner explains that in the cognitive process, every real thing presents itself to us from these two sides, from perceiving and from thinking. The two sides are complementary, as he shows in the following passage:

> The separate facts appear in their true significance, both in themselves and for the rest of the world, only when thinking spins its threads from one entity to another. This activity of thinking is one *full of content*. [...] Thinking offers this content to the percept, from man's world of concepts and ideas. In contrast to the content of the percept which is given to us from without, the content of thinking appears inwardly. The form in which this first makes its appearance we will call *intuition*. *Intuition is for thinking what observation is for the percept. Intuition and observation are the sources of our knowledge.* An observed object of the world remains unintelligible to us until we have within ourselves the corresponding intuition which adds that part of the reality which is lacking in the percept. To anyone who is incapable of finding intuitions corresponding to the things, the full reality remains inaccessible. Just as the colour-blind person sees only differences of brightness without any colour qualities, so can

the person without intuition observe only unconnected perceptual fragments. [Steiner 1964, 73–4; cf. also Note 6, 198]

So, according to these observations, the percept is only one side of the total reality; thinking provides the complementary other side, and full knowledge comes, in a creative act, with a fusion of both. Steiner concludes: The fact that our understanding, or knowledge, of reality involves these two elements, concept and percept, idea and thing, has something to do purely with our own mental organization, not with reality itself. He partly agrees with the dualists, namely on a distinction between percept and concept, thinking and thing, but disagrees with them in that he limits a split between the two to the cognitive level alone while the dualists take this split in consciousness as the ontologically fundamental characteristic of reality itself. For Steiner the split is not an absolute one. In his view it is a natural by-product of our self-consciousness.

> Human consciousness is the stage upon which concept and observation meet and become linked to one another. In saying this we have in fact characterized this (human) consciousness. It is the mediator between thinking and observation. [...] We regard the thing as *object* and ourselves as thinking *subject*. Because we direct our thinking upon our observation, we have consciousness of objects; because we direct it upon ourselves, we have consciousness of ourselves, or *self-consciousness*. Human consciousness must of necessity be at the same time self-consciousness because it is a consciousness which *thinks*. [...] It is just this which constitutes our double nature of man. He thinks, and thereby embraces both himself and the rest of the world. But at the same time it is by means of thinking that he determines himself as an *individual* confronting the *things*. [Steiner 1964, 42–3; cf. also Note 7, 199]

With the help of thinking we can become aware of ourselves as thinking individuals and thereby create a contrast between ourselves and an external world of objects. In a process in which we become conscious of ourselves we begin to distinguish between, and then separate the self from the world, subject from object and the ideal from the material, eventually excluding the one from the other. But since this division is one that occurs in consciousness through thinking it can be reversed again through thinking. Or, in other words, it is the mind itself that provides the link between the ideal and the material, and consciousness, as Steiner puts it, is the "mediator" between the two.

Steiner's reflections in his theory of knowledge on the arrival of self-consciousness through thinking implies the idea of an evolution of consciousness. In *Die Philosophie der Freiheit* he explored this idea on the cognitive level. In subsequent works he investigated it from an historical point of view. *Die Rätsel der Philosophie* (1900/14), for instance, is not a history of philosophy in the ordinary sense. For here Steiner treats the developments in philosophy as evidence of how consciousness evolves in time.

Steiner identifies four phases in history during which he observes a gradual transformation from a more pictorial consciousness to a consciousness dominated by thinking. He locates the first changes in ancient Greece, with the rise of philosophy and the attempt to gain an understanding of the world through thought and thinking. This is, according to Steiner, very different from an earlier type of consciousness, the mythical consciousness, where man related to the phenomena of the world through images. In an important passage in *Die Rätsel der Philosophie*, which will be quoted here in full, he puts it as follows:

> For the thought habits of our time it seems acceptable to imagine that man in archaic times had observed natural elements – wind and weather, the growth of seeds, the course of the stars – and then poetically *invented* spiritual beings as the active creators of these events. It is, however, far from the contemporary mode of thinking to recognize the possibility that man in older times experienced those pictures as he later experienced thought, that is, as an inner reality of his soul life.
>
> One will gradually come to recognize that in the course of the evolution of mankind a transformation of the human organization has taken place. There was a time when the subtle organs of human nature, which make possible the development of an independent thought-life, had not yet been formed. In this time man had, instead, organs that represented for him what he experienced in the world of pictures.
>
> As this gradually comes to be understood, a new light will fall on the significance of mythology on the one hand, and that of

poetic production and thought-life on the other. When the independent inner thought-experience began, it brought the picture-consciousness to extinction. Thought emerged as the tool of truth. This is only one branch of what survived of the old picture-consciousness that had found its expression in the ancient myth. In another branch the extinguished picture-consciousness continued to live, if only as a pale shadow of its former existence, in the creations of fantasy and poetic imagination. Poetic fantasy and the intellectual view of the world are the two children of the one mother, the old picture-consciousness that must not be confused with the consciousness of poetic imagination. [Steiner 1973, 14–5; cf. also Note 8, 199]

Steiner makes an interesting link between the pictorial consciousness of the earliest times and the poetic imagination of later ages. The two are related but not identical. The pictorial consciousness is, according to Steiner, a *dream-like* consciousness in which man does as yet not differentiate himself from the external world. Poetry, in contrast, depends on a *conscious* act of creation. It is a product of the self-conscious individual. Steiner insists that the self-consciousness of later ages must not be read back into the past. Instead we must examine how it developed. The first step towards self-consciousness occurs where man does not any more relate to the phenomena of the world through images. Steiner points out that through the image man is intimately linked to the world, through thinking he begins to set himself apart from it:

> It is in Greece that the aspiration is born to gain knowledge of the world and its laws by means of an element that can be acknowledged as *thought* also in the present age. As long as the human soul conceives world phenomena through pictures, it feels itself intimately bound up with them. The soul feels itself in this phase to be a member of the world organism; it does not think of itself as an independent entity separated from this organism. As the pure pictureless thought awakens in the human soul the soul begins to feel its separation from the world. Thought becomes the soul's educator for independence. [Steiner 1973, 6; cf. also Note 9, 200]

So, thinking leads to autonomy, that is, to an experience by the individual of independence from the external world. Again, Steiner warns that we must not confuse our modern experience of thought and thinking with the experience conveyed to us in Greek philosophy. To modern man thoughts and ideas occur exclusively *in* the mind and are *applied* to the external world. They are experienced as abstractions. In contrast, in Greek philosophy thoughts and ideas appear not as emerging just from within the mind, but as actually emanating from the external world itself. That is, in other words, the outer and the inner are as yet not experienced as entirely unlinked entities; and thought is still experienced as forming a link between the two. Greek philosophy is therefore only the *beginning* of a process leading man to experience himself as an independent, self-conscious individual:

> But the ancient Greek did not experience thought as modern man does. This is a fact that can be easily overlooked. A genuine insight into the ancient Greek's thought life will reveal the essential difference. The ancient Greek's experience of thought is comparable to our experience of a perception, to our experience of 'red' or 'yellow'. Just as we today attribute a color or tone percept to a 'thing', so the ancient Greek perceives thought *in* the world of things and as adhering to them. It is for this reason that thought at that time still is the connecting link between soul and world. The process of separation between soul and world is just beginning; it has not yet been completed. To be sure, the soul feels the thought within itself, but it must be of the opinion to have received it from the world and it can therefore expect the solution of the world riddles from its thought experience. [Steiner 1973, 6–7; cf. also Note 10, 200].[33]

According to Steiner, the whole development in Greek philosophy, beginning, roughly, with Pherekydes of Syros and culminating in Plato and Aristotle is leading up to the experience of an inner life that is separate from the external world. Man begins to experience his thoughts not any more as emanations from nature, but as products of the mind. This is the birth of individual self-consciousness.

---

[33] Cf. T.S. Eliot who expresses a similar idea of the unity of thought and feeling. This unity, in Eliot's view, was still intact in the seventeenth but had disappeared by the nineteenth century: "Tennyson and Browning [...] do not feel their thought as immediately as the odour of a rose. A thought to Donne was an experience [...]." Eliot 1986b, 287.

During the following period, from the rise of Christianity until about the ninth century A.D., the by now self-conscious individual finds himself still thoroughly embedded in a context outside himself – through religious experience. However, a marked change occurs during the scholastic period. By now the experience of thinking as an utterly inner experience is felt so strongly that it becomes increasingly uncertain *how* this inner experience relates to the outer world. The link between thought and world that had been taken for granted in Greek philosophy, and that had not been a philosophical problem in the early Middle Ages, now becomes a matter of philosophical investigation. The question, debated during that period by the nominalists and the realists, as to the nature of universals and their relation to reality, is a clear expression of this new trend. This period is characterized by Steiner as follows:

> The leading philosophers feel the re-awakening of the energy of thought-life. For centuries the human soul had been inwardly consolidated through the experience of its self-dependence. It now begins to search for what it might claim as its innermost self possession. It finds that this is its thought-life. Everything else is given from without; thought is felt as something the soul has to produce out of its own depth, that is, the soul is present in full consciousness at this process of production. The urge arises in the soul to gain in thought a knowledge through which it can enlighten itself about its own relation to the world. How can something be expressed in thought-life that is not itself merely the soul's own product? [...] The human soul attempts to examine its thought-life with regard to its content of reality. [Steiner 1973, 8–9; cf. also Note 11, 200]

These developments lead up to the fourth phase in the evolution of consciousness which Steiner dates roughly from the scientific revolution. In the course of the three previous phases man has become conscious of himself: he has turned his attention to the exploration of his own inner self, and it has consequently become possible for him to experience an independence from nature. At the same time nature has come to be seen as independent from man as well. That is, a view of nature has arisen that strictly divides nature as an outward objective world from the inner subjective world of individual insight. The result is that outer and inner have come to be seen as separate, utterly unrelated entities.

> In the fourth period a picture of nature emerges that has detached itself in turn from the inner soul life. The tendency arises to think of nature in such a way that nothing is allowed to be mixed into its conception that has been derived from the soul and not exclusively from nature itself. Thus, the soul is, in this period, expelled from nature, and with its inner experiences confined to its subjective world. The soul is about to be forced to admit that everything it can gain as knowledge by itself can have a significance only for itself. It cannot find in itself anything to point to a world in which this soul could have its roots with its true being. For in the picture of nature it cannot find any trace of itself. [Steiner 1973, 10; cf. also Note 12, 201]

Steiner traces this tendency of dividing outward observance and inner experience from writers such as Francis Bacon and David Hume to the elaborate, dualistic philosophy of Kant. He further explains that by the nineteenth century the generally accepted view of the world has become the scientific outlook. In this view, reality is considered to be the external world as a self-contained entity that is independent of the human mind. The human being is now just an onlooker, a passive recipient who forms a picture of this reality rather than participating in it *with* his mind. Steiner points out that much of the influential nineteenth century philosophy, such as the English empirical philosophy of Mill and Spencer, for example, depends on this view.

> Spencer and Mill exerted a great influence on the development of world conception in the second half of the nineteenth century. The rigorous emphasis on observation and the one-sided elaboration of the methods of observational knowledge of Mill, along with the application of the conceptions of natural science to the entire scope of human knowledge by Spencer could not fail to meet with the approval of an age that saw in the individualistic world conception of Fichte, Schelling and Hegel nothing but denigration of human thinking. It was an age that showed appreciation only for the successes of the research work of natural science. [Steiner 1973, 347; cf. also Note 13, 201]

Philosophers like Mill and Spencer, according to Steiner, have helped to establish the view that there is no real knowledge outside science. This is a view which has held a strong attraction up to the present day.

G. S. Carter, for example, comments on these developments and their effect:

> Before the middle of the century, the success of the chemists in synthesizing some compounds previously known only from living bodies, and of physiologists in showing that physical laws can be applied to many of the activities of the organisms, suggested that the same materialistic system could be extended to the phenomena of biology. Not merely physiological activities but behaviour, habit and the whole realm of psychology were then assumed to be equally open to the same type of investigation as the phenomena of physics, and it was therefore concluded that they were of the same materialistic nature. From this it was an easy step to the claim that the scientific method is the only means of acquiring knowledge, that there is no real knowledge outside science, a view that has been held by many in more recent times. [Carter, 26][34]

In Steiner's view, then, the evolution of consciousness is an historical process in which man develops through thinking an increasing awareness of himself as an individual. But it is only during the last phase of this evolution, which Steiner roughly dates from the scientific revolution, that man's self-awareness leads him to a definite sense of independence from nature. This sense of independence encourages him to regard his own inner life as something that is not only separate from, but entirely unrelated to nature. At the same time it allows him to interpret nature in materialistic terms. By the early twentieth century, as Steiner observes in his book, materialism is so deeply rooted in consciousness that it is being taken for granted. However, the purpose of his book is precisely to show that it does not need to be taken for granted. He acknowledges its merits, but at the same time he questions its claim to absolute truth by viewing it as part of a larger evolution in which it can have a claim only to partial truth. From the perspective of this larger evolution he concludes that

---

[34] The most popular example of this view in recent times is Richard Dawkins with his fondness for remarks, such as: "We are survival machines – robot vehicles blindly programmed to preserve the selfish molecules known as genes. This is a truth which still fills me with astonishment." Dawkins, v.

materialistic interpretations of the world are not in themselves invalid or wrong but become wrong if they exclude mind and spirit.

> It cannot be the task of an historical presentation to fight materialism or to distort it into a caricature, for within its limits it is justified. It is right to represent materialistically those processes of the world that have a material cause. We only go astray when we do not arrive at the insight that comes when, in pursuing the material processes, we are finally led to the conception of the spirit. [Steiner 1973, xvii; cf. also Note 14, 201]

Steiner's repudiation of a rigid subject-object dualism, based on his philosophical and historical investigations, enables him to criticise both materialism and its opposite without entirely rejecting either. This is why his attitude to contemporary occultism is as ambiguous as his attitude to materialism. In order to clarify Steiner's position further and to understand the actual significance of anthroposophy when it eventually emerged as an independent movement I shall finally consider Steiner's attitude to theosophy, an occult movement to which Steiner was attracted and linked for a certain period.

Theosophy, as it was popularised by the Theosophical Society (founded in 1875), reacted to a general sense of dissatisfaction with Western philosophical and religious traditions in the late nineteenth century, and responded to a vast longing for insights and experiences beyond the merely material. For an experience of such insights it relied on spiritualism, hypnotism and other parapsychological phenomena, and for spiritual illumination it turned to the practices of Eastern religions in preference to those of the West. Steiner made a first acquaintance with theosophy during his student years in Vienna. Amongst the theosophists, whom he called "homeless souls" and "true searchers", he encountered a sympathetic audience for his own ideas, which led him later, between 1902 and 1913, to accept the presidency over the German section of the Theosophical Society [Wehr 1993, 4]. Steiner had much in common with those "true searchers", who, like him, were deeply concerned with an invisible world which they held to be as real as the material world. But in spite of his original sympathies with the Society's cause he became sceptical of its approach.

The difference between Steiner's and the theosophical approach is apparent, for instance, in Steiner's disagreement with Friedrich Eckstein, the head of the Austrian section of the Society and a close friend of Steiner's in Vienna. Eckstein, a convinced follower of Kant, held that knowledge of the extraordinary could not be treated like ordinary knowledge and that it was a matter for initiates to obtain, guard and administer such special knowledge.[35] The philosophical base behind such views is clearly a dualistic concept of knowledge. On the whole, in its outlook theosophy is dualistic. It is anti-rationalistic and anti-materialistic, but has, nonetheless, something in common with the scientific materialism which it rejects: it is as exclusive as its counterpart. It does not allow for any link between the rational and the non-rational, esoteric knowledge and ordinary (exoteric) knowledge, idea and matter, and can therefore account for the one only at the expense of the other.

An approach like that of the theosophists was untenable for Steiner. In contrast, he made an attempt to give his ideas a rational basis. He wanted his approach to be as lucid as that of a science. He objected to spiritualistic practices (such as communications with the other world through mediums in a condition of trance), and insisted that spiritual knowledge must and can be conscious and clear:

> The present task of spiritual knowledge is to bring the experience of ideas, in full clarity of mind, into connection with the spiritual world by means of the will to knowledge. The cognizing human being then has a content of mind which is experienced like that of mathematics. He thinks like a mathematician. But he does not think in numbers or in geometrical figures. He thinks in pictures of the world of

---

[35] For a summary of Eckstein's views cf. Steiner 1951, 295: "Friedrich Eckstein represented vigorously the conviction that esoteric spiritual knowledge should not be publicly propagated like ordinary knowledge. He was not alone in this conviction; it was and is that of almost all experts in the 'ancient wisdom'. [...] [He] wished that what was dealt with publicly by an 'initiate in the ancient knowledge' should be endued with the force that comes from this 'initiation', but that the exoteric should be strictly separated from the esoteric, which should remain within the most restricted circle which understands how to value it fully." Steiner 1951, 295; cf. also Note 15, 202.

spirit. In contrast to the ancient waking-dream cognizing of the spirit, it is a fully conscious standing-within the spiritual world. [...] Within the Theosophical Society, it was impossible to gain a true relation with this cognizing of the spirit. Distrust was aroused as soon as full consciousness sought to enter into a relation with the spiritual world. Full consciousness was known only for the sense-world. No true feeling existed for the development of this up to the point of experiencing the spirit. What was aimed at was really to return to the ancient dream-consciousness, with the suppression of full consciousness. [Steiner 1951, 326; cf. also Note 16, 202]

How Steiner arrived at this conviction was discussed above. In *Die Philosophie der Freiheit*, we saw that Steiner regarded the split between idea and thing, spirit and matter as a split that occurs merely on a cognitive level. The fact that this split is experienced as an objective reality, as Steiner then demonstrated in *Die Rätsel der Philosophie*, is a result of historical changes of consciousness, and should not be trusted as veridical. His conclusion is that if the split occurs in the mind much depends on the mind itself to overcome the very split it has itself created:

Wer die hier angedeuteten Gesichtspunkte zu den seinigen machen kann, gewinnt die Möglichkeit, mit seinem Seelenleben in dem selbstbewußten Ich die fruchtbare Wirklichkeit verbunden zu denken. Das is die Anschauung, zu welcher die philosophische Entwickelung seit dem griechischen Zeitalter hinstrebt und die in der Weltanschauung Goethes ihre ersten deutlich erkennbaren Spuren gezeigt hat. – Es wird erkannt, daß dieses selbstbewußte Ich nicht in sich isoliert und außerhalb der objektiven Welt sich erlebt, daß vielmehr sein Losgelöstsein von dieser Welt nur eine Erscheinung des Bewußtseins ist, die überwunden werden kann, überwunden dadurch, daß man einsieht, man habe als Mensch in einem gewissen Entwickelungszustande eine vorübergehende Gestalt des Ich dadurch zu eigen, daß man die Kräfte, welche die Seele mit der Welt verbinden aus dem Bewußtsein herausdrängt. [Steiner 1985, 601]

Therefore Steiner has no doubt that spiritual knowledge has its root in ordinary thinking. This is why he rejected the idea of having to turn for such knowledge to extraordinary means and to external sources, such as mediums, initiates, or gurus. His idea was that everyone could be his or her own guru – through mental training.

It was inevitable that sooner or later views of the kind which Steiner held would lead to a breach with the Theosophical Society. Over the years the German Section of the Society had taken a new direction under Steiner's influence. In 1913, the Theosophical headquarters answered this change of direction with the exclusion of the German section from the society. The foundation of a separate society, the Anthroposophical Society, followed in the same year. Through Steiner's focus on the individual – man's innate abilities to develop his mind and (re)gain knowledge beyond the material – had gradually transformed *theo*sophy into *anthro*posophy, divine wisdom into human wisdom.

2. A Critical Evaluation of Steiner's Work

Through Steiner's original involvement with the Theosophical Society, anthroposophy has been closely associated with theosophy. By virtue of this association, anthroposophy has been classed with the "theosophical teachings" which were condemned by the Catholic church in 1919 – a condemnation that is still valid [cf. Denzinger, 986]. According to a strict interpretation of Catholic dogma, anthroposophy is a "neugnostische Irrlehre" ("a neognostic heresy") [cf. eg. Simmel vol. i, 631]. In this view, Steiner is guilty of blurring, and eventually confusing the differences between e.g. ordinary thinking and spiritual experience, human knowledge and divine revelation, the merely human and the absolute, to name only a few of the essential distinctions [cf. Grom vol. i, 737–41]. In contradiction to this view, it is possible to show, as I have been trying to do above, that Steiner very well respected the distinctions on which Catholic dogma insists so uncompromisingly, and that he too distinguishes between the two areas very carefully. However, as we have seen, he regards the difference between the two areas as one not of kind but of degree. That is, in Steiner's view, there is a possible not necessarily an easy transition from the one area to the other. From this point of view the criticism of neognosticism is valid to the extent that, in spite of the differentiation, a confusion of the two areas can occur easily and is always latent in anthroposophy.

Sometimes anthroposophy has been described as being a "religious system" [cf. eg. Hooper, 748]. This description is at first mildly surprising. If religion implies dogma, Steiner, with his notably undogmatic emphasis on the "philosophy of freedom" is far from seeking devout reverence to his own insights.[36] Yet the description may after all be justified if Steiner's very individualism, with its appeal to the individual's own powers of discernment and insight, is seen as aspiring to the status of religious dogma. Moreover, even if Steiner was himself possibly fairly liberal concerning his own insights, his followers have not always been as critical and as free-spirited as he would have wished them to be. In fact, almost as soon as the Anthroposophical Society was founded, it was accused of idolizing its mentor (originally Steiner was not a member), and of administering Steiner's work as an orthodox body of beliefs rather than a network of thoughts which is open to criticism and further changes. Such criticism has persisted and has been raised by both anthroposophists and non-anthroposophists.[37]

A final point of criticism that can be raised against Steiner is that his historical outlook appears to glorify a paradisal state, somewhere in a mythical past, of a wholesome integration of man and nature, body and soul, mind and matter – a state from which we seem to have fallen in the course of history. Whether Steiner is correct in his judgement on the individual periods of history which he explores is up to the expert historian to verify. However, even in spite of the necessarily limited perspective of this study, it is, I hope, fair to

---

[36] More often than not Steiner warned his readers and his audience not to follow his own conclusions blindly, but to test his insights against their *own* experiences. Cf. e.g. his reservations in *Occult Science: An Outline*: "The author frankly confesses: he would like readers who will not accept what is here presented on blind faith, but rather put it to the test of their own insight and experience of life. [...] Credulity too easily mistakes folly and superstition for the truth." Steiner 1962–3, 24; cf. also Note 17, 202.

[37] Cf. e.g. Lissau 155–7, and van der Meulen, as examples of an 'insider's' criticism of anthroposophy. For an 'outsider's' view, cf. Badewien.

conclude that the above criticism is justified, but only to some degree. For Steiner's perspective is forward-looking and progressive despite a somewhat conservative and backward-looking aspect to it. That is, he looks into the past not for a remedy, but for points of comparison and contrast with the present. The view of history he thus establishes helps to put into perspective the developments of the present age rather than merely condemning certain aspects of this development without considering their positive value as well. That is, Steiner is able fully to appreciate the development towards the experience of individual self-consciousness while at the same time identifying some of its negative consequences. As a 'remedy' for these negative consequences, he by no means recommends a mindless plunge back into the past. As we have seen, his method, in contrast to that of the theosophists, is not to overcome individual self-consciousness, but to develop it. His approach *starts* from individual self-consciousness, instead of circumnavigating it. He asks the individual to deepen and to expand consciousness, not to abandon it. It must be said, however, that Steiner's approach, like the theosophists', reveals a strong element of cultural criticism. In that respect, he must be seen in one line with the cultural critics of the nineteenth and early twentieth centuries, including the theosophists. For a fair evaluation of the historical importance of anthroposophy, it is therefore necessary, finally, to discuss Steiner's position and his own unique contribution to the cultural criticism of his own time.

3. A Historical Evaluation of Steiner's Work

Steiner lived at a time which marks a turning point in European thought. On the one hand, we encounter in the nineteenth century an optimistic belief in scientific, material and social progress, inherited from the eighteenth century and reinforced by the Darwinian revolution. On the other hand we can observe an increasingly critical attitude to the consequences of this progress. This tendency was, moreover, confirmed and increased by the experience of the First World War and resulted in an unprecedented cultural pessimism [cf. Topitsch, 300, and Carr, 38]. Historical evolution could no longer be uncritically identified with cultural progress. It is in such a context that we must see Steiner's work on the evolution of consciousness, and his concern with the consequences of scientific and technical progress for culture, society and the individual. His thought sprang from an acute sense of crisis which he shared with the more important critical minds of the nineteenth and early twentieth centuries. His thought was influenced to some degree by Friedrich Nietzsche, for example, as is shown by his detailed study entitled *Friedrich Nietzsche: Ein Kämpfer gegen seine Zeit* (1895). The link to Nietzsche is an interesting and important one. For Nietzsche became one of *the* leading figures of a wholly new generation of critical writers and thinkers since the late nineteenth century. With Nietzsche, Jacob Burckhardt and Oswald Spengler, to name only a few, Steiner can be counted among this new generation of cultural critics, and can easily stand comparison with the others.[38] The originality of a thinker, as Eugen Fridell has pointed out, lies not only in his ability to develop a set of entirely new ideas, but also in his gift to recognize, and to incorporate in his ideas what is of urgent general concern to his times and contemporaries [Fridell, 47]. I hope to show that Steiner meets both of these criteria.[39]

The points of interest for Steiner in Nietzsche are numerous. Especially important in this context is Nietzsche's notorious attack on the sciences. By "the sciences" ("die Wissenschaften") he sometimes

---

[38] Cf. Frye, 7–9, on two major views of history. The first is a U-shaped parabola (prominent e.g. in Gibbon): antiquity declines into barbarism but then revives with a new rise to civility. This view grew into a theory of steady progress supported by Darwin's theory of evolution. The second view is an inverted U-shape which Frye conceives as Romantic. Here the peak is in the middle ages to be followed by a steady decline. By Steiner's time, this 'down-we-come' view is beginning to replace the earlier 'up-we go' enthusiasm. According to Frye, Oswald Spengler's "is the most coherent statement of the theory of Western decline".

[39] There is as yet no comprehensive study of Steiner that relates him with other comparable thinkers. One helpful book is Wehr's, *C.G. Jung und Rudolf Steiner: Konfrontation und Synopse* which compares Steiner with the psychoanalyst. Cf. also another book by the same author *Rudolf Steiner: Leben, Erkenntnis, Kulturimpuls*, a study of Steiner that considers the intellectual context in a more general way. For a study that explores work on Nietzsche, including Steiner's own contribution, cf. Hoffmann.

means the natural sciences and at other times, more generally, all other fields of learning and academic study. (The German word "Wissenschaft" has both of these meanings). Consider the following passages:

> (22) Everywhere [there are] *symptoms of a dying* culture, of its complete eradication. Haste, the rivers of religion draining away, the conflicts between nations, the fragmenting and disintegrating sciences, the contemptuous greed and consumer attitude of the learned classes, their lack of care and grandeur. It becomes very clear to me that the learned classes are directly involved in this development. With each new day they become more thoughtless and more careless. Everything serves the approaching barbarism, the arts as well as the sciences – where shall we direct our attention? The Great Flood of barbarism is approaching. –
>
> (23) An age of barbarism is about to begin, the sciences will serve it! –
>
> (24) Proof of the barbarous effect of the sciences. They easily lose themselves in the service of the 'practical interests'. [Nietzsche, Band I, 895; cf. Note 18, 203; my translation]

In these passages from *Leben als Wille zur Macht* (1885-88) Nietzsche criticises some tendencies in contemporary culture that in his view clearly indicate a decline. "The sciences" he sees as directly contributing to this decline. He accuses the administrators of learning of an increasing lack of thoughtfulness and care. And this thoughtlessness and carelessness causes alienation and fragmentation, and is inimical to the unity of culture and of life as a whole. Everywhere Nietzsche discovers tendencies of an alienation of man from nature, from his origins and from his originally creative impulses. Here and elsewhere, as in *Schopenhauer als Erzieher* (1874) and *Die Fröhliche Wissenschaft* (1882), he criticises the dominance of logic and reason over direct experience and dismisses the scientific ideal of objectivity as an arid and sterile ideal. This criticism of objectivity as an arid and sterile ideal may seem mildly surprising in view of Nietzsche's earlier attack on consumerism. Today scientists lament the effects of commercial pressure to produce short-term immediately practical results and contrast this with old-fashioned objective, disinterested science. In fact, Nietzsche too attacked the very same tendencies that are lamented by the scientists of today, as shown by aphorism no. (24) just quoted. While he regards the service of the sciences for "practical interests" as detrimental, he is, nevertheless, equally suspicious of the ideal of objectivity as a value in itself. Whether he envisages a middle ground somewhere in between these two positions is a point that clearly needs clarification. But that would be the aim of a separate, more detailed study on Nietzsche. However, it ought to be recognized in the context of this study that Nietzsche is concerned with an increasing sense of fragmentation and disintegration experienced by modern man. His aim is to expose the sciences as a contributing factor in this development. His prognosis is that if "the sciences" (as he sees them) are further advanced – at the cost of man – mankind will decline in their shade:

> (26) The advance of a science at the expense of man is the most harmful thing in the world. The degenerate human being represents a regression of mankind. He casts his shadow far beyond all times. He disgraces the beliefs and the natural attitude of the individual sciences: the sciences themselves will perish under this attitude. They will have been advanced, but will have no positive but only an immoral effect on life. [ibid., cf. Note 19, 203; my translation]

In his pessimistic outlook, "the sciences" are seen not as contributing to the progress but, on the contrary, to a regress of mankind, as he points out in a chapter entitled "Die Decadence":

> Compared with the artist, the appearance of scientific man is, indeed, the sign of a certain restraining and downgrading of life. [ibid. 881-2, cf. Note 20, 203; my translation]

Nietzsche explicitly rejected the idea of the progress of mankind as inspired by Darwinian theory[40] and as celebrated by some of his more optimistic contemporaries.[41] We have already seen that logic and

---

[40] Cf. eg. Nietzsche's remarks headed "Anti-Darwin. Meine Gesamtansicht / Erster Satz: Der Mensch als Gattung ist *nicht* im Fortschritt." Nietzsche, Band I, 836; "Anti-Darwin. My overall view / First principle: Man as a species is *not* in progress." My translation.

[41] Darwin's views were most effectively, though not uncritically, popularized by T.H. Huxley in England, and, with more complete

reason are, in his opinion, by no means the crown of human evolution, but symptoms of decline. Equally, the arrival of consciousness is interpreted by him as the weakest, not the strongest point in evolution:

> Consciousness is the last and latest development of organic life and is consequently the least perfect and the weakest element of it. Through consciousness come innumerable mistakes which cause an animal, a human being to perish before their time [from *Fröhliche Wissenschaft*, cited in Steiner 1983, 92; my translation; cf. also Note 21, 203]

We recognize these and similar thoughts as echoes in Steiner's writings. In a way, Nietzsche's criticism can be seen as one of Steiner's own starting points. In fact, Steiner regarded the task of a good scholar, that is implicitly his own task, as pursuing Nietzsche's thoughts to their logical conclusion, and as actually 'improving' them.[42] That Steiner identified with Nietzsche to some degree is shown by a leaflet, signed by Steiner and dated 8 February 1892, which had been circulated as some kind of party diversion. In it Steiner answered a number of questions on his personal predilections, and asked who he would like to be apart from himself he said: "Friedrich Nietzsche vor dem Wahnsinn" ["Friedrich Nietzsche before he went mad", rpt in Lindenberg 1993, 51]. It was in Weimar, where he had come to work on Goethe, where he was first (in 1889) introduced to Nietzsche's writings, and where subsequently he laid the foundations of his own "philosophy of freedom" (*Die Philosophie der*

---

agreement, by Ernst Haeckel in Germany. Cf. Carter, 79–80. J.W. Burrow identifies Darwin as "one of the begetters of the strident power philosophers of the later nineteenth century", and he goes on to say: "'The survival of the fittest' in a human context could be all things to all men". Darwinism influenced the essentially optimistic theory of Karl Marx, who dedicated *Das Kapital* to Darwin. It shaped academic sociology, as in the work of Herbert Spencer (Social Darwinism), Walter Bagehot, Prince Kropotkin and William Sumner, to name only a few. It was used by both the political left and the right, and also formed a major element in the rise of racialism, nationalism and anti-Semitism. Cf. Burrow's introduction to Darwin's *The Origin of Species* ...; Darwin, 45.

[42] "I think that true learning recognizes the grandeur of a personality and corrects small errors, or draws incomplete thoughts to their conclusion." Steiner 1983, 94; my translation; cf. Note 22, 204.

Freiheit, 1892, which was discussed above). In 1894 he had a chance to visit Nietzsche at his sick bed. In his book on Nietzsche, published a year later, he reveals an intense admiration for the philosopher, but he also expresses his regrets that Nietzsche, as he believed, suffered from, and finally broke down under the burden of the scientific spirit of the age:

> From my extensive study of Nietzsche I gained the view of a personality whose fate it was to live tragically through the scientific era of the last half of the nineteenth century, breaking down under the impression it made on him. He was a *searcher* in these times, but could not *find* anything in them. [Steiner 1983, 190; my translation; cf. Note 23, 204]

Steiner regarded Nietzsche's personal fate as tragic. But at the same time, he explains, it was *through* Nietzsche that his understanding of the "Problem der Naturwissenschaft" ["the problem of natural science", ibid., 190] was sharpened. Steiner may not have shared all of Nietzsche's conclusions, but he shared the same sense of a crisis of the age, and he had the same awareness of the urgent problems of the time. Such problems include the difficulties that arose with the development of self-consciousness – something that became, as we have seen, Steiner's major concern. Furthermore, the split between the individual and the objective world proclaimed by the sciences (with the consequently increasing sense of alienation) and the failure of contemporary thinking to deal adequately with that split – these are, as we have seen, problems that Nietzsche deals with in his work, and they occur frequently in Steiner's own writings. Like Nietzsche he concludes that an age which suffers from such a failure will eventually result in the individual's and finally cultural decline ("Verkümmerung"):

> Every philosophical thought that is not demanded by this life is condemned to remain barren [...]. [...] An age that is unwilling to think such thoughts shows through this fact merely that it does not feel the need to form human life in such a way that it can really unfold itself in all directions according to its original destination. But, for such a disinclination, a heavy penalty must be paid in the course of human evolution. Life remains undeveloped in such ages, and men do not notice their sickly state because they are unwilling to recognize the demands that nevertheless continue to exist deeply seated

within them and that they just fail to satisfy. A following age shows the effect of such neglect. The grandchildren find in the formation of a stunted life something that was caused by the omission of the grandparents. This omission of the preceding age has turned into the imperfect life of the later time into which the grandchildren find themselves placed. In life as a *whole*, philosophy must rule. It is possible to sin against this demand, but it is inevitable that this sin will produce its effects. [Steiner 1973, xix–xx; cf. also Note 24, 204]

This passage could be taken directly from Nietzsche. It reveals the departure from a blindly optimistic belief in progress. Steiner is an alert witness to this departure, as are many of his contemporaries who express related and similar views to his own and to Nietzsche's. Indeed, we can observe an intellectual development that begins with increasing doubts about the idea of progress and finally culminates in a cultural pessimism.[43] Two other exemplary thinkers, whose work clearly reflects this development, are Jacob Burckhardt and Oswald Spengler.

Burckhardt was profoundly affected by a strong sense of cultural crisis. Like Nietzsche, he could not believe any more in the idea of progress and abandoned it in his historical reflections. His perspective is conservative and backward-looking. As he puts it in his book *Weltgeschichtliche Betrachtungen* (1905), he chose to stress "the repetitive, the consistent, the typical", in favour of the idea of progress.[44] Burckhardt wished to stress the continuity of culture and *Geist* (spirit) at a time which he felt was a threat to them. The idea of progress meant to him a progress in the materialistic tendencies of the time at the expense, not in favour, of culture and *Geist*. He once

---

[43] J.W. Burrow characterizes the course of this development as follows: "The blood-letting of two world wars, and the prospect that organized human aggression, far from improving the species, may actually eliminate it altogether, have dampened interest in the application of Darwin's theory." Introduction to Darwin's *Origin of Species* ...; Darwin 45.

[44] "The philosophers of history regard the past as the opposite and a previous step to us as the advanced: – we observe the repetitive, the consistent, the typical as something we recognise and understand within ourselves." Burckhardt, 6; my translation; cf. Note 25, 204.

explained his attitude in a letter to Nietzsche as being "backward-looking to save the culture of earlier times, and forward-looking in the serene and assiduous defence of *Geist* at a time that might otherwise utterly fall victim to matter" [Marx in Burckhardt, 286; my translation; cf. Note 26, 204].

Spengler went a step further than either Nietzsche or Burckhardt. He rejected the idea of progress, like Nietzsche and Burckhardt before him. But while Burckhardt saw himself as a defender of culture, Spengler, in contrast, became the prophet of its downfall. In *Der Untergang des Abendlandes* (1918-22), he explains that it was Nietzsche (as well as Goethe) who inspired his book, but points out that neither Nietzsche nor any of his contemporaries saw the real extent of the crisis that affected culture.[45] Spengler believed he was able to explain more systematically than anyone before him that Western culture was doomed to come to an end. He had, as Johannes Hirschberger has pointed out, a biological view of history, and believed that a culture, like a living organism, grows and dies again.

> The general philosophical idea behind Spengler's *Weltanschauung* is a brutal biologism. Life as the underlying principle of the processes in history is not any more something like Hegel's idea or Bergson's "élan vital" but a vitality that is more like sheer brute force. [Hirschberger, Band II, 589; my translation; cf. Note 28, 205]

In this view, the fall of Western culture (like the fall of other great cultures) is inevitable. What had for Nietzsche and Burckhardt been signs of decline, were for Spengler symptoms of a definite collapse of culture. Such symptoms include growing urbanisation, mechanization and technical perfection, with the consequent alienation of man from nature. In *Untergang des Abendlandes* and his later book *Der Mensch und die Technik* (1931), he interprets technical progress as the sole

---

[45] "Here, everyone had an idea. But from their own narrow perspective, no one found the sole universal solution that had been in the air since the times of Nietzsche. He was aware of all the important problems, but was too much of a romantic really to dare to face hard reality. In this, however, lies the necessity for the conclusive view that could only be reached in times like these." Spengler, 37; my translation; cf. Note 27, 205.

means in man's strife for control and power over nature. Compare, for instance, the following passage from *Untergang des Abendlandes*:

> Then followed, at the age of reason, the invention of the steam engine, which revolutionised everything and totally changed the economic situation. Up to then, nature had rendered services, now she is forced into slavery. [...] But precisely because of this, Faustian man has become the *slave of his own creation*. His ways and means of living are, through the machine, forced to follow a direction where there is no standstill and no way back. [Spengler, 396–7; my translation; cf. Note 29, 205]

The price we pay for our ruthless pursuit of technical progress, in Spengler's view, is that a split occurs between man and nature which can eventually not be healed any more. Man becomes the "slave of his own creation" – slave to his own struggle for power and dominion.[46] For in this struggle, philosophy, the arts and with them human ideals, such as truth and justice, decline and in their decline herald the collapse of culture. In the end sheer brute force will reign:

> The perpetual principle of history is only life, and always only life, the race, the triumph of the struggle for power, not the victory of truths, feelings or money. World history is world judgement: it has always favoured the continuation of the stronger, fuller, self-confident life form, irrespective of its real right to do so. And it has always sacrificed truth and justice to power and the race. And it has doomed to death those individuals and nations to whom the truth was more important than action, and justice more essential than power. [Cited in Hirschberger, Band II, 589; my translation; cf. Note 30, 205]

---

[46] This is very exactly like C. S. Lewis's *The Abolition of Man* (1943). About man's conquest of nature he writes, for example: "It is the magician's bargain: give up our souls, get power in return. But once our souls, that is, our selves, have been given up, the power thus conferred will not belong to us. We shall in fact be slaves and puppets of that to which we have given our souls." Lewis 1987, 43. In spite of the resemblance to Spengler, Lewis ultimately rejects Spengler's pessimistic vision of an inevitable decline of Western Culture. His solution for the modern crisis is that we must all simply accept the sovereignty of the moral law ("the Tao").

Spengler envisages a world dominated by dictatorship and cruel wars – the end of Western culture, an end that can only be accepted, not escaped. Accordingly his book concludes with the following words: "Ducunt fata volentem, nolentem trahunt" ["The fates guide the willing, but drag along the unwilling", Spengler, 400].

Nietzsche predicted, Burckhardt feared and Spengler regarded the decline of culture as an inevitable fact. Steiner, in comparison, looked for a way out. He made an important contribution to the critical analysis of contemporary life and thought, but became critical of this criticism itself. His thought reveals the consciousness of a crisis in contemporary culture, but *he made this very consciousness itself the subject of his enquiries.* His perspective is philosophical, psychological as well as historical. This approach enables him to show that many of the contemporary assumptions about culture do not need to, and ought not to be taken for granted. That insight alone marks a departure from the sense of resignation, pessimism and even defeat that seems to characterize much of the critical thought of the period.

Northrop Frye regards the view of the decline of Western culture as a mere myth, "a partial insight with a 'seductive simplicity' which is altogether more plausible than the truth'", and he asks for a wider view which would include "a much larger 'truth' about our very complex situation than the mythology of decline affords."[47] Such a view as Frye's does not quite seem to acknowledge the real urgency of the problems caused by the new scientific, technological and social developments. For those, for example, who experienced the atrocities of The Great War, destruction and decline were a real threat. In fact, Spengler's criticism (as well as that of Burckhardt and Nietzsche before him) is a valid and important contribution towards identifying the burning problems of the modern age. There is a difference, though, between a merely 'negative' and a more 'constructive' criticism. Steiner's work clearly belongs to the latter category and goes a step further than either Spengler's, Burckhardt's or Nietzsche's criticism. It would be a gross exaggeration to say that Steiner has a claim to the "larger 'truth' about our very complex situation". But at least he proposes ways of dealing effectively with those problems which his pessimistic contemporaries merely criticise.

---

[47] Frye, 24. The quotations within the quotations are from T.S. Eliot.

Steiner's approach proposes and opens up a new way of rethinking and redirecting the course of development in the sciences, philosophy and the arts. This new way of thinking has had an immediate impact both in the intellectual and necessarily also in the practical field. For the two are, in Steiner's system, absolutely inseparable. In the intellectual field, his great achievement has been to inspire a view of history in terms of an evolution of consciousness. However, Steiner regarded his work in the theoretical field only as a basis from which necessary changes in the practical social and political fields were to follow. His social and political reform ideas are developed in a number of important books and lectures, as for example in *Die Kernpunkte der sozialen Frage in den Lebensnotwendigkeiten der Gegenwart und Zukunft* (1919/20) and *Aufsätze über die Dreigliederung des sozialen Organismus und zur Zeitlage* (1915-21). It was to be the fate of Steiner's social and political reform ideas, that they remained unrealized. What survives, are his small-scale initiatives, which he had set up to demonstrate the practicability of his ideas. Among the practical initiatives which he has inspired and which survive today are those in education, agriculture and medicine, for example.[48]

Steiner's theoretical interest lay in the exploration of consciousness, but he never actually wrote a systematic history of the evolution of consciousness. However, he created an *awareness* of the importance of such a view of history as a counterbalance to the conventional views of the period. It was left to others to do the more systematic work in this field. Among the very first to recognize the importance of this task and to tackle it was Owen Barfield. Others followed the same route, but not until very much later.[49] Barfield's

---

[48] For a discussion of these fields incl. their philosophical base cf. Easton, 253ff.

[49] Cf. Gebser, and Neumann. Some more recent authors in the same tradition include Ken Wilber, *Up from Eden* (1981), and Fritjof Capra, *The Turning Point* (1982), *Uncommon Wisdom: Conversations With Remarkable People* (1987). Other more specifically anthroposophically oriented authors concerned with the same field are Emil Bock, Hans Erhard Lauer and Günther Wachsmuth.

work on the evolution of consciousness in the field of language and literature is a real novelty, considering the conventional intellectual tendencies of the period as I discussed them above. His work must count as real pioneer work in his field. And although he wrote in the wake of Steiner, we must be careful not simply to regard him as a mere epigone. For Barfield developed his thoughts in almost exact parallel to the emergence of Anthroposophy in England. (The English section of the Anthroposophical Society was not founded until 1923). However, the purpose of this study is to determine the exact nature and extent of Steiner's influence on Barfield and to compare Barfield's own original approach with Steiner's. A comparison of the two authors is therefore to follow in the last section.

4. Conclusions: Barfield and Anthroposophy

What are the events that led up to Barfield's acceptance of anthroposophy? When exactly did he become an anthroposophist? And what was the precise significance of anthroposophy for Barfield in those early years of his intellectual development? These are some of the questions which I wish to address in the concluding section of this chapter.

As for the precise date of Barfield's acceptance of anthroposophy, Barfield himself is notoriously vague. This has led to some confusion among scholars. Gareth Knight, for example, has suggested that Barfield became a member of the Anthroposophical Society in 1922 – at a time when the Society had as yet not even been founded![50] Humphrey Carpenter, more cautiously, dates his membership to "about 1922". Walter Hooper, more cautiously still, leaves out the question of membership altogether and simply speaks of Barfield's becoming "a follower of Rudolf Steiner in 1923". [cf. Knight; 220; Carpenter, 255; Hooper, 622]. Who is right? Considering the present confusion, it will be necessary to look at the matter afresh and attempt a more careful reconstruction of the dates and events in question than

---

[50] The precise date of the foundation is 2 September 1923. Cf. Anthroposophical Society in Great Britain 1925, 48–52.

has hitherto been offered. This reconstruction will involve a bit of historical detection work. Let us begin with an account which Barfield gave himself in 1976:

> I must retrace my steps a little. When, in my first term at Oxford, I suddenly decided to attend a class of the English Folk Dance Society, I little knew what kind of a train I had lit. It led to an invitation in the following summer (1920) to join an amateur concert party, touring some Cornish towns and villages for a week or two in September with a programme of music, together with historical dances in costume. The following summer Cecil [Harwood] (who had meanwhile followed me into the E.F.D.S.) joined the same party. A year later, as well as the following year (1923), another friend of the organisers was invited into the party to sing and play the fiddle. This was DAPHNE OLIVIER, who subsequently became Cecil's first wife (she died in 1950) – as another member of the party subsequently became my wife. Whether it was before or after we met, that Daphne, a school-teacher, became acquainted with the work of Rudolf Steiner and attended an educational conference in Stuttgart, I am not sure. But it was through her that we both heard of anthroposophy [...]. [Barfield 1976, 2–4]

Cecil Harwood who is mentioned in this passage was a close friend of Barfield's from school and was up at Oxford at the same time as Barfield, reading Classics at Christ Church. It was, as this passage reveals, through Harwood's future wife, Daphne Olivier, that both men were introduced to anthroposophy. They met her for the first time in 1922. Unfortunately the Anthroposophical Society holds no records about her early activities which makes it impossible to ascertain when (or indeed whether) she actually attended the educational conference in Stuttgart, which Barfield mentions. What we do know for certain is that it was in the same year, when she met Barfield and Harwood, that Daphne first heard Rudolf Steiner lecture. This was at a conference held at Manchester College, Oxford (15-19 August 1922) on "Spiritual Values in Education and Social Life" [cf. Hooper, 676–7]. Daphne Olivier subsequently became a devoted follower of Steiner, and in 1925, together with Cecil Harwood, became one of the first teachers (there were originally five) at the newly established Rudolf Steiner School in London.

It is clear, then, that Daphne Olivier knew about Steiner by August 1922. But what about Barfield and Harwood? Was it in the same year that they learnt from her about Steiner? Barfield himself seems uncertain about this. One other source which may shed some light on this is C.S. Lewis's journal. Here the earliest time we find Steiner mentioned is, not the summer of 1922, but the summer of 1923. It is in an entry dated 7 July 1923 that Lewis records hearing about Harwood's and Barfield's "new philosopher":[51]

> [...] Harwood and I lay under the trees and talked. He told me about his new philosopher, Rudolf Steiner, who has "made the burden roll from his back". Steiner seems to be a sort of panpsychist, with a vein of posing superstition, and I was very much disappointed to hear that both Harwood and Barfield were impressed by him. [Lewis 1993a, 254]

The important word is "new philosopher", which clearly indicates that Steiner had just been newly discovered by Lewis's two friends. Moreover, if either Barfield or Harwood had discovered Steiner as early as the summer of 1922 we would expect them to have discussed this with Lewis much earlier. However, as late as 26 January 1923, when Barfield and Lewis met up, resuming what Lewis calls their usual "dogfight" [ibid., 185], there is no mention of Steiner in his journal entry of that day. This almost certainly means that Barfield had as yet not discovered the philosopher. If he had, he would surely have mentioned him, and Lewis would have made a note of it. Significantly, it is only after July 1923, as Lewis's journal entries reveal, that Steiner became a prominent topic both in his conversations with his two friends and in his own private reflections.[52] All of this suggests, I think, that it was not in the summer of 1922 but some time in 1923 (between 26 January and 7 July) that both Barfield and Harwood learnt about Steiner. This seems to be confirmed by another remark, where Barfield explains that he discovered the philosopher about the same time as he got married. The date of his

---

[51] Lewis knew Harwood. He had been introduced to him by Barfield. From this introduction resulted a lifelong friendship.

[52] Cf. e.g. entries of 19 October 1923, 1 January 1924 (about some time earlier [ca. November 1923?]), 7 March 1924, 18 June 1924. Lewis 1993a, 275, 277, 301, 337–40, etc.

marriage (to Matilda "Maud" Douie) is 11 April 1923 [cf. Appendix, 245].

It seems, then, that Walter Hooper is right in dating Barfield's acquaintance with anthroposophy to 1923, but perhaps not quite right in suggesting that he became a "follower" of Steiner in that year. In fact, Barfield's commitment to anthroposophy was not as instantaneous as that. After discovering anthroposophy, he explains, he and Harwood

> began, rather sceptically, attending together some weekly lecture-readings which GEORGE ADAMS (then George Kaufmann) was conducting at 46, Gloucester Place. This went on for some time and, if my memory is correct, Cecil's detachment lasted a little longer than my own, and it was I who first raised between us the question whether it was not about time we joined the Society. I believe I did actually join a few weeks or months before he did. [Barfield 1976, 4][53]

Initially, then, as this passage reveals, Barfield approached anthroposophy with scepticism. His scepticism, however, gradually gave way, and in 1924 he became a full member of the Society.[54]

---

[53] George Adams, whom Barfield mentions in this passage, was one of the first to promote the cause of anthroposophy in Britain. A graduate in Biology from Cambridge, he came across anthroposophy in 1916. As a pacifist and Labour supporter, he was attracted to Steiner principally for his writings on social and political reform, which seemed to offer new perspectives for war stricken European society. When he met Steiner in 1919 he was persuaded to give up his scientific career in favour of promoting the ideals of anthroposophy. He became a lecturer, interpreter and translator. He gives an excellent, very detailed eye-witness account of the events (the intellectual and social developments) leading up to and following the Society's foundation in, "Rudolf Steiner in England"; cf. also Wicher.

[54] This date is confirmed by Maria Barguirdjian (Membership Secretary of the Anthroposophical Society in Great Britain): "Mr. Owen Barfield joined the Anthroposophical Society in Great Britain in 1924, and is still registered with the number 15. This confirms that he is one of the very early, first founder members of the Society." cf. Barfield 1994.

We may sum up the different stages of Barfield's intellectual development as follows: We saw in chapter one that in 1921 he embarked on his research project "Poetic Diction". As we know, he began his research with a detailed study of the romantic poets and thinkers (Coleridge in particular). It appears that he pursued these studies for two years until he came across Steiner. But he was not fired by Steiner immediately, and it took him another year after that to become a committed anthroposophist. Barfield relates that after reading Steiner for a while, he became impressed with his metaphysic, but did at first not realize the actual connection between his own ideas and those of his predecessor:

> The essence of Steiner's teachings [...] is the evolution of human consciousness, the kind of pictorial consciousness in earlier times. I, in a way, came to the same conclusion on my own before I heard of Steiner, but in terms of language rather, of human beings' experience of language and of nature. In effect, you could say that I came to the conclusion that human beings in earlier stages of evolution had, what you might call, a pictorial consciousness. Steiner, of course, taught that too. He called it sometimes "atavistic clairvoyance". It was rather curious that I was taken by his whole metaphysic, but for a long time they were more or less parallel – his thought of "atavistic clairvoyance" and mine of "original participation", as I called it later. And I didn't connect them. I remember, quite late, after I'd been reading Steiner off and on for a year or two, suddenly saying to myself, this "atavistic clairvoyance" he is talking about *is* what I am talking about. For a time they went on side by side. [Appendix, 186-1]

Barfield suggests in this passage that he was already very far advanced in developing his own approach when he discovered Steiner. Obviously, like many other writers when interviewed, he is anxious to stress his independence. So perhaps his account ought to be taken with a pinch of salt. However, Barfield had concerned himself with an intensive study of the romantics before he came across Steiner. It was therefore in the romantics (Coleridge in particular), not in Steiner, that he had his roots. The idea of an "evolution of consciousness" (and the corresponding idea of participation and wholeness), as we saw in the last chapter, was already foreshadowed in romantic thought. Barfield took this idea from Coleridge and began to develop it into his own linguistic theory of an "evolution of consciousness". But whether or not his theory already stood when he encountered Steiner remains uncertain. At any rate, Steiner himself was so thoroughly influenced by the romantics that in the end it will be difficult to untangle his influence from that of the romantics. It is certain, as Barfield himself has pointed out, that it was only after discovering Steiner that he developed confidence in the value and strength of what he wanted to say. Steiner, he comments, was confirming his own views and

> also strengthening and setting them in a true context, somehow. And also his whole teaching, the detailed account of the evolution of consciousness, the spiritual hierarchies and so forth ... I think I put it once that he began where I left off. All I had done was to establish, in a hostile intellectual atmosphere, that there *was* such a thing as the evolution of consciousness from a more pictorial, more living, if you like, form or quality to our own. He assumes that, to start with, and builds on that this terrific edifice. [ibid., 245][55]

Barfield concluded that what he (and the romantics before him) had been trying to say, Steiner was dealing with far more comprehensively. Anthroposophy, he found, "included and transcended not only my own poor stammering theory of poetry as knowledge, but the whole Romantic philosophy. It was nothing less than Romanticism grown up" [Barfield 1986e, 14]. In what way, then, we may ask, had Steiner, according to Barfield, "transcended" both romantic theory and his own? What, in other words, does Barfield mean when he speaks of anthroposophy as "Romanticism grown up"?

---

[55] Cf. also the following passage: "so far as concerned the particular subject in which I was immersed at the time, that is the histories of verbal meanings and their bearing on the evolution of consciousness, Steiner had obviously forgotten volumes more than I had dreamed. It is difficult to lay my finger on what convinced me of this. As far as I know there is no special treatise on semantics or semasiology among his works. Rather it was a matter of stray remarks and casual allusions which showed me that some of my most daring and (as I thought) original conclusions were *his* premises [...]." Barfield 1986e, 13. It is worth noting that Steiner *did* give a course of lectures on language and evolution of consciousness in Stuttgart in 1919–20. Barfield does not seem to have been aware of this. But then, these lectures were not published until 1940; cf. Steiner 1981.

One of the clues for answering these questions lies in his essay "Romanticism and Anthroposophy" (1926), where he makes the following criticism:

> What one cannot help noticing to-day about Romanticism is that it is all a little vague and vast and shadowy. Perhaps it is for that very reason that the word *romantic* has long been the nucleus, together with such counter-terms as *classical* or *realism*, of violent and heated discussions in aesthetic circles throughout Europe. And perhaps it is partly as a reaction against all this that there should be abroad at the moment a fairly pronounced feeling that Romanticism, at any rate as metaphysic, is a failure. Its potentialities seem to have been left hanging in the air, its numerous loose threads ungathered [...]. [Barfield 1926b, 118]

Barfield's chief criticism, as this passage shows, is that the romantics, in his view, failed to develop their ideas into a comprehensive and solid philosophical system. This is not quite true. We only have to remind ourselves of Hegel's *Phänomenologie des Geistes* (1807), for example, to convince ourselves that some romantics at least developed the most extraordinarily compact thought systems.[56] However, Barfield's criticism seems to be directed mainly at the English romantics, Coleridge in particular. And Coleridge's philosophy is indeed notoriously unsystematic.[57] However, Barfield's criticism is not only concerned with systematic philosophy, but also with the question of how this philosophy relates to the practical world. When he said that the "potentialities" of romantic philosophy "seem to have been left hanging in the air" he indicated that he felt that what was lacking in romantic philosophy was a proper footing of its ideas in the world of practical affairs. This at least is how he certainly felt about

---

[56] For a discussion of Hegel's aim in his *Phänomenologie* to develop a "total system of *Wissenschaft*", cf. e.g. Abrams 1971, 225–37.

[57] Barfield shrewdly observes that what actually made Coleridge so incoherent was his exaggerated desire for coherence: "His extraordinarily unifying mind was too painfully aware that you cannot really say one thing correctly without saying everything. [...] His incoherence of expression arose from the coherence of what he wanted to say. It was a sort of intellectual stammer." Barfield 1986d, 146.

Coleridge. Comparing Coleridge to Goethe, for example, he comments:

> Goethe had his feet firmly planted on the earth. As a scientist, as a knower, he largely confined himself to the realm of natural science and his regular industry combined with his great genius had by the end of his life illuminated this realm with a steadily increasing flood of light. Coleridge never succeeded in finding his feet on earth at all. Look at the portrait of him in the National Gallery in London [...]. Compare the majesty of the forehead and the eyes with the pathetically weak mouth. He himself said that he had "power without strength" [ibid., 161–2]

"What does it mean to have power without strength?", Barfield immediately goes on to ask, and continues: "Power is of heaven. Strength is the faculty of applying it on earth." That is, in his view, Coleridge had powerful ideas, but was unable to put them into realization, to demonstrate their effectiveness outside the purely mental sphere. This lack of application in Coleridge's work has provoked heavy criticism in Coleridge scholarship. Marilyn Butler, for example, comments:

> All along, his work internalizes: it moves the sphere of significant action from the world of event to the world of thought, from system to experience, from the literal and scientific to the imaginative and moral. [Butler, 91]

Moreover, the essence of Coleridge's "literary strategy", according to Butler, is this:

> It is frequently the function of an intellectual jargon that those who have once learnt the tone and language remain of the party. Coleridge is surely the first example, in England at least, of the sage who turns himself into a cult-figure for the next student-generation. [...] With all its incidental weaknesses, Coleridge's oeuvre succeeds impressionistically in validating the experience of the individual intellectual, and in refuting the notion that the isolated, alienated thinker is either worthless or without influence. However unmethodical, his thinking is directed towards emotional solutions for the loneliness of his type. [ibid., 91–2]

This is a very cynical view, which spots only Coleridge's weakness but ignores his potential strength. Surely, Coleridge's views about wholeness and participation are too important to be reduced to the mere level of compensation for intellectual loneliness and eccentricity. Abrams adopts a wider view. He has shown that the romantic vision of wholeness and participation went hand in hand with the vision of a "total and enduring transformation of man *and his world*". In other words, the imagination as an integrative faculty was seen as a power of liberation, enabling man to "remake his *physical and social environment* into a form adequate to human needs" [Abrams 1971, 343, and 334 (my italics)]. Indeed, as Nigel Leask has shown, Coleridge's interest in the imagination, his interest in the ideals of wholeness and participation, were originally part of a wider interest in a political transformation of society along the lines of "an egalitarian commonwealth" [Leask, 3]. He shared these interests with many of his fellow writers and thinkers, who in the early stages had been keen supporters of the political ideals of the French revolution. However, it is a notorious fact that, as disappointment with the actual events of the revolution set in, these writers' original interest in outer revolutionary change dwindled, and increasingly shifted to a preoccupation with an inner revolution of man's moral and intellectual world. In other words, the early romantics were revolutionaries who were looking not only for intellectual and moral, but also for practical social and political change. The later romantics became conservative, withdrawing from the public sphere, internalizing social and political ideals.[58] Coleridge's development clearly reflects this shift. Indeed, as Nigel Leask has pointed out, what can be observed in his work is a

> mounting tension [...] between a theory of imagination as an integrative agency dissolving and dissipating social divisions and hierarchies, and as an otherworldly *consolation* which removed the practice of virtue from a public to a private sphere. [Leask, 3].

Leask has shown that Coleridge increasingly gravitated towards this latter position of internalization. Marilyn Butler, as we have seen, criticises this tendency to internalize as a weakness. And she is fully

---

[58] For a detailed discussion of this complex development in Romantic thought, cf. Abrams 1971, 325–72.

justified, I think, in doing so. Nevertheless, her view is very one-sided, for she ignores, as I said earlier, Coleridge's potential strength. Barfield, in contrast, recognizes both Coleridge's weakness and his potential strength. He comments, using an analogy:

> A flash of lightning is in many ways a very weak thing. As soon as it has come down from heaven and discharged into the earth it is diffused through the whole earth and vanishes from sight. You cannot direct it into channels. A flash of lightning will not run an electric tram. But still it is a flash of lightning. [Barfield 1986d, 162]

In other words, it was Coleridge's achievement to have sparked off a number of important, fresh ideas. These ideas, however, in Barfield's view, clearly needed to be developed further. What they needed was the strength of application. To use Barfield's lightning analogy, the flash of lightning had to be transformed into a strong current, which could then be channelled into positive action.

If we return from here to Steiner, it will not be difficult to see why Barfield thought that anthroposophy was "Romanticism grown up". Steiner had clearly both of the things which Barfield thought so important: power of thought and strength of application. Steiner, as we know, had given his ideas of wholeness and participation a strong philosophical framework. This at the same time served as a basis for wider changes: e.g. in the cultural, the social and the political spheres. This is where anthroposophy had transcended romanticism. The ideas of wholeness and participation, which Coleridge and other romantic thinkers had developed, needed to be rescued from the merely mental sphere and made accountable again in the public sphere. Barfield obviously believed that Steiner had succeeded in this. But what about himself? Did Barfield ever engage in any questions of public interest? And did he himself ever attempt to *apply* any of his ideas in the public sphere? The answer, as I already indicated at the end of the last chapter is clearly yes. So far we have only got to know Barfield as a theorist. But, as we shall see, from the mid 1920s, he, like Steiner, took on two other roles as well: that of the cultural and social critic, and that of the cultural and social reformer. I shall concern myself with these two roles, and with the question of how successful Barfield was at them, in my third and in my last chapters.

III.
Barfield as Cultural and Social Critic

What will come as a surprising novelty to most readers of Barfield is the fact that the philosophical and literary issues, which he debated with with C. S. Lewis for example, interlock with much broader issues of a wider public interest. It is not generally known that his thought responds directly not only to the intellectual but also to the practical concerns of the time. A number of Barfield's earliest essays, leading up to and following the publication of *Poetic Diction*, reveal a thinker who was involved very deeply indeed in the contemporary discourse on many of the burning issues of the period. Apart from philosophical and literary topics, he discussed, for instance, social, political and economic matters.

This side of Barfield's intellectual activity has been ignored in Barfield scholarship. His philosophical and literary reflections have been divorced from the concrete situation to which they respond, with the effect that the real urgency and relevance of his ideas have been lost. In this and the following chapter I shall explore the practical aspect of Barfield's thought. I hope thereby to readjust our usual 'placing' of Barfield by clarifying his principled position not only as a philosopher of language and consciousness, but also as a critic of modern culture and society.

I shall begin with a few general preliminary remarks about the historical context of Barfield's early work. The beginning of Barfield's intellectual career falls into the decade following the Great War. It is important to remember that this time was in many ways a time of crisis. The 1920s were a period of great economic instability which culminated in 1929 in a world wide economic crisis, the Depression. Throughout the period preceding and following the Depression, levels of unemployment in Britain (and elsewhere in Europe) were very high and poverty was increasing. At this time of social and economic instability politicians seemed to have no immediately effective solutions to offer. And thus, in an atmosphere of social and economic instability as well as political insecurity, fascism could grow and gain a foothold in Europe. The world of culture did not remain unaffected by these developments either. Much of contemporary thought, art and literature, for example, can be seen as reflecting the instabilities, insecurities and anxieties which mark the general *Zeitgeist* of the period following the Great War.

These conditions, of which I have just given an outline, are the setting of Barfield's early publications. In these publications many of the above points find a careful consideration. In fact, his essays of the 1920s reveal a sense of crisis as strong as that of many of his contemporaries. Consider, for example, the following passage from an essay of c. 1925 (characteristically) entitled *Danger, Ugliness and Waste*:

> At a time when this country, if not all Europe, if not civilization itself, needs more urgently than ever before the assistance of the clearest brains it possesses, I do not apologise for trespassing on your time. Nor will I waste it by quoting opinions in support of the foregoing assertion. There is no need to. The last twelve months have heard a quick crescendo of warning, and it is no longer only the politicians or writers, such as the author of "The Four Horsemen of the Apocalypse" from whom the omens are forthcoming; financiers, economists, scientists, philosophers, artists – almost every day some fresh mind speaks out, corroborating the panic without apparently shifting the load of hopeless apathy beneath which it is suppressed. Professor Graham Wallas has drawn a close comparison between the years 1923 and 423 A.D., and there is scarcely a general conversation among intelligent people which does not end on the note of precariousness and insecurity. When Cassandra *is* silent, it is generally because she is afraid of being dull. [Barfield 1925c, 1][59]

In this essay, then, Barfield conveys a vivid awareness of the sense of "precariousness and insecurity" which affects the time. He himself goes on to show, in the following paragraph, that post-war society is in a state of great confusion, suffering from high unemployment, poverty and a stagnating economy: "The confusion alone of post-war European society", he observes, has led to an

---

[59] Tennyson 1976, 230, gives 1929 as the date of publication. This date must be wrong, for the Bodleian Library (which, as a copyright library, receives a copy of every newly published book in Britain) holds a published copy of Barfield's essay which was acquired in 1925.

hypnotic state in all but the strongest-minded. As for the latter, they look around them and see – in this country more than one million permanently unemployed, supported, and inadequately supported, by a state whose 'solvency' is only to be maintained by grinding taxation; they see half the population living on a bare subsistence level and many actually starving: poverty is not difficult to comprehend. But they also see the factories lying idle that could absorb the energy of all the unemployed and more; the ships rusting in dock that could bring them food, and the food and clothing which actually are produced or imported as often as not rotting in barns and warehouses because 'there is no market' for them. [ibid., 2]

In this situation Barfield notices that the common attitude is one of helpless resignation. Financiers, economists, scientists, philosophers and artists, as he points out, are all alarmed by this situation, and are highly critical, but with their criticism they seem to be aggravating the sense of "precariousness and insecurity", rather than alleviating it; they are, in his words, merely "corroborating the panic without apparently shifting the load of hopeless apathy beneath which it is suppressed" [ibid., 1]. Barfield here reflects in some respects the current criticism, but his remarks show that in other ways he goes a step further. In some degree he is critical even of the contemporary criticism itself. He sees it as being insufficiently aware of its own fundamental weakness, that is, he sees its failure to go to the root of the problem, its inertia. With his observation that modern criticism is merely "corroborating the panic", he suggests that contemporary thought itself, clogged by inertia, may inadvertently be one of the propelling forces of the crisis.

Barfield suggests, therefore, that not only modern thought, but also modern society is in a state of crisis. Indeed, as we can see from the above observations, he sees the crisis in contemporary thought and the crisis in modern life at large (including politics, economics and social affairs) as linked phenomena. That is, he assumes a causal connection between the two. In his early work he therefore essays a thorough investigation of this. There is evidence that he perceived something of such a connection as early as 1921. In his essay "Some Elements of Decadence", where he defines his specific task as that of analyzing "the spirit of the age",[60] he argues that modern thought is essentially decadent. He holds it to be decadent because it lacks, in his view, the rigour and vitality to deal with decisive changes which occurred in the recent past. Consider, for example, the following passage (earlier in the essay Barfield introduced a hypothetical intellectual called John to illustrate all the failures he attributes to modern intellectuals and artists):

> Perhaps this not wholly symbolic connection between John and his environment is the key for which we are searching. The Western world had only just emerged from the two intensest universal experiences it had ever known, experiences which had quickly and roughly changed all its body and soul. In less than a hundred years it had had to assimilate industrialism and the Darwinian Theory. Then came the war. No wonder then, if like John it is a little tired, if, for the time being at least, it seems to have reached the same stage of premature maturity and hollow wisdom; for it was not spiritually old enough for any of these things. [...] [T]he common intellectual attitude to-day is sceptical with Hume and Voltaire, impersonal with Mr. Bernard Shaw, or dilettante with the Platonists and George Santayana. Thomas Hardy has apparently monopolised the only personal dogma which a powerful intellect can hold, without needing to be ever up in arms to defend it with fierce, brilliant paradoxes and overwrought mysticisms. The Western world is like Pope's *Essay on Man:* it knows much, but it has not felt what it knows. [Barfield 1921c, 345]

What Barfield suggests here is that industrialization, Darwinian Theory and the Great War produced vast changes which have as yet not been properly digested or coped with. That is, he suggests that the modern mind is, in many ways, lagging behind these changes (which is what is implied in the phrase that the Western World is "not spiritually old enough for any of these things"). It is interesting to note that with this view he anticipates by one year the theory of "cultural lags", formulated by William Fielding Ogburn in his book *Social*

---

[60] "It is a pretentious and thankless task to attempt to analyse even a small part of the spirit of the age which we ourselves have condescended to adorn, and wise men never do it aloud. But perhaps one element of decadence is an exaggerated fear of looking foolish." Barfield 1921c, 345.

Change, With Respect to Culture and Original Nature (1922). A. J. Jaffe defines the phenomenon of "cultural lags" as follows:

> Adjustment is the final factor producing cultural evolution. Since all elements of a culture are interrelated, any pronounced change in one element will of necessity result in changes in other elements. Each time an invention is made, some social change has occurred that requires adjustment. An invention (material or nonmaterial) in one part of a culture may create an adjustment in a related part of the culture. "These adjustments do not take place instantaneously but are made after a delay and are called 'cultural lags'".[61]

Barfield, it will be noticed, identified the primary problem of his time as just such a delay in adjustment to the changes in recent history (which is what Ogburn later called a "cultural lag"). This was the point in his essay "Some Elements of Decadence" (1921): that modern thought had failed to adapt (and to respond adequately) to the changes caused by industrialization, Darwinian Theory and the Great War. With this failure it was evident for Barfield that modern thought was in a crisis. In *Danger, Ugliness and Waste* (c. 1925) he then concluded, as we have seen, that the crisis in modern thought not only mirrored, but actually also exacerbated the crisis in other spheres of modern life, e.g. the political, social and economic spheres. In this chapter I shall therefore examine in detail, first, what, according to Barfield, had caused the crisis in modern thought, and, secondly, what were, in his view, the consequences of this intellectual crisis for the other spheres of modern life. In this chapter I shall be particularly concerned with the consequences for politics. I shall then, in my last chapter, also discuss the consequences for the social and economic spheres.

---

[61] Jaffe, vol. xi, 279. The quotation within the quotation is from Ogburn's work *Social Change ...*, (1922).

1. Dualism and the Intellectual Roots of the Crisis:

Barfield's earliest essays reveal that the intellectual roots of the contemporary crisis lay, in his view, in the dualism which he felt was dominating modern thought. There is, in fact, hardly any essay from the 1920s which is not, in one form or another, preoccupied with dualism and its consequences. His earliest criticism of dualistic thought can be found in a review written in 1921 of works by George Santayana. (Santayana, we remember, is one of the authors whom, in "Some Elements of Decadence", he dismissed as "decadent"). Barfield begins this review by quoting what he considers to be a sufficiently representative statement by Santayana: "Things are interesting because we care about them, and important because we need them" [Barfield 1921b, 730]. He then proceeds to give us a summary of what he believes to be the philosopher's essential views:

> the philosopher, like the lady who so exasperated Carlyle, must "accept the Universe". Value is not the property of things, but an imposition of man, whose preferences are ultimately irrational; the task, and the only true task, of philosophy is to accept the human values it finds here, to see where they are incompatible, and to decide what reconcilement and combination of them will secure the most permanent joy. To do this and live accordingly is to live the Life of Reason [...]. [...] [E]motion exists and is good, but it is hypocritical to suggest that it can "transcend" reason, which must never, never fall asleep on that perch, where it sits holding the reins of religion, art, and love, and saying to them firmly: "thus far shalt thou go and no further." Only the lunatic is of imagination all compact; lovers and poets are not, or should not be, lunatics, but men who (as he somewhere says) "hold a lunatic in leash", and though it may be a long leash (if the lover is ardent or the poet great) *they must never quite let go.* [ibid.]

In this passage, as we can see, Barfield makes two complaints. The first is that Santayana, as Barfield understands him, declares values to be of an entirely subjective nature. The second is, that, in Barfield's view, the philosopher has created a gulf between reason and emotion and unduly emphasizes the superiority of reason over emotion; this is perhaps an echo of the point Barfield made in "Some Elements of

Decadence" when he complained that the "Western world is like Pope's *Essay on Man:* it knows much, but it has not felt what it knows" [Barfield 1921c, 345]. With these complaints Barfield does perhaps not make his general point very clear. Nevertheless, I think we can sense the direction in which he is heading. His criticism, it seems, is mainly directed at a tendency in dualistic thought to confine the experience of the individual knower to complete subjectivity. Santayana's philosophy, he points out, assumes that there is no objective knowledge of any kind; it assumes, to be more precise, that while there may be an objective reality outside the human mind, this reality remains essentially unknowable. Barfield comments:

> Thus, matter may or may not have an objective existence – but why trouble to discuss the question, for, in any case, to human beings (and philosophers are in this class) matter can only present itself as an experience of their own consciousness and nothing more? [Barfield 1921b, 729]

What Barfield mainly objects to, then, is a tendency in Santayana's philosophy to divorce ideas from a supposedly unknowable reality. In subsequent essays, Barfield demonstrates that this tendency to divorce idea from reality is not an isolated instance confined to Santayana's philosophy in particular, or even to philosophy in general. It has flourished and grown, for example, as he points out in a much later essay which is relevant here, into an entirely new discipline, that of psychology. In this essay, entitled "Psychology and Reason" (1930), he argues that a certain feature of psychology provides a striking parallel to the dualism of philosophy. For the chief interest of psychology, according to him, lies not so much in considering ideas on their own merit but in explaining the motives which have prompted them:

> The person with a true reverence for Psychology does not reply *to* his opponents' arguments; he talks *about* them. He considers not what you say, but why you say it. He does not give *reasons* for his own point of view, but the *causes* of yours. You suggest tentatively that the square on the hypotenuse of a right-angled triangle is equal to the sum of the squares on the other two sides, and immediately you blush and wilt and your knees tremble as you feel his deep eyes penetrating right through the dark unconscious motives which led you to make that absurd remark. After all, you say to

yourself, if I am really that sort of self-deceiving noodle, it *cannot* be true. [Barfield 1930b, 611]

There is, as this passage is obviously designed to bring home to us, something extremely absurd in the tendency (encouraged by psychology) to consider ideas not in terms of their *telos* – significance or force – but in terms of their psychological genesis. But there is something more serious to this, as Barfield is anxious to show. The really important point he is attempting to make here has a pre-echo in a piece he had written some nine years earlier. In this piece entitled "Milton and Metaphysics" (1923) he traces the same tendency of divorcing idea from reality also in the field of literary criticism, and begins with the following remark:

> There can be few more stimulating literary studies than to watch the way in which attitudes towards *Paradise Lost* have been veering and changing since its birth. [...] [C]ritics have reacted to the force [of the poem] in different ways; and the way in which they have reacted to it, hated it, loved it, explained it to themselves, is extremely interesting, for it concerns the history of our minds. [Barfield 1923b, 524]

Barfield observes the following historical changes in the attitude towards Milton's ideas: Johnson in the eighteenth century could, according to Barfield, still accept Milton's theology. This was no longer the case in the nineteenth century when, as he claims, Milton's theological conceptions were increasingly losing their appeal. Consequently, by the early twentieth century, he then observes, *Paradise Lost* was considered to be no more than a "monument to dead ideas" [ibid.]. He sums up this development as follows:

> The twentieth century has come more and more to see in *Paradise Lost* merely what it calls a 'sublimation' of Milton's personal character, a kind of vast Brocken-shadow of his private life. The 'ideas' in the poem have come to seem more and more dead and the personality of the man more and more vivid and alive. [ibid. 524–5]

The phenomenon of the "Brocken-shadow", mentioned in this passage, is a visual effect that is especially associated with a mountain called Brocken in the German Harz mountains. It is caused by the figure of the observer when at a certain angle of light his shadow is cast on a bank of mist where it then appears as a figure of gigantic size. Barfield might have been influenced here by Coleridge, who had himself seen the phenomenon, and who uses the Brocken spectre as an image of self-projection.[62] Barfield draws on this image to illustrate the twentieth century attitude to Milton's poetry. In the twentieth century critics tend, according to Barfield, to treat Milton's ideas as mere projections of Milton's mind with no real substance to them; that is, his ideas are seen (in the words of Sir Walter Raleigh, quoted by Barfield) as indicating "nothing but the character of the artist" [Barfield 1923b, 524]. Compare this with another significant passage from "Psychology and Reason":

> Our biographies are cleverer and cleverer collocations of striking anecdotes, designed to illustrate the romantic personal quality of the subject, and we are frankly bored if anything is said about the man's work or his thoughts. [...] All of us know that Milton was a disappointed husband, and that therefore he was the sort of man who *would* write a pamphlet on divorce. Which of us has read the pamphlet? And that reminds me that literary criticism bids fair to become as bad an offender as any in this romantic-personal-psychological-Gaderene rush down hill into intellectual chaos. The modern critic is no longer capable, it seems, of conceiving that a work of art has an existence of its own and apart from its creator. He is no longer approaching it as an object in itself, *per se, auto kath auton monoeides*, and considering its value for all time. [Barfield 1930b, 610]

In this context, it is interesting to note that C. S. Lewis, like Barfield, but in his own different way, attacked the idea that poetry was valuable only in so far as it reflected the mind of the poet. Lewis attacked this idea in *The Personal Heresy* (1939) – a dispute with E. M. W. Tillyard which again started from Milton. Lewis's dispute with Tillyard arose precisely from the fact that Tillyard had said we read Milton to find the mind of Milton. Lewis, in contrast to Tillyard, maintained that in so far as we can "know" a poet, it is "by sharing his consciousness, not by studying it":

---

[62] Cf. Coleridge's poem "Constancy to an Ideal Object", Coleridge 1912, 455–6, and Coleridge 1957ff, vol. i, 430. For a discussion of the Brocken-spectre as a Coleridgian image of self-projection, cf. Prickett 1970, 20ff., and Davidson, 142ff.

> I look with his eyes, not at him. He, for the moment, will be precisely what I do not see, for you can see any eyes rather than the pair you see with, and if you want to examine your own glasses you must take them off your nose. The poet is not a man who asks me to look at *him*; he is the man who says 'look at that' and points; the more I follow the pointing of his finger the less can I possibly see of *him*. [Tillyard and Lewis, 11][63]

This criticism by Lewis of the modern "psychological approach" to literature serves well to illustrate what Barfield, nearly twenty odd years before Lewis (beginning with "Milton and Metaphysics" in 1923), was himself most seriously concerned with. He was concerned with a tendency, not only in Miltonic criticism, but in literary criticism in general, to ignore the thing behind the idea and to focus instead on the personality of the thinker himself. In his essay "Psychology and Reason" he presses this point further by drawing a parallel to a similar development in philosophy:

> Modern philosophy (I mean that part of it which is generally recognized and spoken of as such by those who do not read it) ended with Kant in severing the knower from his universe and confining knowledge to the categories and forms of perception by which he schematizes for himself an unknown and unknowable cosmos. We have only carried this process one stage further, by not even believing in the objective reality of the categories. Now we are not even interested in the activity of knowing – only in the pitiful empirical personality of the knower. [Barfield 1930b, 611]

Barfield, he assures us, does not intend by remarks like these to condemn generally the new developments in the fields of philosophy and psychology. His aim is, not to discredit these developments, but to gain a thorough understanding of their possible implications and consequences.

> Now there is no question here of 'attacking' Psychology or any other nonsense of this sort. I wish only to consider one or

---

[63] The entire argument, as presented by Lewis, is an interesting pre-echo of what would later become the standard New Critical position on the irrelevance of authorial intention.

two points in connection with its increasing popularity and a corresponding inevitable tendency to apply universally certain rather trite formulas, to erect if I may say so, a complete, if vague metaphysic upon them, to see all experience included in the circle of abridged Psychology instead of seeing Psychology included in the circle of all experience. In short, spectacles are a very fine thing – provided that one is able to take them off. [ibid., 607]

"What", he asks himself, then, "does it signify, this perpetual, prurient prodding back to the personality behind the idea?" The answer he gives us is this:

It signifies, first and foremost, that we have lost all sense of the reality of ideas. Thought – and indeed *anything mixed with thought* – we feel now to be no more than a shadow hovering over the surface of something more solid – "these Thoughts" (as the author of *Trivia* once put it) "dipped up that phantasmagoria or phosphorescence which, by some unexplained process of combustion, flickers over the large lump of soft gray matter in the bowl of my skull". [ibid., 610]

These observations by Barfield about the loss of "the reality of ideas" coincide in some ways with a criticism that had arisen in the field of psychology itself. This criticism was voiced by the prominent psychiatrist Carl Gustav Jung. Jung, too, in his own different way, had recognized what Barfield called the loss of "the reality of ideas". That is, he had recognized this loss in the tendency in modern psychology to explain all human activity (including that of mind and spirit) deterministically, in terms of biology. It is interesting that just one year before Barfield's critical essay "Psychology and Reason" (1930) appeared, Jung had published an article in which he had criticised the current determinism and called for an urgent reevaluation of the activities of mind and spirit (*Geist* – the German word implies both meanings):

We moderns need to revive mental and spiritual experience, that is, we need to regain an existential experience. This is the only way of breaking the vicious circle of biological processes. [...] Anyone who does not see this aspect of the human soul is blind, and anyone who attempts to dispute it, or even to explain it away has no sense of fact. [Jung 1991, 56; my translation; cf. Note 31, 206]

The person at whom this obvious attack is directed, of course, is Freud. Jung's major criticism of Freud here and elsewhere is precisely that Freud had, in his view, diminished the sense of "the reality of ideas" by attempting to explain human activity, including the activity of *Geist* (that is, of mind and spirit), wholly in terms of biological instinct. Compare, for example, the following account by Jung of his difference with Freud:

> Above all, Freud's attitude towards the spirit seemed to me highly questionable. Wherever, in a person or in a work of art, an expression of spirituality (in the intellectual, not the supernatural sense) came to light, he suspected it, and insinuated that it was repressed sexuality. Anything that could not be directly interpreted as sexuality he referred to as 'psychosexuality'. I protested that this hypothesis, carried to its logical conclusion, would lead to an annihilating judgment upon culture. Culture would then appear as a mere farce, the morbid consequence of repressed sexuality. 'Yes', he assented, 'so it is, and that is just a curse of fate against which we are powerless to contend". [Jung 1977, 172–3; cf. also Note 32, 206][64]

Jung, in contrast to Freud, believed neither that *Geist* was powerless, nor that culture (as an extension of *Geist*) was a "farce". He denied that man was determined by instinct, and stressed instead the importance of mind and spirit (*Geist*) as vital driving forces of human activity.[65]

This – the re-discovery and re-evaluation of mind and spirit as vital driving forces of human activity – became a life-long task, not only for Jung but also for Barfield. Having said this, I nevertheless think that a comparison of the two authors should not be carried too far. For various comments by Barfield show that he was in some ways critical of the psychiatrist's views. Indeed, although we have noted Jung's affirmation of the "reality of ideas", it appears that Barfield

---

[64] Apart from these reflections in his memoirs, Jung explores his differences with Freud in more detail in Jung 1990.

[65] For the significance of *Geist* in Jungian psychology, cf. e.g. Samuels et. al., 81–3.

still found him insufficiently objectivist. Consider, for example, Barfield's comments on Jung in *Poetic Diction* (1928). On the one hand, he praises Jung for his rediscovery of the importance of myth, but, on the other, he criticizes him for restricting myth to the purely subjective sphere, thereby denying it any external significance: "the myths are seen [by Jung] as a sort of unconscious 'projection' of the inner life of feeling upon an inanimate outer world" [Barfield 1987, 203, (cf. also 38)]. Barfield makes a similar criticism in various other places, as for example in an interview he gave in 1976, where he accuses Jung of denying that mind, or the unconscious mind, is something "which transcends the separateness of an individual human being's physical body." Here, however, he admits that Jung is ambiguous on this point and that elswhere he allows a more transcendental understanding of the unconscious mind:

> The collective unconscious is really understood only if you see it not as something which arose out of the aggregation of a number of experiences had by individual human beings but as something out of which the human individual and his physical body originally arose. There are other passages in Jung where he does speak of archetypes as if he meant it that way. [Barfield in Sugerman, 14]

This is not the place for a detailed discussion of the differences between Barfield and Jung [For more details, cf. Avens]. The essential thing for us – whatever the differences – is to recognize the single-minded aim of both thinkers to re-evaluate the activities of mind and spirit. It cannot be overemphasized just how important this aim was to both thinkers at a time which seemed to endorse an increasingly deterministic view of human affairs. The comparison with Jung shows, I think, that Barfield – with his criticism of dualistic thought – was at the forefront of establishing new views to counteract this determinism. In the following two sections I shall explain this further by tracing Barfield's critical views on the consequences of contemporary dualism for the individual, culture, and, above all, politics.

2. Dualism, Individual and Culture

Let us recapitulate what we have learnt so far about Barfield's views on dualism and its effects. Barfield suggested, as we saw earlier, that the changing attitudes towards the poet Milton tell us something about the history of our minds. That is, he suggested that certain trends in literary scholarship reveal something about the evolution of our consciousness. Now, as Barfield has shown, not only literary scholarship, but other academic disciplines as well (e.g. philosophy and psychology), are in the twentieth century characterized by an essentially dualistic perspective. Dualism, however, was for Barfield clearly not confined to the academic level. If we consider his fictional writings as well as his writings on practical affairs (which is what I propose to do in this section) we quickly realize that his concern with 'academic' dualism was part of a far wider concern with current cultural, political and social processes, as well as with individual self-consciousness in the twentieth century. That is to say, contemporary dualism was not at all merely a matter of dry academic thought. On the contrary, in Barfield's view, it affected the *whole* of contemporary life and experience, and therefore profoundly influenced and shaped modern self-consciousness, culture and society.

In which way, then, has dualism, in Barfield's view, influenced and shaped modern consciousness? Now, the first thing we have already seen is that dualism, with its divorce of idea from reality, has, according to Barfield, resulted in a loss of "all sense of the reality of ideas" [Barfield 1930b, 610]. One of the things which he notices about the consequences of this loss is that it has created in the twentieth century a profound feeling of (spiritual) isolation, loneliness and alienation: "To-day", he comments,

> we see ourselves as a community of somnambulists, ships that pass in the night, uncommunicative and that by necessity, each hopelessly imprisoned in a misty aura of his own phantasies, men like trees walking. [ibid., 611]

If we now turn our attention to Barfield's fiction we shall find there an expression of precisely such feelings of intense loneliness, isolation and alienation. The themes explored in his fiction of the 1920s are all concerned with the consequences of an outlook which separates

individual thought (and experience) from reality. His short story
"Dope" (1923), already mentioned in chapter one, is perhaps the most
impressive illustration of an alienating outlook which reduces the
individual to a passive spectator of an external reality, whose
processes are increasingly felt to be slipping out of control. "Dope" is
about a young factory worker who experiences life, not as meaningful
interaction, but as a mechanical succession of disconnected scenes. It
begins like this:

> At 6:30 P.M. the wheels of the factory stopped turning, and
> five hundred minds, which had been turning with them all day,
> were set suddenly adrift. One of them belonged to Henry
> Williams, unskilled labourer, aged twenty, who flowed out
> through the gates in the long chattering stream and plodded on
> alone toward his Underground station with nothing particular
> in his thoughts except a row of the little bright screws he had
> been sorting all day. [Barfield 1993a, 78]

The rhythm of the story is that of the big city and the machine. Life,
including the mental life of the protagonist, appears to be entirely
mechanical. The individuals in the story are doomed to lead, as the
title "Dope" suggests, the drugged existence of human automata.
There is a very interesting parallel to this in the silent film *Metropolis*
(1926), in which Fritz Lang portrays a modern urbanized mechanical
life founded on slave labour. We may also compare C.S. Lewis's
gloomy (unfinished) short story "The Dark Tower" (1939) where
Lewis envisages a totalitarian state in "Othertime", in which an all-
powerful ruler transforms people into will-less 'automata'. It is
interesting that the setting of the perverse ritual of dehumanization
exercized by the ruler, the "Dark Tower", is "an almost exact replica"
of the new university library in Cambridge – an image which not only
expresses Lewis's apparent dislike of that particular modern building,
but also suggests that totalitarian perversion may have its root in the
"dark tower" of perverted intellect and learning (which is one of the
things the modern library building seems to stand for).[66] Moreover,
the imagery connected with the ruler's desire for absolute power has

---

[66] For an interpretation of *The Dark Tower* in its context of contemporary totalitarianism, cf. Kegler, 125–6.

strongly sexual implications – a (possible) reference to Freud and his claim that human motivation is based on sexual instinct.

It is likely that Lewis's story "The Dark Tower" was influenced by Barfield's writings, both fictional and non-fictional, of the 1920s, for it is more than obvious that in this story (dated c. 1939) Lewis, in his own different way, brings together many of the themes explored by Barfield more than a decade earlier. However, independently from the question of literary influence or debt, we can recognize both in Barfield's short story "Dope" and in Lewis's "Dark Tower" a spirit which is common to both authors and which they share with their age. As to Barfield's own story, considered in the light of similar works of art and literature such as Lang's or Lewis's, it is clear that it represents something more than a simple case study of a young factory worker. In fact, it embodies twentieth century fears about the predicament of modern man in an increasingly mechanized world: fears, for example, about the loss of meaning in a world where individuals feel they are doomed to coexist without relating to each other or the world around them. It also embodies fears about the loss of freedom as man increasingly feels dominated and enslaved by the machine.[67] By giving expression to such fears, especially fears about the loss of freedom, Barfield adumbrates, in some ways, the dawning of the age of totalitarianism and fascism. To this latter point I shall come back later, in my discussion of Barfield's political views. Meanwhile, I shall return to my original investigation of the influence of dualistic thought on modern consciousness.

The short story "Dope", as I hope the above interpretation has shown, is a good example of the consequences of dualistic thought. It illustrates how a divorce of idea from reality and the subsequent loss of the "reality of ideas" plunges the individual in intense feelings of isolation and alienation. The depths of human isolation and alienation are further explored by Barfield in a short story entitled "The Devastated Area" (1924). This story, too, has as its theme the impotence of thought and feeling over against a hollow, this time not literally mechanical, but spiritually empty world. It is about a shell-

---

[67] About the loss of meaning and the loss of freedom through technical progress as persistent themes in 20th century literature, cf. Segeberg 1887.

shocked soldier, called Stephen, who is so completely devastated by the horrors of war that he has very nearly lost the ability to communicate his experiences. Returning from the war to a world which seems to him to have nothing much to offer but superficial sympathy at the very best, he suffers from an intense spiritual loneliness. Consider the following juxtaposition of his own war experience and his girl friend Muriel's reaction:

> Three days in the shell-hole – looking straight into the top of that man's head – he and another fellow. And not even horrified – at the time – they had joked: How are you feeling now, Henry? Top-hole! thank you! ... "Oh, Stephen!" said Muriel, when he told her, "Oh, Stephen!" – just what she had said when little Freddy cut his thumb so deep. Well, what else could she have said? Did he expect her to faint? Yes, but he could still draw a map with his eyes shut of the inside of that head! Oh, what funny patterns!
>
> "The workings of men's brains ..."
>
> Matthew Arnold
>
> [Barfield 1993b, 78]

The first thing we notice in this passage is that, in spite of Muriel's apparent sympathy, Stephen remains essentially alone with the horror he has experienced. It is worthwhile pointing out that there is an interesting parallel to this in Barfield's remarks of 1921 about the poet Wilfred Owen:

> To this poet war seems to have meant above all things loneliness; he must have been haunted continually by a horrible sense of spiritual isolation, which kept whispering to him that his friends – above all, that the women – at home, loving, sympathetic, imaginative as they might be, had never once been at the threshold of *sharing* his experiences. He felt with anguish that he was gradually slipping further away from them, *isolated by his own suffering.* [Barfield 1921a, 454]

There is something much darker and more terrible in this experience of loneliness than is fully spelt out in the Owen review. The short story is more revealing in this respect. Here one cannot help feeling that the really shocking thing is not the *horror* of war alone, it is the actual *reaction* to that horror of those who stayed at home. Of course, one cannot reasonably expect anyone to share *fully* in an experience which they have not gone through themselves. Perhaps in this respect the protagonist Stephen expects too much of his girl friend Muriel. However, there *is* something deeply shocking about her reaction to Stephen's account of the terrible death of one of his fellow soldiers. As is evident in the passage quoted above, Muriel seems to consider the cruel loss of a soldier's life on the same par with a small injury inflicted on a boy. Her sympathy, therefore, resembles something more like indifference than real sympathy and understanding. To put it in a slightly extreme form, there seems for her to be no difference between a small accident in everyday life and organized mass destruction in war. Death in war, being considered on a par with an injury in ordinary life, looks as if it were simply accepted as part of ordinary life – accepted as the norm rather than the exception. Surprisingly, perhaps, Stephen's attitude to the war, although it appears different, is more similar to Muriel's attitude than might at first be suspected. The only difference between them is that Muriel reacts to the horrors of war with indifference, and Stephen with despair. But they both seem to *accept*, though not approve of war as part of the normal conditions characterizing human life. This needs further illumination.

We can find some illumination if we place Barfield's short story in the contemporary context of Western thought about the war. If we do so, we shall immediately recognize that the story exemplifies in many ways what Paul Crook has termed the "schizoid tendencies" that often – since the publication of Darwin's *Origin of Species* (1859) – prevailed in Western thought about the war. According to Crook, war was, on the one hand, condemned, but on the other, accepted as an inevitable expression of a "pugnacious human nature" [cf. Crook, 1]. That is, in other words, it was condemned, but at the same time accepted on the assumption that man's conduct was inevitably guided not by reason but by aggressive animal instinct. This seems to be the approach which characterizes both Stephen's and Muriel's attitude. Crook terms this approach to war "war biology" or "animal reductionism". The whole point of Crook's book, however, is to show that there were also certain attempts to establish a "peace biology", or what he also calls "elevationism" [ibid., 9ff]. As I hope to show later, on the whole, Barfield has to count more as an "elevationist" than a "reductionist". However, the spirit of this particular short story is unquestionably "reductionist". That is, it draws on a philosophy which divorces idea from reality and subsequently, with the help of Darwinian Theory, reduces reality to the level of physical or biological processes. This marriage of dualism with ideas from Darwin results in a very narrow view of human nature and life, as is well illustrated in the short story. For the protagonist accepts as a fact the futility of all dreams and ideals and resigns himself to the view that life is inevitably and ultimately a brutal animal struggle for existence. Note the rat imagery in the following passage:

> Dreams rushing faster and faster, round and round, like the furious colours on a soap bubble just before it bursts. Rat swimming madly in a cage plunged in water, legs kicking, the will to live. "Hi! I must get out of this!" said the rat bursting his lungs. Life is a cart on the way from Newgate Street to Tyburn. I must get out of this. Plenty of people do, you know ... found with his head in a gas oven. "Poor Boy! Life was too much for him!" Muriel would know he hadn't been callous. A catch in her throat. A catch in my throat – eyes hot. Good Lord! Stop this! Tom Sawyer. (Selfpity Limited.) You baby! Muriel – Muriel! O my darling. "Yes, yes! Poor little Stevy!" No. No use. Well then, write something! Write – write? What's the good of writing? The only people who'll read it are the people who feel it already. The nice, gentle people you want to get at, who go on deceiving themselves all their lives, they'll just read the first page and put it away. They'll think you have made a faux pas. [Barfield 1993b, 84]

It is clear that the narrator of this passage, as indeed of the whole short story, is the protagonist himself. But the narration uneasily oscillates between first and third person narration, indicating the narrator's confused perception of himself both as subject and as object, as agent and as patient – indeed more as patient than as agent. I say patient, because of his intense suffering and his helplessness. The experience of war and the insight into the apparently inevitable structure of our life as an animal struggle for existence – these have left the protagonist completely disillusioned. Ideals have lost their power for him to create or re-create meaning in a world he has come to accept as utterly meaningless: "Life is a cart on the way from Newgate Street to Tyburn. I must get out of this.", as he puts it in the quotation above. However, it isn't all as bleak as that.

In spite of his extreme despair, the hero has not lost or given up his ability to communicate. Even though he wearily questions "the good of writing", he actually goes on writing and tells us his story. He is still able and willing to give expression, at least, to his despair. The story does therefore not actually document the final *breakdown* of communication and meaning. Some form of communication is still maintained, however fragmented it may be. The fact that the hero has not stopped communicating means that he has as yet not abandoned himself entirely to his despair and is struggling to come to terms with his suffering. There is still hope that he might succeed. In this context, Barfield's remarks about Wilfred Owen are again interesting:

> It is when he is giving expression, either in his lines or between them, to this misgiving [loneliness and isolation] that his poetry rises to its greatest height, greatest of all, perhaps, when his loneliness is striving to find comfort in a new philosophy, and his shocked affections are actually putting out poor tendrils to clasp the mud and blood about him. 'Greater Love' is a stern, almost cruel, renunciation, but it is not a joyous one: [...]. In 'Apologia Pro Poemate Meo' he tries to rejoice in his new faith [...]. But he soon returns to the old note [...]. These two poems – the finest in the book – are alone enough to suggest that he might have gone far and found the something he seems to be searching for in his tentative metrical innovations, could he only have lived through into more tranquil days. [Barfield 1921a, 454]

As this passage suggests, Barfield perceived in Owen's poetry not only an effort to cope with intense suffering, but also gropings for a "new philosophy", that is, gropings perhaps for a more hopeful, more meaningful perspective on life. Barfield may have intended to convey a similar impression in his short story. For by still communicating his suffering, the protagonist continues to reach out to other human beings. And in this alone there might be the beginning of a recreation of new meaning and new relationships in a world shattered by war. However, we must be careful not to be too optimistic. The story remains ambiguous and disturbing. It ends abruptly, and there is no way of knowing what will happen to the hero in the end: will he choose a philosophy of life and relations? or will he abandon himself to a philosophy of death and destruction? that is, will he choose to live or to die? or choose a dim existence between life and death? Any of these options are open.

It is important to remember at this point that in the same year (1921) when he claimed that Owen was "striving to find comfort in a new philosophy" [ibid.] Barfield was himself beginning to explore a "new philosophy". That is, he embarked on his research project *Poetic Diction*. *Poetic Diction*, of course, was later to be published as a book with the significant subtitle *A Study in Meaning* (1928). It is perhaps slightly surprising to find that Barfield should be building up a learned theory about the "rediscovery of meaning" in *Poetic Diction* while at the same time composing short stories which suggest the opposite: the breakdown of meaning. Of course, none of his stories, not even the bleakest of them, "The Devastated Area", ever end in a complete breakdown of meaning. But we have to admit that these stories, that is the ones which I have discussed, come pretty close to such a breakdown. There is, therefore, an odd discrepancy between the views held in his theoretical work and those coveyed in his fiction. It should be noted (I shall discuss this in more detail later) that Barfield eventually resolved the discrepancy and abandoned the pessimistic outlook of his short stories. However, the stories provide evidence of the fact that for a certain period he was, in some respects at least, thoroughly in line with the accepted literary fashion of the period, and therefore shared to some extent its outlook. Both the tone and the style of his short stories invite comparison, for example, with the work of T. S. Eliot, who is considered as one of the most eminent and perhaps most representative literary figures of the period. It is, of course, Eliot's *The Waste Land* (1922) which immediately comes to mind as a good example for a comparison. Consider, for instance, the following lines:

> What are the roots that clutch, what branches grow
> Out of this stony rubbish? Son of man,
> You cannot say, or guess, for you know only
> A heap of broken images, where the sun beats,
> And the dead tree gives no shelter, the cricket no relief,
> And the dry stone no sound of water.
>
> [Eliot 1987b, 61]

> 'Trams and dusty trees.
> Highbury bore me. Richmond and Kew
> Undid me. By Richmond I raised my knees
> Supine on the floor of a narrow canoe.'[...]
> 'On Margate Sands I can connect
> Nothing with nothing.

> The broken fingernails of dirty hands.
> My people humble people who expect
> Nothing.'
>
> [ibid., 70]

The perspective of the speaker in this poem resembles that of the protagonist in Barfield's "Dope". This perspective, as I have already pointed out in my comment on "Dope", is characterized not by meaningful interrelation, but by fragmentation and disintegration. Again we recognize in this a way of thinking which divorces idea from reality. As Eliot puts it in his poem "The Hollow Men" (1925):

> Between the idea
> And the reality
> Between the motion
> And the act
> Falls the shadow.
>
> [Eliot 1987a, 85]

The result of this divorce, as is illustrated by the previous quotation, is an experience of the complete impotence of thought. Individuals are doomed to live in a world in which they can "connect/ Nothing with nothing". A. D. Nuttall has shown that the above lines from Eliot's "The Hollow Men" depend on "a metaphysic which makes ordinary thought and intercourse impossible" [Nuttall 1974, 242]. This is in my view true for *The Waste Land*, as much as for "The Hollow Men", which is Nuttall's example. And it is not difficult to see that the same is also true for Barfield's "Dope" and his other story "The Devastated Area". Both Barfield's stories and Eliot's poetry, which I have discussed, give each expression to a sense that we are all "uncommunicative and that by necessity, each hopelessly imprisoned in a misty aura of his own phantasies, men like trees walking." This, we remember, is in Barfield's view *the* characteristic of modern self-consciousness [Barfield 1930b, 611].

There are, as we can see, strong parallels in Barfield and Eliot. But there is another element in Barfield which is not quite so strong in Eliot. In Barfield the modern experience of isolation and alienation is combined, in his story "Dope", with specific fears about the alienating and dehumanizing effects of technical progress. There are a number of passages in *The Waste Land* which reflect similar fears.[68] However, there is in the poem a more *general* sense of the transformation of individuals into a faceless mass and of life into a meaningless existence,[69] and this is seen not primarily as an effect of technical progress, but of more general processes inherent in modern civilization as a whole.[70] A perhaps more typical expression of the fears about the effects of technical progress can be found in the reflections of another contemporary of Barfield's, those of Arthur J. Penty.[71] It is evident that Barfield was acquainted with Penty's views but that his attitude to Penty was ambivalent [cf. Barfield 1925a[72]]. In some ways he agreed with Penty, in others he vehemently disagreed with him. Barfield's disagreement with Penty will be explored in the next chapter. At the moment I am mainly concerned with what is common to them both. Let us consider the following observation by Penty of 1925 about the effects of industrialization on modern life:

> [M]achinery exercises an influence akin to magic, putting men into a kind of hypnotic trance, causing them to act in ways they do not entirely approve. Indeed, I incline to the opinion that machinery is on the material plane what magic is on the spiritual, because the attitude towards both phenomena[l][73] is

---

[68] One example comparable with Barfield's vision in "Dope" of men as human automata is Eliot's image from *The Waste Land*, "when the human engine waits / Like a taxi throbbing waiting" Eliot 1987b, 68.

[69] Cf. e.g. the following lines: "Unreal City, / Under the brown fog of a winter dawn, / A crowd flowed over London Bridge, so many, / I had not thought death had undone so many." Eliot 1987b, 62.

[70] About Eliot's criticism of modern civilization in *The Waste Land*, cf. e.g. Gordan 1977, 29–30, 93–4, 108–9, etc.

[71] Penty, an architect, is the author of the book *The Restoration of the Guild System* (1906). This book inspired a movement, which began effectively in 1912, called "Guild Socialism". Barfield himself was, as I shall discuss in more detail in the next chapter, actively interested in a different movement called "Social Credit".

[72] The reply is addressed to Penty's article "The Line of Least Resistance".

[73] The 'l' here must be a printer's error.

mechanical. This is the great difficulty of dealing with it. [...] The man who accepts the permanence of machinery as the first tenet in his creed ends in getting nowhere. For he finds himself obliged to sacrifice every standard of thought, every belief and ideal at the behest of progress, and therefore spiritually and mentally he goes to pieces and ends his days in a maze of conflicting ideas in which he comes to doubt everything except that machinery has come to stay. [Penty, 200]

This passage reads a little like a comment on Barfield's "Dope". Both "Dope" and Penty's article express a strong sense almost of resignation over the process of mechanization. The individual is depicted as a more or less helpless cog in the wheel of the machinery he has himself created. Machinery is seen as creating a form of existence in which man is being deprived of his essential freedom and his humanity. The result is a sense of complete alienation and loss of meaning. For in the end, mind and spirit are felt to be completely overruled by the force of the technical development, and there appears to be no way of stopping this process. Such criticism of the alienating and dehumanizing effects of the machine has, of course, a root in the criticism, which arose in the nineteenth century, of the effects of industrialization.[74] However, Penty's article contains more than a 'simple' criticism of the effects of technical progress and industrialization. His views culminate in an apocalyptic vision of the actual breakdown of civilization:

> instead of being used for constructive purposes it [machinery] is only used for destructive ones, and therefore must end in destroying the civilisation which nurtures it; and therefore machinery and civilisation are involved in a common ruin. [Penty, 200]

These reflections by Penty are easily recognizable as yet another variant of the divorce of idea from reality and spirit from matter. Here the divorce expresses itself as a polarisation of culture and civilization – culture being identified with the world of ideas and ideals (e.g. art

---

[74] About the criticism of the alienating and dehumanizing effects of industrialization since the nineteenth century, cf. e.g., Marx 1964, Feuer, Pappenheim, and Fromm.

and literature) and civilization with the world of material processes (e.g. technical progress and industrialization). Historically, this polarisation can be traced back well beyond the nineteenth century, but it is generally agreed that it was in the nineteenth century that it took on a special urgency [cf. e.g. Segeberg 1987???, and Ott]. It has also been said that in England this sense of polarisation was never as strong as in Germany [Schwanitz, 391]. Yet Penty definitely felt very strongly indeed that there was an antagonism between culture and technological civilization and that the two were mutually exclusive. "The man who accepts the permanence of machinery as the first tenet in his creed [...] finds himself obliged to *sacrifice* every standard of thought, every belief and ideal at the behest of progress", as Penty puts it in the passage quoted above (my italics). This feeling of the mutual exclusiveness of ideal and (material) reality, culture and civilization resulted for Penty (and also for Eliot) in a sense that modern civilization was on the verge of a decline. For Penty (though not so much for Eliot) this sense of decline was fired above all by his fears about the adverse effects of technical progress. In his words again, "machinery and civilisation are involved in a common ruin". With this view, Penty's outlook very strongly resembles that of the influential German cultural historian Oswald Spengler.

As I have already discussed in my chapter on Steiner, it was Oswald Spengler who in the early twentieth century expressed the perhaps most coherently pessimistic views on the consequences of technical progress. To Spengler the process of mechanization appeared as a process that was increasingly getting out of control and was therefore threatening civilization. Machinery, according to Spengler, had turned into a machinery of destruction, and Western civilization was heading towards its inevitable decline. Spengler had completed (but not published) his book *Untergang des Abendlandes* before the outbreak of the Great War. In retrospect, when the book appeared in 1917, the events of the war seemed to confirm his gloomy views, as he notes in the introduction: "Die Ereignisse [des Krieges] haben vieles [dieser Einsichten] bestätigt und nichts widerlegt." ["Many (of these views) have been indisputably confirmed by the events (of the war)." My translation; Spengler, ix].

Penty, as we have seen, came to remarkably similar conclusions. As to Barfield, it ought to be stressed that he actually never completely subscribed to an extreme pessimism such as that of Penty and Spengler. Nevertheless, from what we have seen so far, it is clear enough that at least at some early stage of his intellectual career he held certain views in common with these authors. At one point, he admits, for example, the notion of a "monstrous energy which we can organise for the destruction of civilisation, but not for its maintenance and development" [Barfield c. 1925, 6]. Moreover, there is a curious parallel in Barfield's and Penty's choice of the word "hypnotic". Penty, we remember, spoke of machinery as "putting men into a kind of hypnotic trance, causing them to act in ways they do not entirely approve" [Penty, 200]. This is the state of drugged apathy and involuntary passivity to which the individuals in "Dope" are condemned. Barfield, in his essay *Danger, Ugliness and Waste*, uses the same word, "hypnotic" to describe the state of social, political and economic stagnation which in his view characterized post-war Britain [Barfield c. 1925, 2; full quotation above, 102.]. That is, the word "hypnotic" describes a condition suffered not only by individuals, but by society as a whole.

It can be safely concluded, then, that to some extent Barfield shared with his contemporaries a strong sense of crisis. This sense of crisis, being rooted in an essentially dualistic world view, expressed itself variously as visions of alienation, stagnation, disintegration and decline. However, although Barfield shared with his contemporaries a sense of crisis, he eventually came to completely different conclusions and rejected the pessimism of his contemporaries. This is evident most clearly for the first time in his vehement disagreement with Eliot.

Eliot (as I pointed out in chapter one) approved of Barfield's short story "Dope". We do not know whether Eliot also knew "The Devastated Area" (it had been published in *New Age*) and whether or not he liked it (one would expect him to have done so had he known it, but there is no evidence for this). What we do know is that Barfield had sent him a number of other stories, which apparently were markedly different from "Dope" (and therefore implicitly also of "The Devastated Area"). Of these Eliot did *not* approve. The stories, which Barfield sent to Eliot, do not survive, but Eliot's critical response to them is preserved in a letter to Barfield, where Eliot wrote: "I believe in a fundamental rhythm, of which one's original work gives variations, and I think that this is very much stronger in "Dope" than in anything else of yours I have seen" [Eliot 1924]. In an earlier letter, which is not preserved, Eliot had praised the rhythm of "Dope" and had apparently asked Barfield to keep working on it. Barfield who, meanwhile, had resolved to abandon the pessimistic theme of "Dope" (and implicitly also of "The Devastated Area") made the following reply:

> I think that the rhythm which you noticed in "Dope" was really something adapted to that particular sketch. I mean it worked itself out from the subject, and was an expression of the sort of passivity with which undeveloped 20th century minds (as far as I can see) watch a mechanical world clicking past their limited field of vision. To repeat the rhythm, it would be necessary to repeat the subject, and I believe at present that it is a waste of energy to record an impression of that sort more than once. I am a little tired of a literature which can do nothing but point out ironically that there is nothing much going on but disintegration and decay. At the same time thank you very much for your kind suggestion that I should work on it. [Barfield (1924-48), fol. 25, Letter to T.S. Eliot dated 30 April 1924]

As is evident from this letter, Barfield clearly objected to a dualistic world view which fostered pessimistic visions of "disintegration and decay". Barfield objected to it because it was essentially reductionist in its interpretation of human nature and activity. He believed that a pessimistic world view, which dwelt on decline and denied positive change and improvement, was essentially damaging and destructive. Barfield makes this absolutely clear in an article, which followed six months after his letter to Eliot, in which he discusses the link between dualistic thought and the rise of fascism.[75] Although in this article Eliot is not actually mentioned, it is nevertheless clear from its content that Barfield objects to Eliot's views for very similar reasons that he objects to fascism. It ought to be emphasized, though, that Barfield never directly accused Eliot of being a fascist. It may well be that he was right to withold the charge. Certainly Eliot, like other writers of the period, employed terms such as 'race' in a manner which can easily grate upon modern sensibilities: In *After Strange Gods* (1934)

---

[75] Barfield 1924, 9. The letter responds Levy's "The Spiritual Basis of Fascism".

he wrote of the inhabitants of Virginia "you have been less industrialised and less invaded by foreign races". In *Notes Towards the Definition of Culture* (1948) he applauds efforts made by Welsh and Scottish nationalists not "to lose their national character" [Eliot (1933), 16; Eliot 1948, 57]. His views about Jews and Jewishness are more elusive, less definitely ascertainable than many recent writers suppose.[76] What is clear is that we can say of him what has been said of T. E. Hulme: "he says nothing in support of semi-divine leaders, the deification of the nation-state, or militarily organized mass movements" – all of which are essential features of fascist doctrine.[77]

Eliot, as is well known, had much in common with Hulme. He (Eliot) "cultivated a state of mind that was the very antithesis of the eclectic, tolerant democratic mind that had surrounded his late-nineteenth-century Mid-Western childhood" [Gordan 1977, 71]. And this attitude he essentially shared with Hulme. Zeev Sternhell comments:

> Hulme [wrote] that "man is an extraordinarily fixed and limited animal whose nature is absolutely constant. It is only by tradition and organization that anything decent can be got out of him." [...] The young philosopher thus concluded that there was a necessity for a strict religious discipline and obedience to the state. [...] Such was the conceptual framework that, in the years before the Great War, Thomas Hulme passed on to Yeats, Pound, Lewis, and Eliot. They were all agreed in rejecting the humanistic tradition, and they all rebelled with extreme violence against democracy. [Sternhell, Snajder and Asheri, 240–1]

Sternhell concludes that Eliot's own pessimistic and antidemocratic attitude, like Hulme's, resembles the "revolutionary conservatism, which in some cases is synonymous with fascism" [ibid., 240]. Recent scholarship, then, recognizes in Eliot's ideas certain features which compose a definite ingredient of fascist ideology. For this not only

---

[76] For an example of the recent revival of the picture of Eliot as anti-Semitic, cf. Julius.

[77] Quinton, 117. For an explicit rejection by Eliot of certain elements of fascist doctrine, cf. e.g. Gordan 1989, 22–3, and, more recently, Scott, 65.

Eliot, but also Hulme, Pound and Lewis, among other writers of the period, have been considered by Sternhell, not directly as fascists, but as "fellow travellers of fascism" [ibid., 239]. From here it is now necessary to return to Barfield and to discuss his own views on fascism and his reasons for rejecting it.

3. Dualism and Politics

Barfield airs his views about fascism in his response to an article entitled "The Spiritual Basis of Fascism" (1924) by one Dr Oscar Levy, "Editor of the authorised English Edition of Nietzsche's work", as the author introduces himself. After this introduction the author immediately adds a quotation – "Il n'y a de supportables que les choses extremes" – which is, disappointingly, not from Nietzsche, but from one Robert de Montesquiou, and which sets the tone of his own article [Levy, 305]. The tone is that of an extreme admiration of an extreme political movement, Italian fascism. Levy, who appears to have known Mussolini personally, laments the sluggish reception of Mussolini's fascist doctrines "by a thoroughly senile public all over Europe" – a lamentation to which, as Levy reports, Mussolini replied: "I shall write no more. They [the public] are too stupid! They don't understand a word." Thus Levy feels called upon to take upon himself the heroic task of defending Mussolini and his doctrines:

> I myself am still of the opinion that people ought to be made to understand. It is important for them to do so. It is also important for present-day Italy not to be misunderstood. I shall, therefore, try to explain that Fascism is not a "brutalitarian", not even "utilitarian" creed, but one inspired by a very high ideal – an ideal which only labours under this one disadvantage that it is a New Ideal. [ibid., 306]

This "New Ideal", of which Levy seems so completely convinced, and which is designed to guarantee "the guidance and progress of mankind" [ibid., 307] is hopelessly vague and remains oddly undefined throughout the article. Levy seems satisfied that this ideal has its "spiritual [meaning ideological] basis" in the philosophy of Nietzsche, and for this reason alone it seems in his view totally acceptable, requiring no further justification. Levy consequently offers none. This is where Barfield at once takes issue. He accepts that fascism may have its "spiritual basis" in Nietzsche, but this is in his view not an automatic reason for admiring it. On the contrary, he warns of the danger of blindly and uncritically accepting Nietzsche as an authority, and gives the following reasons for this:

> I was particularly grateful, if I may say so, for his [Dr. Levy's] information concerning Mussolini's debt to Nietzsche. But to understand Nietzsche properly, it is surely necessary to place him in his own intellectual setting of late nineteenth century thought. The idea of a struggle for existence and the survival of the fittest had bitten deeply enough into thousands of European minds, but deepest of all, perhaps into Nietzsche's, who followed the example of innumerable contemporaries in applying this theory – evolved to account for certain definite phenomena in Natural Science – to all sorts of spheres outside it, notably to the political, economic and spiritual activities of human beings. The more I read of and about Nietzsche, the more convinced do I become that that ghastly suspicion of all human activity being automatically predetermined by rigid, extra-human laws was gnawing at his intellectual and emotional vitals, much as it gnawed at the milder vitals of men like Arnold and Clough. In them it produced an incurable melancholy. In Nietzsche it produced, not tears, idle tears, but the strained fury of his paeans in praise of strength, will, self-assertion of any sort. [Barfield 1924, 9]

In the passage following these remarks, Barfield draws our attention from philosophy to contemporary politics and illuminates the link between the two. In order to understand the suggested link it will be necessary, first of all, to place the above remarks about Nietzsche in the larger context of Barfield's discussion of the effects of dualistic thought. As we have seen, the effect of dualism with which Barfield is mainly concerned is the loss of "all sense of the reality of ideas" [Barfield 1930b, 610; cf. also above 111 and 114-3]. Now, in his response to Dr Levy just quoted, he considers the special role of Darwinian theory, where it is applied to areas outside the strictly biological sphere, in deepening this sense of the loss of "the reality of ideas". In Barfield's view, as we saw earlier, this loss had diminished the individual's sense of being able to participate, with his ideas, actively and creatively in the world around him; it had reduced him to a passive spectator of reality. Where it is applied to social processes, as Barfield argues here, the idea of a struggle for existence and the survival of the fittest helps to remove the individual even further, to plunge him still more deeply in the passive role of the mere spectator. For he comes to believe that he is governed by extra-human laws over which he has no control.

From here Barfield makes a sweeping link to contemporary politics, demonstrating that it is this marriage of dualism with Darwinian Theory which forms the ideological backbone of the authoritarian politics of fascism. It ought to be noted, however, that Barfield does not reject Darwinian Theory itself; he only warns of the disastrous effect of applying it uncritically, as he believes Nietzsche does, to other spheres.[78] For the effect of such extraneous application, according to Barfield, is this: Darwinian Theory is being abused to "justify an ideal that seeks to turn the many into a sort of power-fodder for assisting the spiritual development of the few" [ibid., 9]. The phrase "spiritual development of the few" sounds perhaps a little vague, but I think it is clear what Barfield is getting at. With his observation that fascism endorses an "ideal" which "seeks to turn the many into a sort of *power-fodder* for assisting the spiritual development of *the few*" (my italics), he recognizes two of the essential features of fascist ideology: its élitism and its authoritarianism. In other words, Barfield believes that the reductionist interpretation of human nature, based on Darwinian Theory, has stripped humanity of its essential freedom, and has thereby paved the way for a minority élite to assume power of control. Or to put it more clearly, Barfield suggests that the body of ideas based on Darwinian Theory has created a mental climate, which has made the individual and society on the whole vulnerable to authoritarian control and manipulation.[79]

---

[78] This, of course, is a very narrow interpretation of Nietzsche, who, as I have discussed elsewhere, has shown in many places that he is anything but a blind follower of Darwin. Cf. above 82.

[79] For a scholarly discussion of the connection of Darwinism with élitism and authoritarianism, cf. e.g. Sternhell 1979, 344ff., and Crook, 7–8.

Barfield, we may say, grasps the full implications of Levy's article. It is the tone of his article which betrays Levy's cause. Levy's enormous priggishness strikes one at first as slightly comic. Only at a second glance does it become obvious what is hidden behind this priggishness. His condescending remarks about the "senile public", together with his reference to Mussolini's condemnation of the public's "stupidity" reveal an only thinly disguised contempt for "the mass". Levy's missionary zeal appears thus to be based on an ingrained sense of élitism, which he prides himself of sharing with Mussolini. This zeal for enlightening a dumb public rests on an unquestioned assumption of superiority. And in this sense of superiority lies of course the justification for élitist, authoritarian leadership and politics. It is therefore not surprising in the end to find that Levy's essential attitude is fundamentally anti-libertarian, anti-egalitarian and anti-democratic. The enlightenment ideals of Liberty, Equality and Fraternity are identified by Levy with contemporary Bolshevism and are therefore rejected as a cause of upheaval and chaos.

> Fascism is not only an antidote, but likewise a remedy against Bolshevism. For Bolshevism is not so much a revolutionary as a reactionary creed. Bolshevism wishes to put the clock back to the old principles of the French Revolution: it even stands up most shamelessly for Liberty, Equality and Fraternity. These ideas, however, have decayed, nay, have become idols which are as good as dead: it is for the new fascist movement to bury them altogether and to enthrone in their place other ideals and living aspirations for the guidance and progress of mankind. [Levy, 307]

The present-day reader of this passage is alarmed by the apparent ease with which Levy is prepared to sacrifice the fundamental human rights of freedom and equality for the vague and undefined ideal of "the progress of mankind".

It looks as if the view of human nature underlying Levy's views rests on the pessimism, which, as I discussed above, also characterized the 'fashionable' outlook of artists and philosophers like Eliot and Hulme. Hulme's words, "man is an extraordinarily fixed and limited animal whose nature is absolutely constant. It is only by tradition and organization that anything decent can be got out of him", may stand as representative for this pessimism [quoted in Sternhell 1979, 240]. There is a big step between making certain (pessimistic) assumptions about human nature, and actively seeking to install a politics which bases its measures on these assumptions. It does not look as if either Eliot or Hulme took that step. Levy, in contrast, with his blind admiration for Mussolini, and his uncritical support of the practices of the fascist movement in Italy, is prepared, I think, to take this step. It is clear, that in Levy's view, the 'dumb mass' had to be chastised and curbed for its own good. Even extreme measures, which would normally be condemned as "brutalitarian", were in his view justified for the promotion of "the progress of mankind", which is the ultimate end of all political endeavours. The action taken by the Italian fascist movement for achieving this end, could of course never be condemned as "brutalitarian", as Levy protests, but it had, naturally, to be considered as pure idealism. This is the message Levy puts across in his article.

Barfield reacts very strongly against all of this. His philosophical insights had made him suspicious of the élitism implied in Mussolini's "one man show", and had made him suspicious also of the authoritarian practices of the Italian fascist movement, which he likens to the practices of the "Ku Klux Klan" [Barfield 1924, 9]. Nevertheless, his objections to fascism, as is obvious from my discussion above, are not systematic. It is obvious that he is far from grasping the full significance of this very complex political movement. But such complete understanding was, of course, virtually impossible in 1924 when fascism was still 'young' and its complex effects in the public sphere not yet fully visible [cf. Hayes 1973, 37]. As we have seen, even as fervent an admirer of fascism as Dr Levy had reason to complain about the sluggish reception of fascism. But even while Barfield could hardly grasp the *full* significance of fascism, he at least had a good grasp of some of the philosophical principles on which fascist ideology rested. It is on the basis of his philosophical insights that Barfield was able at once to recognize fascism as a threat to human freedom and equality. This early diagnosis of the fundamental dangers of fascism remains in fact a remarkable achievement. With his warnings therefore, Barfield has to count as probably one of the earliest critics of Mussolini and his fascist movement in Italy.

4. Conclusions

In this chapter I have discussed Barfield's objections to dualistic thought as representing one of the roots of the crisis experienced in contemporary life. We have seen that Barfield identified dualism as one of the roots of the crisis not only in modern consciousness, but also in modern culture and society. It is in his discussion of fascism that the perhaps most disconcerting effect of dualistic thought becomes evident. Barfield, it is to be concluded, is unequivocally critical of dualistic thought. Yet, as we have also seen, his own thought did not remain unaffected by dualism: it is in his fiction that we recognize that, for a certain period, his own outlook was 'infected' by the very dualism which he rejected intellectually. From this emerges a question which needs an urgent answer. It is clear that Barfield criticised dualism, most severely in his discussion of fascism. But what is not so clear is whether he succeeded in moving beyond a mere criticism by transcending dualism with a *constructive* outlook of his own. An answer to this question will be the essential concern of my final chapter.

IV.
Barfield as Reformer

In the last chapter I discussed Barfield's criticism of dualism and of what he identified as its destructive effects. What remains to be assessed now is the significance and effect of his own outlook. The question which I shall address in this chapter is whether Barfield merely criticised dualism or whether he also succeeded in transcending it: in other words, whether he merely opposed dualism, or whether he was also able to offer a real alternative to it, not only on an intellectual but also on a practical level.

One way of approaching an answer to this question is to compare Barfield to and contrast him with those authors whom he opposed. One of the most obvious candidates for such a comparison and contrast will be T. S. Eliot, with whom, as we saw in the last chapter, he disagreed most vehemently. But before I turn to a re-assessment of Barfield's relation to Eliot I shall be concerned with another writer of whom he was nearly as critical. This writer is Matthew Arnold, an important predecessor both of Barfield and of Eliot.

Arnold was one of the most influential writers and critics of the nineteenth century. He left a heritage which was so impressive that for the following generation of critics it was very difficult to escape from his influence. He made a weighty contribution to the field of cultural and social criticism and, more specifically, to the question of the relation between culture and modern civilisation.[80] It is for this reason that Arnold's position ought to be considered with some care in relation to Barfield's own position.

Barfield's reaction to Arnold was simply to dismiss him, without second thoughts. His completely unqualified criticism suggests a radical break with his predecessor. But the question which I want to

---

[80] For a general discussion of Arnold's significance as a cultural and social critic and his influence on twentieth century critics, among them T. S. Eliot, for example, cf. Dickstein, 8–34; Davis and Schleifer, 35–41; also Williams, 110–29. About Arnold's views on the relation between culture and civilisation, cf. Schwanitz, 389–91.

ask in this chapter is whether he really is as radically different from Arnold as his criticism suggests, and whether he actually succeeds where he seems to believe that his predecessor had failed.

Usually he presents his own views with such confidence that he creates around himself an air of unquestionable superiority. In fact, his reaction to other authors, including Arnold and Eliot, is sometimes quite condescending, and at other times extremely aggressive. Aggression and condescension, however, are not normally taken to be signs of strength and superiority, but rather of weakness and insecurity. This should make us perhaps a little suspicious. The questions which will therefore be asked in this chapter are: How much can we really trust Barfield's judgement of others or even of himself? And will he ultimately be able to convince us that his own views are more constructive than the views held by those authors whom he criticised so severely?

1. Barfield, Arnold and Eliot

Barfield's criticism of Arnold is to be found in the article on fascism, which I discussed in the last chapter. There he mentions Arnold in one breath with Nietzsche as one of those writers who uncritically resigned themselves to a dualistic world view. Both, in his view, blindly accepted Darwin's theory of the struggle for existence, and uncritically applied it to other spheres outside the strictly biological:

> The idea of a struggle for existence and the survival of the fittest had bitten deeply enough into thousands of European minds, but deepest of all, perhaps into Nietzsche's, who followed the example of innumerable contemporaries in applying this theory – evolved to account for certain definite phenomena in Natural Science – to all sorts of spheres outside it, notably to the political, economic and spiritual activities of human beings. The more I read of and about Nietzsche, the more convinced do I become that that ghastly suspicion of all human activity being automatically predetermined by rigid, extra-human laws was gnawing at his intellectual and emotional vitals, much as it gnawed at the milder vitals of men like Arnold and Clough. In them it produced an incurable

melancholy. In Nietzsche it produced, not tears, idle tears, but the strained fury of his paeans in praise of strength, will, self-assertion of any sort. [Barfield 1924, 9]

As far as Nietzsche is concerned, as I have already pointed out, this judgement by Barfield is too one-sided to count as a just evaluation of the philosopher's views. Nietzsche, as I suggested earlier, was everything *but* a blind and uncritical follower of Darwin [cf. above, 82-1 and 131]. If we take a closer look at Barfield's judgement of Arnold we again detect a certain degree of imbalance in his views. In the lengthy passage which I have just quoted he sums up the effect of Darwinian Theory as having produced in Arnold's mind an "incurable melancholy". There is no doubt some truth in this. But everyone who has a passing acquaintance with Arnold's work will at once protest that Barfield here represents only *half* the truth. It is generally agreed that part of Arnold's work – his poetry – is often melancholy in tone. But the same can hardly be claimed of his prose writings. There is, in fact, as has often been noted, an odd tension between his melancholy poetry and his more optimistic prose [cf. e.g. Dickstein, 23; cf. also Altick, 281].

As a poet Arnold gives expression to sometimes intensely melancholy feelings, as when he reflects on loneliness and isolation, writes about his longing for happiness, and laments the powerlessness of ideals in a world which seems hostile to them. In a passage of his "Stanzas from the Grande Chartreuse", for example, he describes himself as "wandering between two worlds, one dead,/ The other powerless to be born,/ With nowhere yet to rest my head" [Arnold 1950, 302, ll. 85–7] And in "The Scholar Gypsy" he mourns for a half-mythical, imagined seventeenth century: the

> days when wits were fresh and clear,
> And life ran gaily as the sparkling Thames;
> Before this strange disease of modern life,
> With its sick hurry, its divided aims,
> Its heads o'ertaxed, its palsied hearts, was rife [...]
>
> [Arnold 1950, 261, ll. 201–5]

The concluding lines of "Dover Beach" provide another moving example of Arnold's despair over an incomprehensible and essentially hostile universe, where human love and ideals seem powerless:

> Ah, love, let us be true
> To one another! for the world, which seems
> To lie before us like a land of dreams,
> So various, so beautiful, so new,
> Hath really neither joy, nor love, nor light,
> Nor certitude, nor peace, nor help for pain;
> And we are here as on a darkling plain
> Swept with confused alarms of struggle and flight,
> Where ignorant armies clash by night.
>
> [ibid., 211–2, ll. 29–37]

Lines like these – many more examples could be given – are undoubtedly deeply melancholy in their outlook. Arnold admitted as much himself. In 1853, for example, he wrote to his friend Arthur Hugh Clough:

> I am glad you like the *Gypsy Scholar* – but what does it *do* for you? Homer *animates* – Shakespeare *animates* – in its poor way I think *Sohrab and Rustum animates* – the *Gypsy Scholar* at best awakens a pleasing melancholy. But this is not what we want. [Arnold 1932, 54]

As these remarks suggest, Arnold did by no means resign himself uncritically, as Barfield implies, to the melancholy outlook conveyed in his poems. And I think he would have resented Barfield's suggestion that his "melancholy" was "incurable". In his rather offhand condemnation Barfield seems to have ignored the fact that Arnold *did* look for a "cure". The search, however, was conducted not so much in his poetry as in his prose. It has been pointed out that as a poet

> Arnold provides a record of a sick individual in a sick society. This was 'actuality' as he experienced it – an actuality, like Eliot's and Auden's, representative of his era. As a prose writer, a formulator of 'ideals', he seeks a different role. It is the role of what Auden calls the 'healer' of a sick society, or as he himself called Goethe, the 'Physician of the iron age'. [Abrams 1993, vol. ii, 1346]

We should not too hastily conclude from his abrupt dismissal of Arnold, then, that Barfield had absolutely nothing in common with the earlier writer. As we saw in the last chapter, for example, up until

1924 Barfield himself produced some fictional work which was, like Arnold's poetry, largely pessimistic in its outlook; at the same time, again like Arnold, he strove in his theoretical work for an outlook which was decidedly more optimistic. There is, in fact, a certain tension between his fiction and his theoretical writings, which is not so very unlike the tension inherent in Arnold's work. Moreover, Barfield, like his predecessor, defines his own role not only as that of a critic, but also as that of a "'healer' of a sick society". This double resemblance suggests a certain kinship between the two authors. If we make a close comparison it emerges that Barfield's break with Arnold is not at all as radical as he would like us to believe. This will make it necessary to examine the actual similarities between the two authors in some detail. From there I shall return to a fresh assessment of Barfield's claims to superiority over Arnold and to the question of whether they can ultimately be maintained.

I have hinted that there are certain parallels between the themes of Arnold's poetry and those of Barfield's prose fiction. These parallels should be obvious enough. Here I want to concentrate on a comparison of their theoretical writings. As soon as we take a closer look at Arnold's theoretical writings we discover in them a wealth of ideas which recur in a similar form in Barfield's work. Let us begin our comparison with a simple example. Barfield, we remember, was deeply concerned with what he called the loss of "the reality of ideas". This loss, as he explained, was reflected in the twentieth-century attitude towards the ideas of the poet Milton, for example. Twentieth-century critics, he believed, were interested no longer in the significance of Milton's ideas, but only in their psychological genesis. Modern art critics, he concluded, were no longer capable of approaching a work of art "as an object in itself [...], and considering its value for all time" [Barfield 1923b, 610; cf. above, 108–7]. There is a striking parallel to this in an essay by Arnold, entitled "A French Critic on Milton". This essay also focused on Milton, and placed the following demand on the literary critic: "Sooner or later the question: How does Milton's masterpiece really stand to us moderns, what are we to think of it, what can we get from it? must inevitably be asked and answered" [Arnold 1972, 187]. Here Arnold, like Barfield, pulls away from an investigation of genesis to the efficacy of Milton's poetry. It may be said that Barfield's special emphasis on 'reality' is absent, but this in its turn appears where Arnold writes: the critic's task is to "see the thing as it really is" [Arnold 1970b, 84] and to "press the sense of the thing itself with which one is dealing, not to go off on some collateral issue about the thing" [ibid., 89]. "The 'thing itself' with which one is here dealing", Arnold explained further, is "the critical perception of poetic truth" [ibid.]. If we didn't know that this last phrase was from Arnold, we should have thought it had been copied straight from Barfield's *Poetic Diction*.

Arnold, as Barfield after him, was interested in works of art as *living* works. Both demanded of the good critic that he be able to assess the value and the significance of a work of art. Art and poetry (the two words are used by both authors synonymously) – these represented to Arnold and Barfield more than 'simple' objects of aesthetic appreciation. Their stress on the value and significance of works of art indicates that they attributed to art a more important role: art, as I hope to show, was conceived by both authors as a centre of defence against the disintegrating tendencies of the modern age. This role is outlined by Arnold in his idea of 'culture' and by Barfield in his theory of 'poetry' and the 'imagination'. It is worthwhile comparing the two authors' ideas about culture and poetry. Such a comparison reveals some even more significant parallels in the two authors' works than those which I have already identified.

Arnold's idea of culture is most fully developed in his essay *Culture and Anarchy*. In his essay, he explains in the preface, he proposes to

> recommend culture as the great help out of our present difficulties; culture being a pursuit of our total perfection by means of getting to know, on all matters which most concern us, the best which has been thought and said in the world; and through this knowledge, turning a stream of fresh and free thought upon our stock notions and habits, which we now follow staunchly but mechanically, vainly imagining that there is a virtue in following them staunchly which makes up for the mischief of following them mechanically. This, and this alone, is the scope of the following essay. And the culture we recommend is, above all, an inward operation. [Arnold 1995b, 190]

As this passage suggests, Arnold defines culture as a standard of perfection – a standard which is to be reached by "getting to know [...]

the best which has been thought and said in the world". The stress on study – on a "getting to know" – seems to suggest that culture merely refers to an established body of learning, and that to reach the standard of perfection would be the same as aspiring to a high degree of learnedness. Moreover, the stress on culture as "above all, an inward operation" seems to suggest that culture refers to nothing more than a merely egoistic personal cultivation. Arnold's position would be very narrow indeed had he not taken his defintion of culture one important step further, as, for example, in the following passage:

> culture, which is the study of perfection, leads us [...] to conceive of true human perfection as a *harmonious* perfection, developing all sides of our humanity; and as a *general* perfection, developing all parts of our society. [Arnold 1995b, 192]

Raymond Williams comments:

> Culture, then, is both study and pursuit. It is not merely the development of a 'literary culture', but of 'all sides of our humanity'. Nor is it an activity concerning individuals alone, or some part of society; it is, and must be, essentially *general*. [Williams, 115]

Arnold, as we can see, does not, after all, confine culture to the narrow spheres of abstract learning and aesthetic appeciation, where it would remain socially impotent or merely decorative. The ideal which culture holds up before us is an ideal of human life. It is an ideal of perfection conceived as "the general harmonious expansion of those gifts of thought and feeling, which make the peculiar dignity, wealth and happiness of human nature" [Arnold 1995b, 62]. In short, culture is a standard of human wholeness. It might be thought that the wholeness to which Arnold refers is the wholeness of the individual human subject. But Williams is right when he says that it concerns not only the individual but society as a whole. In Arnold's words:

> And because we are all members of one great whole, and the sympathy which is in human nature will not allow one member to be indifferent or to have a perfect welfare independent of the rest, the expansion of our humanity, to suit the idea of perfection which culture forms, must be a *general* expansion. [ibid., 62]

Arnold's idea of culture is clearly not narrow and élitist, but broad and general. He insists that where it remains narrow and élitist it is a mere "caricature". The explicit aim is therefore to divest culture of all that is "harsh, difficult, abstract, professional, exclusive; to humanise it, to make it efficient outside the clique of the cultivated and the learned" [ibid., 61 and 79].

For Arnold, then, culture is a whole way of life to which everyone is entitled. As has often been pointed out, this ideal of culture is a direct response to the growing sense of fragmentation and loss of wholeness experienced in modern industrial society [cf. e.g. Davis and Schleifer, 119]. He observes, for example, that

> the mere unfettered pursuit of production of wealth, and the mere mechanical multiplying, for this end, of manufactures and population, threatens to create for us, if it has not created already, those vast, miserable, unmanageable masses of sunken people, to the existence of which we are [...] absolutely forbidden to reconcile ourselves [...]. [Arnold 1995b, 79]

Arnold insists that such "degradation and wretchedness" must not be tolerated and concludes: "So all our fellow-men, in the East of London and elsewhere, we must take along with us in the progress towards perfection, if we ourselves really, as we profess, want to be perfect" [ibid., 78]. Perfection, therefore, means, in very concrete terms, the creation for *everyone* of such conditions which make possible a life of wholeness and dignity. Thus Arnold's idea of culture offers a criticism of and an alternative to the dehumanising and fragmenting processes of industrialization. And his stress on the need to make culture "efficient" clearly indicates that he is concerned to give his ideal of wholeness a practical bearing in a society where this ideal is felt to be under threat.

Arnold, it has been said, "is the harbinger of modernism precisely because he felt so acutely the breakdown of the 'whole and unified life of man' in Britain" [Davis and Schleifer, 37]. Barfield, although he is not a modernist, seems to share with Arnold this sense of a breakdown. What he also seems to share with him is a felt need for a remedy. Indeed even the remedy which he recommends is very similar to Arnold's own. Arnold, as we have seen, recommended 'culture' as "the great help out of our present difficulties". 'Culture' was his standard of human wholeness and social health. Now, if we turn to Barfield, we shall see that he makes certain claims for poetry and the imagination very similar to the claims made by Arnold for 'culture'.

The key idea, for both writers, is that of unity. Poetry and the imagination, therefore, have a very special function in Barfield's system of thought: they are guarantors of unity and antidotes to dualism. Barfield, as we saw in the last chapter, objected very strongly to dualism. He objected to it because of what he believed were its alienating and disintegrating effects on modern life and consciousness. In *Poetic Diction* and elsewhere he links this sense of alienation and disintegration to certain developments in the history of language. We saw, however, that language reflects not only the present fragmentation, but also a past unity. It can thus, in Barfield's view, become a healing agent: an instrument by which unity and wholeness can be restored, with the help of poetry and the imagination.

Barfield's concept of the imagination, then, like Arnold's concept of 'culture', represents a standard of wholeness. For Arnold, as we have seen, it was a standard to be reached by study, by a "getting to know"; culture was defined "above all, as an inward operation". Much the same can be said of Barfield's concept of the imagination. For unity and wholeness are created "conceptually", as Barfield puts it in *Poetic Diction* [Barfield 1987, 86–7]. That is, unity and wholeness occur first and foremost *inside* the human mind, on the level of consciousness. This stress on the imagination as an "inward operation" (to use Arnold's very appropriate phrase) makes it look as if Barfield was some kind of champion of a merely egoistic cultivation of the human mind. As we have seen, exactly the same suspicion with regard to Arnold arose earlier. At a closer look, it rapidly emerges, however, that 'culture' was for Arnold not only study, it was also a way of life: that is, Arnold was also interested in giving his idea of 'culture' a practical bearing in society. Can we say the same about Barfield's concept of the imagination and the standard of wholeness it represents?

This last question can certainly be answered in the affirmative. It is evident that Barfield was quite aware of the fact that his concept of wholeness – if it was to have any meaning at all – had to be translated into 'reality'. He insists, for example, that imaginative activity, which he also calls "living", "creative" or else "concrete thinking", is an activity whose value and whose "existence can only finally be *proved* by experience" [Barfield 1986b, 77]. The imagination, as he demands elsewhere, must become *"operative* in the practical scientific sense" [Barfield 1986a, 60]. It must extend "from mere wondering contemplation of an inexplicable *result*, towards something more like sympathetic participation in a process" [Barfield 1987, 132]. This, we remember (cf. Chapter II, above), is where he claims the romantics failed: their theory of the imagination "was never grounded satisfactorily in reality. As a result the modern reader or critic is apt to feel, as he approaches even some of their noblest and completest productions, 'Yes, it is all very fine, very exciting, very noble – but as a philosophy of life, it really will not do!'" It is further evident that Barfield was thinking not only of experience (which might after all be continued as private), but also in terms of utility or efficacy:

> In the legend of Parsival tragic consequences follow the failure of the hero to ask the crucial question at the crucial moment. The question he should have asked when he saw the Holy Grail was *'Of what is it served?'* The same question should have been asked by the Romantic Movement, when it saw the visionary Grail of the human imagination. But it was not asked – not at any rate in this country – except by Coleridge [...]. And in the state of Romanticism, as it exists today we see the tragic consequences that followed. The charm faded. The mirror cracked from side to side. Just as Coleridge, who had indeed had a vision of imagination as the vessel by which divinity passes down into humanity – just as he fell back from *this* kind of imagination into the fantastic dreams of the opium-slave; so the metaphysic of Romanticism has gradually fallen sick, lost faith in itself. Imagination is still accepted, but it is accepted for the most part as a kind of conscious make-believe, or personal masquerade. [Barfield 1986c, 28–9; my italics]

As this passage suggests, Barfield is aware of a danger (inherent, as he believes, in romanticism) of reducing the imagination to the mere contemplative or aesthetic level, where it would remain impotent or merely decorative. He perceives his own theory of the imagination not as an aesthetic theory, but as a theory of knowledge; and in so far as he insists that knowledge must become "operative" and translate into "experience", his theory of the imagination is also, as he puts it in the quotation above, a "philosophy of life".

Barfield's theory of the imagination, then, can be summed up as follows. Imagination is, in the first instance, an intellectual activity. But it is also a force of transformation. It represents a standard of human wholeness. And wholeness is not only a state of mind, but also a form of being, a way of life, a process. Having established all that, it will be necessary finally to consider not only the significance but also the effect of Barfield's theory.

As to its significance, it will be helpful, I think, to remind ourselves briefly of Barfield's objections to dualism. Dualism, as we saw in the last chapter, represents, in Barfield's view, a reductionist, and therefore essentially pessimistic view of human nature and activity. It divorces idea from 'reality' and denies thought any validity as an active power of transformation *within* reality. Such an outlook, Barfield concluded, is essentially inhumane and destructive. It reduces the individual to a passive spectator of reality. And when allied to Darwinian Theory, as Barfield suggested, it deprives humanity of its essential freedom; for it assumes that man is automatically predetermined by extra-human laws over which he can have no control. Thus Barfield associated dualism with élitism, inequality and authoritarianism, for it provides, in his view, a justification for a minority to assume the power of control over the majority. Now, placed over against all this, the concept of wholeness – of a unity of idea and reality – represents a potentially more positive and optimistic view of human nature and activity. By conceiving thought as an *active* force *within* 'reality', it can be seen as ascribing to the individual a more active and creative role in directing his own affairs. Man is thus not a passive spectator of, but an active participant within 'reality'. In some sense, therefore, the idea of wholeness suggests the absolute opposite to the élitism, inequality and authoritarianism implied in dualism.[81]

We conclude: Barfield's imagination represents a standard of wholeness which implies a genuinely humane conception of human nature and activity; it thus offers an important criticism of the reductionist and pessimistic world view of contemporary dualism.

---

[81] It is worthwhile noting that something like this was suggested also by Arnold when, as we have seen, he insisted that culture is not élitist, but general – a way of life to which *everyone* is entitled.

But, and this is the really important point, it offers an important criticism not only of dualistic *thought*, but also of its *practical effects* on contemporary life and experience. Further, it is conceived not only as a criticism but also as a real alternative. For Barfield did not stop at a mere diagnosis of problems. As we have seen, he wanted his theory to become effective in a practical way. What we must therefore finally ask, then, is how effective his theory really is.

The reader of *Poetic Diction* and Barfield's other writings about the imagination may readily agree with Barfield that his concept of wholeness offers a genuinely humane view of human nature and activity; he may also agree that it should become operative in practical ways. But he will at once ask: How is this to be effected; that is, how can 'wholeness' become an actual experience? And what will this experience mean in concrete terms? As soon as we start looking for an answer in the writings considered so far we come up against a big blank. We search for concrete suggestions but what we get are passages like the following:

> [T]he period which culminated in the Industrial Revolution and the Great War has altered the world out of all recognition. Is it not painfully obvious on all sides that, if the continuity of Western civilisation is to be preserved, we need fresh creative thinking, the power to create fresh forms out of life itself, that is to say, out of the part of Nature which is still coming into being, the spiritual world?
>
> Not that this power to think life into the world has ever been wholly lost from Europe. As religious inspiration, as art, as poetry, it has continued to manifest itself sporadically right down to our own day. But it is a very long time since it appeared anywhere with strength enough to be *operative* in the practical, scientific sense. [Barfield 1986a, 59–60]

By now we know Barfield's turn of mind well enough to recognize these remarks as his typical reaction against the contemporary cultural pessimism. What is implied here is his usual criticism of modern thought and its damaging consequences in the practical sphere. This passage also contains his characteristic demand for an urgent change of consciousness, which is to be followed by appropriate practical changes. What is under threat, as he explains to us, is "the continuity of Western civilisation". However, civilisation, he suggests, can be "preserved", and what we need in order to preserve it is "fresh creative thinking", which must also become *"operative* in the practical, scientific sense". This is all very well, we may think, but what exactly is this "fresh creative thinking" supposed to do? In precisely what way is it supposed to preserve Western civilisation? By "creat[ing] fresh forms out of life itself", and by "think[ing] life into the world"? But what is this supposed to mean? The reader who demands some more concrete suggestions will inevitably be disappointed. Certainly, we recognize that the change of consciousness, effected by the imagination, is meant by Barfield only as a first step – to be followed by the actual *transformation* of those structures in contemporary life which are felt to be unsatisfactory, damaging and destructive. However, as soon as we ask *how* this transformation is to be achieved – and *how* our "fresh creative thinking" is supposed to become effective – Barfield's language becomes characteristically evasive.[82] Clearly, Barfield *means* his theory to be translated into practical experience. But the effect of his style and argument in all his theoretical writings – there is not a single exception – is that his ideal remains essentially vague and abstract for us.[83] It seems, then, that Barfield the diagnostician is himself incapable: the doctor is also the patient. Indeed, it seems that Barfield's theoretical work suffers serious weaknesses – weaknesses,

---

[82] Cf. also the following passage: "And at last let him [i.e. the reader] ask himself: What does it mean, to 'build Jerusalem in England's green and pleasant land'? And what *can* it mean except this, which is not the concern of England alone, but of all humanity, to rise from the Consciousness Soul to the Imaginative Soul? – The other Jerusalem – the visible one – can only arise as an outward form of this invisible City of the mind. The 'Satanic Mills', which have arisen over England since Blake's time, will never be thrust down from their hideous tyranny, until those of which he actually sang – the dead thinking of Newton, Locke, and Hobbes – have been burst asunder from within." Barfield 1986b, 83.

[83] This charge of vagueness and abstraction can be partly removed, when we read Barfield's theoretical work side by side with his essays on practical affairs. I shall discuss these essays at a later stage. Here I am exclusively interested in the effect of his theoretical work. And the effect is, indeed, that the link between Barfield's ideal of wholeness and practical experience remains absolutely obscure. Thus, if we judge his theoretical work on its own terms, the charge of vagueness and abstraction stands.

moreover, which, if we look back, we find are already foreshadowed in Arnold's work.

For Arnold, as we saw above, culture is both study and pursuit, knowing and doing. This is his doctrine. However, as Raymond Williams has pointed out,

> his emphasis in detail is so much on the importance of knowing, and so little on the importance of doing, that Culture at times seems very like the Dissenters' Salvation: a thing to secure first, to which all else will then be added. There is surely a danger of allowing Culture also to become a fetish. [Williams, 125–6]

Consider, for example the following passages:

> The idea of perfection as an *inward* condition of the mind and spirit is at variance with the mechanical and material civilisation in esteem with us [...]. [Arnold 1995b, 62–3]

And:

> The pursuit of perfection, then, is the pursuit of sweetness and light. He who works for sweetness and light, works to make reason and the will of God prevail. He who works for machinery, he who works for hatred, works for confusion. Culture looks beyond machinery, culture hates hatred; culture has one great passion, the passion for sweetness and light. [ibid., 78]

Although, as we saw earlier, Arnold professes concern about culture as a wider process and a way of life, passages like these suggest the opposite, that culture is in fact not rooted in any ordinary processes at all. This is clearly indicated by phrases like culture "is at variance with", "looks beyond", "hates". Another example is Arnold's demand that the critic who is concerned with culture "must keep out of the region of immediate practice in the political, social, humanitarian sphere" [Arnold 1995a, 42]. In passages like these culture appears to be something highly exclusive. As an "inward condition" it appears to be generally opposed to all external processes. It thus looks as if it were not part of, but opposed to the processes of modern civilisation: social, political, industrial or otherwise. There is obviously an odd tension between Arnold's concept of culture and the effect of his argument. His doctrine is that culture, as a standard of wholeness, is an active force. But the effect of passages like those I have just quoted is that for us his ideal remains curiously inactive and sterile. Raymond Williams has pointed out that Arnold's concept of culture is open to the charge of vagueness, and comments: "Culture was a process, but he [Arnold] could not find the material of that process" [Williams, 127]. In other words, Arnold holds an ideal (of wholeness) but does not, and perhaps cannot, demonstrate to us in detail how this ideal can be realized within the processes of our ordinary experience. Williams therefore concludes: "The result seems to be that, more and more, and against his formal intention, the process becomes an abstraction" [ibid., 127].

Barfield's heavy criticism of Arnold, as we can now see more clearly, is quite misleading. It suggests a radical break with his predecessor; but in reality it obscures some genuine continuities. It obscures, above all, the fact that his theory, as I have shown above, is open to the same charges as Arnold's theory: those of vagueness and abstraction. If we accept this it becomes increasingly difficult to excuse Barfield from the very same faults which he finds, as it turns out, not only in Arnold but also in Eliot. This will become more obvious when we examine his relation to Eliot more carefully.

One thing they have in common, for example, is that both authors seem to share a strong sense of the disintegration of modern life and consciousness.[84] This, as we have seen, has a pre-echo in Arnold. Moreover, both twentieth-century thinkers react very strongly against Arnold. Eliot, like Barfield, is very careful to distinguish himself from Arnold. Yet again, he, like Barfield, obscures certain genuine continuities between himself and his predecessor.[85] Let us pause for a moment to consider what this implies for Eliot.

---

[84] About Eliot's preoccupation with the disintegration of modern life and consciousness and his search for wholeness, cf. e.g. Frank.

[85] On the continuities between Eliot, Arnold and other Victorian writers, cf. e.g. Smidt 1994; Christ; Stead.

Eliot criticizes Arnold's concept of culture for its "vagueness" [Eliot 1986a, 432]. At the same time, in spite of this criticism, he appears himself to move even further in the same direction. This is indicated by his rejection of Arnold in favour of the more sceptical and pessimistic philosophy of F. H. Bradley.[86] He explains that he prefers Bradley for the "unity" of his thought, as opposed to Arnold's apparent "inconsistency", and illustrates his preference with the following quotation from the philosopher's work:

> "How can the human-divine ideal ever be my will? The answer is, Your will it never can be as the will of your private self, so that your private self should become wholly good. To that self you must die, and by faith be made one with that ideal. You must resolve to give up your will, as the mere will of this or that man, and you must put your whole self, your entire will, into the will of the divine. That must be your one self, as it is your true self; that you must hold to both with thought and will, and all other you must renounce." [quoted in Eliot 1986c, 452]

This passage actually reflects, I think, a certain tendency which is already inherent in Arnold, but goes an important step further. Arnold, as we have seen, endorsed an ideal which he meant to be effective within the processes of our ordinary life. Against his formal intention, however, his ideal remained abstract and vague. In comparison, in the passage from Bradley, the ideal is not only abstract and vague, it has become absolutely unattainable; the ideal, on the one hand, and ordinary experience, on the other, have become radically incompatible. Thus, while Arnold (still) thought that the ideal could and should be "humanised", to use his own phrase, the opposite is the case in Bradley, who insists that it is the human being who must subject himself to the ideal. Bradley, in other words, has removed the ideal so thoroughly from all ordinary life and experience that it is conceived no longer as something to be developed from within but as something to be imposed from the outside. In Eliot this attitude, as has often been noted, translates into an extremely reactionary concept of art [Brooker, 6]. Compare, for example, the famous passage about James Joyce's "mythic method":

---

[86] For a discussion of this, cf. Scott, 63; cf. also Kojecky, 31.

> It is simply a way of controlling, of ordering, of giving shape and significance to the immense panorama of futility and anarchy which is contemporary history. [...] It is, I seriously believe a step toward making the modern world possible for art. [Eliot 1975, 177–8]

Art, as this passage suggests, reflects an ideal which is drastically incompatible with the reality of modern life – a reality which is portrayed as a "panorama of futility and anarchy". The movement into a conception of utility is pre-empted, it would appear, by Bradley's assertion of the unattainable, transcendent character of the Absolute. In Eliot, this translates into an extremely pessimistic view of modern life. At the same time, the role in modern life given to art is essentially élitist and even authoritarian. As Peter Brooker comments, what Eliot "came to prescribe is a 'modern' art which would administer to and correct the 'modern world', not collaborate with it" [Brooker, 6].

Barfield, as we saw in the last chapter, was deeply opposed to the pessimism as well as the élitism and authoritarianism which are implied in Eliot's divorce of the ideal from ordinary life and experience. However, even though he rejected Eliot's dualism it is not at all clear that he was able to offer a convincing alternative in its place. It is true, of course, that Barfield, in his attempt to refute dualism, is at great pains to develop a philosophy of 'wholeness' – of a unity of mind and matter, of ideal and reality. But the crux is that while he pays lip service to an ideal of 'wholeness' he has, as we have seen, failed in his theoretical writings to present any convincing evidence of how this ideal can be realized in the practical world. Because of this failure his ideal remains as unattainable and as remote as Eliot's. Thus while formally rejecting Eliot's dualism Barfield in fact inadvertently corroborates and sustains it.

It appears, then, that his heavy criticism of Arnold and Eliot is far from proving his own superiority over them. On the contrary, it disguises a serious weakness inherent in his own theoretical work: failure of application. As a result, he seems to acquiesce in not only the very world view to which he objects, but also in its practical consequences. However, there are signs, even as early as 1922, that he became increasingly aware of the weakness in his own approach, realizing that his theory could only be considered a serious alternative if he could prove its validity in practical life. Subsequently, from 1924 or 1925 onwards he began to concern himself seriously with questions of practical reform.

2. The Turning Point: Towards Reform

Barfield's growing awareness during the early 1920s of the need for a practical application of his ideals is most prominently reflected in his little-known fairy tale *The Silver Trumpet* (published in 1925). This book raises some very important issues, and ought therefore to be examined in some detail before we turn to his ideas of practical reform. It is about a pair of identical twin sisters. The two sisters, although they look exactly alike, are completely different in character. The first is an extrovert, worldly wise and active (Barfield compares her to a "box office") [Barfield 1925b, 9]. The latter is introverted, unworldly and contemplative (she is compared to a "church"). The former becomes jealous of the latter, kills her and eventually takes over the power over the whole kingdom. As a result of her brutal regime of terror everything living and beautiful becomes paralysed.

The contemplative sister had a daughter. At first, the terror created by the second sister drives this girl to seek seclusion. Paralysed and inactive, she pines away in an isolated tower. But then one of the king's servants rediscovers a beautiful silver trumpet (the evil sister had hidden it away), which, as soon as he plays it, has the extraordinary effect of awakening the girl and the rest of the kingdom, from lethargy. The effect, unfortunately, does not last very long, and as soon as the sound of the trumpet ceases, everyone relapses into their old passivity.

> As the note died slowly away, everybody in the castle stirred slowly, like a man waking from sleep, and looked mazedly round him. Many of them opened their mouths to ask what had happened, but just as they were about to speak, they seemed to change their minds, they looked away, they dropped their eyes to the ground as though they were ashamed of something, as though they all knew something which they were all pretending they didn't know. [ibid., 120]

What had originally caused everyone's reawakening was the trumpet's conjuring up memories of a past, harmonious and fulfilling life. The trumpet made everyone dream of their lost freedom and happiness. (One is reminded of the effect attributed by Barfield in his theoretical work to poetry and imagination.) But this is what finally propels the girl into action.

> Once more the sound floated from the the stable across, and in at the windows of the castle. Once more Princess Lily began to wonder, and then suddenly she knew that she was very unhappy.
>
> "I must help myself!" she cried [...]. [ibid., 121]

The girl remembers, moreover, the wise words of a (good) witch – a genuine precursor of Terry Prachett's shrewd Granny Weatherwax whose witchcraft mainly consists in giving very down to earth advise. This witch had reprimanded the girl for failing to meet her responsibilities as a young princess. "Silence gives consent", the old lady had warned her [ibid., 127]. The girl takes this very seriously and resolves not simply to go on dreaming, but to act on her dreams. As a consequence, she descends from her isolated tower back into the world, and with the help of the obligatory young prince, who has in the meantime arrived, frees the kingdom from the tyranny of her evil aunt.

What are the implications of all this? First of all, what springs to mind immediately is that Barfield portrays the twin sisters' relationship in the very Coleridgian terms of polar opposites. It ought to be noted that, originally, the more active sister is not actually portrayed as being evil, nor is the more contemplative sister portrayed as being wholly good. But both are depicted as suffering each from her own particular weakness: the active one tends towards being a bit of a bully, the contemplative one to being a little too dreamy and therefore a bit feeble. Either of them, in a way, balances the other's weakness. Neither of them is properly complete without the other. Balance, in fact, is the very principle of their existence. But this balance between them is from the beginning a very precarious one. Without the active energy of the one, the beauty and idealism of the other has no power; and without the beauty and idealism of the other, the energy of the first sister turns into an exercise of sheer brute force. This is what happens when the strong sister ruthlessly overthrows the balance and seizes power by killing her weaker sister. It is only then that she becomes really evil.

What prevails, even though only temporarily, is the Darwinian principle of the survival of the fittest. These developments in the story are deeply disconcerting, suggesting that the world of ideals has no real chance of survival. In the end, however, Barfield reassures the reader that this is not his final verdict on the scheme of things. He allows one character, the young girl who is a representative of the ideal world, to gather the strength to act and thereby to bring the ideal back to life.

The girl's initial failure to engage with the horrible realities around her, and her withdrawal, instead, into an imaginative world turns out to be deeply irresponsible. For her escapism helped to *maintain* a brutal regime which should have been resisted and overthrown. "Silence gives consent", as the wise witch had said. In a way, Barfield's criticism of her irresponsibility (which happily, of course, she eventually overcomes) reflects his awareness of his own weakness: the failure of application. It also echoes the criticism which has been made by him and others of Coleridge. Coleridge, we remember, has been accused of failing to match his ideals to social realities. As Nigel Leask comments: "What began as a critical stance, the adoption and application of an integrated life-style and ideology in opposition to the contemporary order, became a tacit complicity with that order" [Leask, 13]. This comment on Coleridge reads like a very good interpretation of the events in Barfield's story: for in the tale, the girl, by withdrawing from her responsibilities, becomes an involuntary accomplice of her evil aunt.[87]

Moreover, the narrative reflects Barfield's awareness not only of his own personal weakness or that of his predecessor Coleridge, it also reflects his awareness of more general feelings (inherent, for example, in the philosophy of the early twentieth century) – feelings of resignation over the powerlessness of ideals. We remember Barfield's discussion of the ideological roots of fascism in this kind of

---

[87] Cf. Lewis's *The Siver Chair* (1955) which also deals with idea and reality. Lewis knew Barfield's *Silver Trumpet* [cf. Lewis 1993a, 275] and was perhaps half-consciously infuenced by it.

sensibility. His fairy tale *The Silver Trumpet*, with its illustration of the mechanism of a brutal authoritarian regime of terror and repression, is an uncanny anticipation of what was to occur in European history. In this respect, the story is a powerful plea for the absolute and acute urgency to counteract these developments – a plea for doing so by bringing the world of ideals back to life. This ultimately meant for Barfield, as I finally hope to show, a fundamental change in the contemporary social and economic system.

It is in a short story of 1922 that Barfield for the first time explores the social consequences of the divorce of the ideal from the real made in contemporary philosophy. This story is most important as it contains the principal ideas of Barfield's social criticism, and anticipates his later concern (from 1924 onwards) with details of a social and economic reform. In other words, it sets the agenda for all his reform ideas, and ought therefore to be examined in some detail. The story, entitled *Seven Letters*, explores what a society looks like in which social ideals are being neglected, and the Darwinian principles of the "struggle for existence" and "survival of the fittest" are allowed to dominate instead.

As the title suggests, the piece consists of seven letters. The central figure is an unemployed, middle-aged female worker called Mrs. Gitting. Barfield does not *tell* her story but leaves it to the reader to piece the details together from the contents of the letters, one of which is written by the worker herself. The first three letters are exchanged between the owner of a company that produces fur gloves and the owner of a shop that sells these items. The shop owner tells the producer that he had been dissatisfied with the quality of a certain type of glove and therefore wished to withdraw his order. As a consequence, production is stopped, with the following recommendation by the producer to his production manager:

> Kindly get improved quality fur only. I should suggest that you choose your women more carefully. [...] [I]t ought to be possible to effect the requisite improvement without increasing payment in the present state of the market. This is important. [Barfield 1922, 16][88]

---

[88] The story is only one page long. All subsequent quotes are from that page.

The fourth letter seems at first quite independent of the previous correspondence. It is written by the unemployed and semi-literate Mrs. Gitting who begs in her letter for some financial help from the "East London Relief Fund". This is followed by the instructions of the organizing secretary of the Fund to a care assistant, asking her to examine the situation of the applicant, and to "make strict inquiries, as the trustees are dissatisfied with the rate of depletion of the Fund." The reader has by now developed a suspicion that the situation of the applicant is somehow connected with the "improvement" made by the businessmen of the first three letters. Indeed, the suspicion is confirmed in the sixth letter – a private communication of the mentioned care assistant to a friend in which she relates details of her work experiences, in particular her experience with the unemployed Mrs. Gitting:

> I had to go and see a Mrs. Gitting this morning, who is fifty-five years old and has lived all her life by pulling the fur out of rabbit-skins. I opened the door and could hardly get into the room, it was so blocked with dirty clothes and old cardboard boxes – and a good deal of vegetable refuse – and the smell! My dear, she told me she hadn't had work in for three weeks, and the room simply *reeked* rabbit! [...] Didn't know why they hadn't sent her any more skins [...]."

The reader is now able to form a fuller picture of the fate of the central character, Mrs. Gitting. She appears to have been an employee of the firm which has, according to the owner's instructions, ceased the production of those items from which she seems to have made her living. Without any prior warning, she, as the sole breadwinner of her family (in her letter she mentions that her husband is dead), has lost the source of her income, and has consequently sunk into deep poverty.

The contrast between what the reader has learnt so far and the last letter of the short story could not be more drastic. It is written by a student of an imaginary "Radcliffe College" at Oxford and contains an elaborate report on the activities and worries of student life, such as the following:

> I have been so busy this term that I haven't had time to turn round and think. Moreover, I have been rather troubled about

myself lately. Enormous changes have been going on somewhere inside me [...].

Did I tell you I was writing a paper for the Plato Society? It is taking up a dreadful lot of my time and interfering with those long, solitary walks which I think so important. It is on "Divinity in Mind and Matter" – a pretty deep subject, what?

This last letter appears to have no direct connection with the previous letters. Yet, there is a concrete element which connects the student directly with the fate of the worker in the story, namely, a pair of "woolley bear gloves" which the student has just purchased, as he reveals in a postscript. He is probably able to afford the item easily. What he ignores, though, is the human cost involved in its production. He is oblivious of the human tragedy (as in Mrs. Gitting's case), caused by the fierce competiton for a "market" (i.e. people like the student himself) and the ruthless exploitation of the workers by their employers.

What are the implications of this story? The first, most striking thing is that it portrays a society which is deeply divided. This division, as is obvious at once is the result of a social system which is based not on ideals of social justice, but on the selfish economic interests of a powerful ruling class. Their sole interest seems to consist of financial profit-making and economic gain without consideration for the social consequences. This self-interest, moreover, is disguised as an immutable economic law – the law of supply and demand – to which everyone is made to believe they are subject without control.

The result of this ruthlessly exploitative thinking is that the economic system is not used as an instrument for the purpose of creating human well-being. But it is exactly the other way round: it is the human beings who are being used, or rather abused as instruments. That is, they are being abused as instruments of a production of whose benefits they are ultimately deprived. Those, like Mrs. Gitting, who are at the lowest scale of the social ladder become elements within an economic system whose "laws" they do not understand. Mrs. Gitting clearly does not know why she is experiencing all this misery. She has become the victim of a system which has failed to provide the foundations of a dignified life for all its members. Thus degraded she sinks to the status of a helpless dependent on society. The reaction – in terms of social policy – to this dilemma is the generation of a "Relief Fund". However, the story clearly suggests that this fund has merely the function of a "fig leaf", so to speak, disguising the real problem, and diguising, above all, the urgent need for a fundamental change in the whole system.

Moreover, there is a shocking irony in the fact that the student in the story should toy with ideas about "the pretty deep subject" of "*Divinity* in Mind and Matter" [my italics], while on the other end of the scale there are people like the worker who are in fact doomed to lead a life of material *deprivation*. The form of this story – a series of more or less disconnected letters – is very clever and most effective in portraying a deeply divided society. The society which Barfield decribes is a society dominated by an economic and intellectual élite whose fundamental attitude is characterized by indifference and irresponsibility towards the needs of society as a whole. The student's *carefree* existence mirrors the businessmen's *careless* treatment of their employees. The only '*caring*' people are the care workers for the Relief Fund, but they are confined to the more or less passive role of distributing some means from a slender fund, and have no real power to alter the actual situation. In a way, all of them accept the system as it is. They tacitly accept the principle that is governing society as Barfield portrays it: the principle of a "struggle for existence" and "the survival of the fittest". Any reflections on the ideal of "Divinity in Mind and Matter" appear to be of no consequence in this overall accepted scheme of things.

Placed against the deep problems of the worker, then, the student of the story is evidently an absurd figure with his airy 'unanchored' reflections. At the same time it is impossible to escape a sense that Barfield himself is that student. After all, he could hardly claim not to be interested in the student's topic "Divinity in Mind and Matter". In fact, this topic could be said to be one of Barfield's own major interests. But again, as in his novel *The Silver Trumpet*, this earlier piece contains a strong element of implicit self-criticism. What is criticised as being so absurd is not the student's topic as such, but the way he is handling it. If he took his philosophy of "Divinity in Mind and Matter" really seriously he could not possibly tolerate the material deprivation of another human being like Mrs. Gitting. On the contrary, the philosophy of unity and integration, with which he is evidently preoccupied, could and should be a direct challenge to an unjust social system which is based on a philosophy of division and fragmentation. But as a result of the student's preoccupation with a mere self-cultivation this larger vision remains unrealized.

Barfield's criticism (from which he evidently does not exclude himself), then, is mainly directed at the complacent detachment of an educated class who appear to pursue their intellectual interests with a complete disregard for social realities – the social realities of a system which is in Barfield's view brutal and exploitative. In a way, as is implied in the short story, their apathy allows them to continue their leisurely existence at the expense of the rest of society. In this story (as well as in his later story *The Silver Trumpet*), then, Barfield exposes the discrepancy between the pursuit of philosophical ideals on the one hand and the reality of material deprivation on the other and suggests that it is high time to take a positive step forward and effect *real changes*.[89] Otherwise, he then concludes in his essay *Danger, Ugliness and Waste* (1925), "the world of culture must remain for ever the bitter farce it sometimes seems":

> "[...] [W]e may talk of education and of university extension, and we may be rightly proud of these things; but we know all the time in our hearts that without a general spread of means and leisure the world of culture must remain for ever the bitter farce it sometimes seems – an everlasting Decameron set in an everlasting plague. This social conscience of ours may be a comparatively recent addition to our hearts, but it is a permanent one, and now that it has evolved in us, there is no greatness without it. Until its pangs are allayed, the sincerest

---

[89] Notice the parallel of Barfield's criticism of the powerlessness and ineffectivity of contemporary thought (combined with his social criticism and his demand for real changes) with Marx's famous eleventh thesis on Feuerbach: "Die Philosophen haben die Welt nur verschieden *interpretiert*, es kömmt darauf an, sie zu verändern." – "The philosophers have only *interpreted* the world in various ways; the point is to *change* it." my translation; Marx 1962, 317. Barfield does not consciously appear to draw on the ideas of Karl Marx. A comparison of the two authors should therefore not be taken too far. Nevertheless, the parallel is interesting and deserves in my view further attention. This, however, would be the task of a separate study, and cannot be attempted here.

works of art will also be the most tortured and preoccupied, sacrificing spirit to idea and life to propaganda. (...) I believe that for the future we have to face either a world without these things or a world in which the leisure and refinement which alone make them possible are not drawn in dividends from half-educated millions to whom all chance of knowing them, or even the value of them is denied. One of two things is true. Civilisation is either a ghastly accident, or it is a means to the end of freeing the human spirit in this world. If the former – so; but if the latter, there can be nothing more than a fluttering of wings, until humanity has established its place in the sun." [Barfield c. 1925, 14]

This passage is again a good example of Barfield's rejection of an uncritical application of Darwinian theory to social affairs. Barfield concludes that the idea of a "struggle for existence" and "the survival of the fittest" is not the only way of understanding evolution. Evolution is also the evolution of a "social conscience", the evolution of minds that take control of the situation and create an environment for the benefit of all. Where such an understanding is not gained, culture, in Barfield's view, will remain a macabre farce[90] (- like the jolly pursuits of the young aristocrats in Bocaccio's *Decamerone*, which is set in a plague context). For it will back up an unjust and inhumane social system.

In contrast to this, Barfield employs a concept of culture which is, even if he does not admit it, very similar to Matthew Arnold's. Arnold, as we know, saw culture not only as self-cultivation, but as a process, a way of life. Culture was his ideal of wholeness and human well-being, both of which, he insisted, were not reserved for an élite, but must be extended to all. We recall his words:

> And because we are all members of one great whole, and the sympathy which is in human nature will not allow one member to be indifferent or to have a perfect welfare independent of the rest, the expansion of our humanity, to suit

---

[90] We are reminded of Jung's objection to Freud that by explaining all human action in terms of biological instinct Freud reduced culture to a mere farce – a position with which Jung vehemently disagreed. Cf. above, 112.

the idea of perfection which culture forms, must be a *general* expansion. [Arnold 1995b, 62]

Like Arnold, Barfield envisaged changes in the world of practical social affairs. And these changes were to be based on the ideals of wholeness and human well-being. But in contrast with the earlier writer, Barfield then concerned himself seriously with concrete details of the ways in which such changes could be effected. It is in his discussion of the function of industry in society that his suggestions for practical change – a reform of the contemporary social and economic system – become apparent.

3. The Function of Industry

It will be noticed that Barfield's views on technical progress and industrialization are more positive than those held by other contemporary critics of industrial civilization. Ultimately, as I would like to suggest, his positive approach depends on a radically different world view from that underlying the views of these contemporaries. Earlier (in Chapter III) I discussed Barfield's criticism of a world view which reduces the individual to the role of a passive spectator – a world view in which reality is supposed to be predetermined by rigid laws over which man is thought to have no control. This sense of a loss of control characterized, as we have seen, some of the contemporary views on the developments caused by technical progress – views, such as Spengler's or Penty's, of the machine as a new force that is threatening human freedom and integrity, and indeed threatening civilization itself. In accordance with his criticism of contemporary philosophy, Barfield challenges such views and dismisses them as a "fallacy". He claims, in contrast to his more pessimistic contemporaries, that the

> New Economics are proving more and more succinctly every day that it is physically possible to set each individual, irrespective of his strength or weakness, and of his moral or aesthetic value in the eyes of his contemporaries, free to work out his own destiny – or, at least, subject to no control other

than that of Nature, and the laws of his own being. [Barfield 1924, 9][91]

Barfield's own world view – he maintains, as we know, that man is not in the least doomed to be a passive spectator of reality but can play an active and creative role in shaping his destiny and the world around him – enables him to assign to man a fairer measure of control over the industrial developments than his more pessimistic contemporaries are prepared to allow. This is not to say, however, that he looks at these developments through a pair of rose-coloured spectacles. He is realistic enough to recognize – with his contemporaries – also the negative aspects of these developments. He admits, for example, that the events of the First World War have revealed "the monstrous energy which we can organise for the destruction of civilization, but not for its maintenance and development" [Barfield c. 1925, 5]. He also makes the grim prediction that "there is absolutely no doubt that without a change in our economic system [...] the next war is as inevitable as the last". Here Barfield is uncannily prescient; but he hastens to add that this change is "a change that could be made easily and to everybody's immediate advantage" [ibid., 5]. For Barfield, a recognition of the actual and possible negative consequences of industrialization is reason not for resignation but positive action. And such action, he suggests, is urgently required:

> we as a nation, as an empire, or as a community of many nations, should bring about consciously and of our own will those changes that are being thrust upon us in any case, in order that, working with knowledge, we may avoid the incalculable disasters which Nature will otherwise use to bring about the same end. [Barfield 1929b, 794]

This passage seems to suggest a hint of determinism in Barfield's thought when he speaks of "Nature" as a somewhat ominous, potentially destructive force. What he seems to mean is that in the process of industrialization forces of transformation were set free which have radically altered the course of previous developments.

---

[91] Cf. Barfield 1925a, where Barfield again argues for the positive role of machinery in liberating society. This letter is a critical response to Arthur J. Penty's article "The Line of Least Resistance, where Penty had condemned machinery as detrimental, and argued for its abolition.

However, he also suggests that the direction of these changes can be controlled and channelled in constructive ways; only when such control is not exercised, he implies, will disaster ensue: man would be controlled by his own inventions, rather than the other way round.[92] Barfield, meanwhile, appears to be absolutely convinced that it is possible to exercise such control. This conviction, as I have pointed out before, ultimately rests on the assertion of man's creative ability to direct in his own favour those developments which he has himself initiated. All depends, then, as he proposes, on the attempt to form new ideas and to "seize the opportunity to hammer them into *shapes* which are at the same time *realities*" [Barfield 1929b, 749; my italics].

These observations demonstrate clearly the fundamentally dynamic character of Barfield's thought. His concept of organic wholeness, in contrast to that of Penty and Spengler, does not exclude, but includes the machine. In the modern world 'organic' is commonly seen as the simple opposite of 'mechanical'. But Barfield, in accordance with his own philosophy, brings together the two fused meanings in the Greek word *organon*, which originally meant 'tool' or 'instrument' *as well as* 'living organ'. Barfield, in other words, does not reject the machine, but sees it as an intrument for the creation of conditions of wholeness and integration.

Such observations and proposals are still more or less abstract. But Barfield is prepared to go a step further. He makes a very careful analysis of the ways in which industrialization has changed society and economics. Based on this analysis he then proposes his own ideas about the ways in which society can control and use the new technical developments for a positive transformation of the social system.

---

[92] This is very like the argument of C.S. Lewis's *The Abolition of Man*. Lewis, however, does not have the practical (political) reform side. His 'solution' is simply that we must all accept the sovereignty of the moral law ("the Tao", as he calls it).

4. Social and Economic Reform

About the effects of industrialization on society and economics, he makes the following observations: industrialization with its new inventions and new techniques of productive organisation had transformed a world of shortage into a world of material plenty within only one hundred years. The high level of technical perfection enabled a productivity of the utmost efficiency. Moreover, the war had stimulated this increase in the power of production. "We are", Barfield concludes, "far wealthier than before the war", but, paradoxically, he adds, "there is no corresponding improvement in human well-being" [Barfield c. 1925, 7.][93]. What Barfield addresses here is what social historians of the period have termed the paradox of "poverty amid plenty". John Stevenson, for example, comments:

> While the social investigations carried out between the wars demonstrated that there had been significant advances in average living standards and levels of material comfort, even using the most stringent standards, they also revealed that a considerable proportion of the population remained in poverty, with its attendant problems of poor housing and ill-health. [Stevenson, 70]

When Barfield claims that there was "no improvement of human well-being", he exaggerates the situation. For, as Stevenson and other historians have shown, average living standards actually were improving. Barfield is possibly deliberately polemical here, focussing on the fact that a large number of the population were, in spite of these improvements, still excluded from them. There were 1.25 million (i.e. 12% of all wage earners) unemployed before the depression and 3 million after, and there were certain areas, the coal-mining and ship-building areas, e.g. in Wales and Scotland, as well as the working class areas in London, that were hit especially hard. As Peter Wende has pointed out, even when after the depression the economy began to

---

[93] Barfield, who had learnt Latin at school, perhaps alludes here to Sallust's famous phrase "publice egestatem, privatim opulentiam" ["poverty in the public sphere, wealth in the private"]. This is from Cato's big speech, contrasting the degenerate Rome of his own day with the better older time; cf. Sallust, 104, l.ii, 22.

recover, a large part of the population still remained in poverty, in spite of a general upward trend in the economy [Wende, 303]. This is the paradox that Barfield addresses here.

Barfield then investigates why, in spite of the vast potential for increasing the wealth of the nation, a large part of the population was still excluded from that wealth. In his attempt to identify the root of the problem, he makes the following point:

> The first thing that strikes us about this industrial civilisation is its youth. It has been *growing* ever since we have known it, ever since it was born. Moreover, it has grown fast – so fast that economic and social theory have had to keep up with it as best they could. They may possibly be abreast of its development. They are certainly not ahead. [Barfield 1929a, 216–7]

In this passage Barfield makes a similar point to the one he had made in 1921 in his essay "Some Elements of Decadence" when he said that contemporary thought was lagging behind the recent changes in history. As to the rapid changes caused by the industrial revolution, he comments critically, social and economic theory are only just keeping up with the problems caused by these changes, instead of looking ahead for a long-term solution. He particularly objects to the way in which the problem of unemployment and poverty is handled. Thus he speaks dismissively of the "hugger-mugger way" of dealing with the problem "through the Poor Law guardians and an annual deficit of 15,000,000 l. on the Unemployment Fund" [ibid., 221]. He believes that the current efforts of grappling with unemployment are "hardly even touching the problem [ibid., 215]. What is needed – this, we remember, is the same point he made in his short story "Seven Letters" – is not short-term relief, but a long-term solution. With reference to the severity of the unemployment problem in the coal-mining area of South Wales, he comments:

> The miner who, finding himself in a situation as hopeless as this, is politely informed that it is permanent is surely entitled to ask the outside world at any rate to think, and to think rather harder than usual, even if it involves revising some first principles. [ibid., 216]

A revision of "first principles", as he makes immediately clear, implies a complete revision of the basic understanding of the function of industry in society. The current, accepted view, according to him, is this: industry is held to be "an institution 'to provide labour', which, like the ant, many [...] seem to regard as an end in itself" [Barfield c. 1925, 6]. However, as Barfield observes, industry, while increasing productivity, had at the same time created unemployment. Consequently, in a system of increasing technical perfection "any unemployment that existed would clearly be permanent, while the introduction of every fresh piece of labour-saving machinery must necessarily increase it" [Barfield 1929a, 219]. The first thing that needs to be recognised, then, is that unemployment is not a negative, but a positive and highly desirable result of industrialization. Such a recognition depends on an altogether completely different understanding of the function of industry, namely:

> Its object, surely, is to provide not employment but leisure – by replacing human labour to provide the mass of people, instead of as formerly only a small minority, with economic freedom. [...] In terms of the capacity to produce goods and services, Europe is a very wealthy continent, and it is her wealth, not her poverty, which is choking her. It is thus not employment which needs to be increased but unemployment. Unemployment without its accompanying poverty is leisure. [Barfield 1925a, 306]

As this passage suggests, Barfield envisages a transformation of unemployment into leisure, that is a complete tranformation of society in its current state:

> I said earlier that there is an obligation on the outward world to think. This article is an attempt to fulfill my part of that obligation, so far as I am capable. The essential suggestion it makes is that the causes of this ugly problem [unemployment] may be regarded in two ways. On the one hand they may be seen as the last sickness of an old and excessively complex organisation; and on the other, by shifting the eye a little to one side, they can actually appear as the infant gropings of a new order of society, which has hardly yet begun. [Barfield 1929a, 221]

What Barfield anticipates is, in fact, the arrival of the leisure state. The transformation of unemployment into leisure, which he envisages, is in his view not at all an utopian ideal, but a practical possibility. For the wealth which would create leisure is potentially available through the increasingly efficient industrial production. This wealth, Barfield then suggests in accordance with his philosophy of unity and participation, should be regarded as communal wealth, that is, it ought to be regarded as something from which everyone is by right entitled to profit. For, as he claims, the efficiency created by technical progress is "a communal but intangible asset, representing the accumulated thought and labour of many generations of scientists and others" [Barfield c. 1925, 6]. As he puts it more poignantly elsewhere:

> The wealth of the twentieth century is compounded of many factors, among which there is one that takes a very high place. I refer to that imponderable increment that arises from the *development* of industry in the past, from the inventive genius of scientists and the devotion of all manner of nameless men to problems of industrial administration. Whatever may be said of the other factors, I challenge everyone to deny that this increment belongs *to us all*. The law at any rate signifies its tacit assent to this proposition by refusing to grant patents in perpetuity. You may keep your estate in your family as long as you please, but not your genius. What is so little realised as yet is the enormous importance which this imponderable increment has at length attained. There is – or there could be – plenty for all. Anyone who keeps a weather eye open for statistics of productivity can convince himself of the fact in a few months. [Barfield 1929b, 799]

Barfield concludes, then, that the nation should be able actually to profit from the fruit of its common endeavour. The key lies in an adequate mechanism of distribution.

> Money is the chief agent for the distribution of the common wealth. In other words, when we speak of the "financial credit" of a person or a group, we mean the power to claim so much of that wealth for his own particular use. It follows that the total "financial credit", the total purchasing power, of the community should be enough to purchase all the wealth it can produce. [ibid.]

Barfield observes that at present this is not the case and therefore suggests that it is necessary to look for a way to enable the nation to profit from its common wealth. The solution that would enable the nation to do so would depend on a reform of current financial and economic policy. Here he follows the proposals of a (now very little known) movement called "Social Credit".

The "Social Credit Movement" was initiated by the engineer and economist Major C. H. Douglas (1879-1952). Douglas's proposals involve the application of a new financial theory based on the so-called A + B theorem. Barfield appears to rely heavily on the Major's theory, which is why it is necessary here to consider its basic points.[94] Its premises are formulated in the mentioned A + B theorem which reads thus:

> Payments may be divided into two groups: Group A – All payments made to individuals (wages, salaries and dividends). Group B – All payments made to other organizations (raw materials, bank charges, and other external costs). Now the rate of flow of purchasing power to individuals is represented by A, but since all payments go into prices the rate of flow of prices cannot be less than A + B. The product of any factory may be considered as something which the public ought to be able to buy [...]; but since A will not purchase A + B, a proportion of the product at least equivalent to B must be distributed by some form of purchasing power which is not comprised in the descriptions grouped under A. It will be necessary at a later stage to show that this additional purchasing power is provided by loan credits (bank overdrafts) or export credit. [Douglas, 22, cited in Finlay, 107]

Douglas concluded: since the rate of flow of purchasing power to individuals is represented by A, but the rate of flow of prices always involves more than A (namely A + B), the public can never buy the whole product. A system of industrial expansion, where the rate at which B payments were being incurred was greater than that at which they were being transformed into A payments, was bound to create increasing poverty amid plenty. For the rapid distribution of an

---

[94] In the following account of the Douglas scheme I am heavily indebted to Finlay.

increasing amount of goods was clogged rather than enhanced by a mechanism in which the prices of the end product continuously superseded the amount of purchasing power available to the public. In such a system the continuance of the productive system depended on and was controlled by those who provided the supply of B payments: the financiers.

> Consequently, as the rate of flow became bigger and faster, these providers of credit came to exercise an ever-increasing dictatorship over the organization of industry. In step with the quickening of the rate of flow went the hardening of financial monopoly. [Finlay, 111][95]

Douglas profoundly disagreed with the existing economic system which created poverty and what he termed its "twin evil ... servility" by means of "the constant filching of purchasing power from the individual in favour of the financier." He believed that continual physical want created "servility", and "servility" was "a definite component of a system having centralized control of policy at its apex" [quoted in Finlay, 106 and 112]. Douglas was ultimately motivated by a fear that such a system would eventually result in totalitarian control of power. He was convinced, however, that a careful understanding of the existing economic system would show the way how this could be prevented from happening.

His own preventative solution was a half-way house between capitalism and socialism. One aspect of Douglas's socialism, which we find almost literally taken over by Barfield, is his idea of a "Cultural Heritage". With the socialists he believed that "natural resources are common property, and the means of exploitation should also be common property." Moreover, he held that "the industrial machine is a common heritage, the result of the labours of untold generations of people whose names are for the most part forgotten ... therefore ... society as a whole ... has a right to the product" [quoted in Finlay, 112]. Based on this idea of a "Cultural Heritage" is his notion of real and financial credit – a notion that is also found in Barfield. Financial credit is merely one, usefully visible expression of the real wealth of a nation. The real wealth is ultimately identical with the

---

[95] This summary of Douglas's conclusion is Finlay's.

"Cultural Heritage" and the use made of it by society. Therefore financial credit should like its basis, real credit, be a communal possession. In short, Douglas wanted the society to be in control of economics through its control of financial power.

The chief criticism raised against "Social Credit" is that it was technically more complicated to put into practice than Douglas admitted.[96] Nevertheless, the scheme was received very well and enjoyed a large following between the two wars and after. It had the largest following in the Dominion economics of Canada, Australia and New Zealand. The province of Alberta had a "Social Credit" Government between 1935 and 1971, and British Columbia one from 1952 to 1972. In England, followers include, among many others, R. H. Tawney (economist and historian), William Temple (later archbishop of Canterbury), Bertrand Russell (the philosopher), and, of course, Owen Barfield.

5. Conclusions

It is not difficult to see why "Social Credit" would appeal to Barfield both intellectually and practically. Barfield's philosophical investigations had alerted him to a tendency in contemporary thought towards intellectual impotence, inertia, and pessimism – a tendency that was reflected in the practical sphere by a growing sense of impotence in handling the changes and problems caused by the industrial revolution. In Douglas he encountered a thinker who offered practical suggestions as to the ways in which the power of control over industrial developments could be regained. "Social Credit", Barfield was convinced, offered a solution that was realistic and practicable. Just how practicable it really was, and whether Barfield's judgement of it is at all realistic, remains for the expert in the social and economic history of the period to assess. What is important to stress here is that Barfield made an attempt to identify what he

---

[96] For a critical assessment of "Social Credit", cf. Clark, and McConnell.

considered to be the dilemma of his times, and that he was prepared to look not only for an intellectual, but also for a practical solution.

As we have seen, Barfield was aware of an aspect in contemporary thought that generated a mental climate inclining to fascism and totalitarianism. In particular, he exposed Darwinian theory as a doctrine that, when applied outside the sphere of biology, could create a system in which the power of control was being delivered into the hands of a minority. As we have seen, his portrayal of contemporary society is that of a society that is deeply divided and vulnerable to exploitation. Moreover, he showed that current economic theory and practice (with their divorce of consumption from production, and their focus on an expansion of foreign markets, without first satisfying home demand) were deepening social divisions, and were creating an atmosphere of international rivalry through an increasingly fierce competition for markets.

Barfield's philosophical, social and economic analysis, despite certain weaknesses at the level of fundamental theory, creates an insight into a highly explosive mixture of elements in contemporary life that foreshadowed the arrival of fascism and the dangers of an impending Second World War. The urgency with which he applied his thought to possible ways of counteracting impending disaster is impressive. His suggestions never came to fruition in a practical way. Nevertheless, his acute sense of observation and his gift for addressing the central issues of the period, as well as his courageous attempt to offer practical solutions to the problems that characterized the time, earn him a high place among the twentieth-century analysts of that period. And perhaps it would not be too much to say that Barfield's vivid and forceful approach to opening up alternative ways of thinking and acting remains as relevant now as it was when he developed it.

General Conclusions

Barfield's theory of imagination, as I hope to have shown, is both a theory of cognition and a philosophy of life. His key concept was unity (together with the associated ideas of wholeness and participation). Unity was the standard by which not only modern thought, but the whole of modern life was judged. Barfield developed his philosophy in deliberate opposition to the then prevalent dualistic world view which, in his opinion, had a detrimental effect on individual, culture and society. On the psychological level, he held dualism responsible for the increasing feelings of alienation in modern life. On the social level, he identified dualistic thought as one of the roots of social division and inequality. On the cultural and political levels, he believed dualism to have fostered a pessimism which (together with many other factors) contributed to the emergence of fascism.

At this point, however, he took an important further step: he did not stop at a mere criticism of dualism, but conceived his own philosophy as a constructive alternative; based on his ideal of unity, he envisaged a complete transformation not only of culture, but also of society at large. The project, evidently, has a certain grandeur. Barfield, however, has difficulties convincing us that it is really practicable and effective. The matter may be summed up in a twofold observation: Barfield makes himself the champion of the ideal of wholeness, but in his theortical work he fails to demonstrate in detail how this ideal can be realized. It therefore looks as if he was content, in practice, to solve the problem of dualism on an exclusively mental level. The fact, moreover, that he adapted his ideal from the past inevitably makes him look conservative, if not reactionary. We gain the impression that his efforts boil down to the simple restoration of an allegedly more unified and holistic past. All in all, it appears that his approach is essentially backward-looking and anti-rationalistic, and serves as an escape from the actual challenges and complexities of modern life.

Although Barfield does not blatantly express any extreme anti-rationalistic or indeed reactionary views, it cannot be denied that there is a certain danger in his approach to expose him to criticism of this kind. This danger, as we have seen, already lurks in romantic thought by which Barfield is heavily influenced. It is thanks to C.S. Lewis, however, that he was alerted to this danger. With the additional help of Rudolf Steiner, moreover, he discovered the progressive element in romanticism. As a result of Lewis's criticism, on the one hand, and Steiner's influence, on the other, Barfield began seriously to concern himself with an application of his philosophy in the world of practical affairs. This new direction of his thought is reflected in a series of publications (from the mid 1920s onwards) which deal with questions of social and economic reform. These writings reveal an author who, in contrast to many of his more pessimistic contemporaries, welcomed change and technical progress. He welcomed them as positive means to the end of creating those conditions which would make the experience of wholeness and participation possible in modern life. For this reason, despite the weakness in the area of practical detail already noted, Barfield ultimately has to count as an essentially progressive and modern thinker.

Unfortunately, his practical reform writings have so far been completely neglected in scholarship. This is perhaps not surprising. Indeed, our present inability to appreciate the practical reform aspect of his thought may itself result from the dualism which he himself had hoped to overcome. The consequence of our partial view of Barfield is that he has become obscure and esoteric and has lost his concrete relevance in the practical world of our daily experience. He has thus suffered a similar fate to that of Rudolf Steiner – a fate which neither he nor his predecessor deserves.

Afterword: Owen Barfield Today – Elmar Schenkel

Owen Barfield's death in 1997, at the age of 99, went largely unnoticed by the intellectual community. Some scholars remembered him as the author of a 1928 book on *Poetic Diction*, others may have recalled his study *What Coleridge Thought*, but most will probably have assumed that he had died many decades before. Only in his later years, upon his retirement from the law, did Barfield begin to formulate his own philosophy in a systematic way, though the origins of his thought are latent in his early literary studies. It was in *Saving the Appearances – A Study in Idolatry, Worlds Apart, Unancestral Voice, History, Guilt, and Habit*, or *Romanticism Comes of Age* that he voiced his own philosophical ideas, which were both indebted both to German and English romanticism, to Goethe and to Steiner, and yet altogether unique. Even the anthroposophical community has scarcely paid attention to this British thinker, who himself was shocked to see how much of his own philosophy had been anticipated by Rudolf Steiner. It is the aim of the present study by Astrid Diener to discuss these parallels and resonances, but also Barfield's original contribution to and confrontation with contemporary discussions. Barfield's reputation has suffered under the hands of those whose cast of mind was his very target, the specialists. He could also have been taken up by the so-called New Age, but he may not have been fashionable enough for this branch of thought, or, alas, frequently of thoughtlessness, for he was too much of a seriously committed thinker and scholar who enjoyed the subtleties of differentiation and philology. Unimpressed by faddish phrases and catchwords, he avoided easy fusions and confusions such as a 'tao of physics' or a global amalgamation of science and mysticism. Yet chances are that his ideas may turn out to be more seminal in the long run than most short-lived and easily marketable slogans.

Of course, there are notable exceptions to the aforementioned silence regarding Owen Barfield, such as T.S. Eliot, who helped him find a publisher for some of his philosophical works, the American poet Howard Nemerov or the physicist David Bohm. The American novelist Saul Bellow, while on a spiritual quest himself, discovered Barfield, who introduced him to Rudolf Steiner's anthroposophy. Bellow actually visited him in Kent in 1975, and though this visit was disappointing in some respects, Barfield retained his importance for him as a thinker. The blurb of Barfield's *History, Guilt, and Habit* (1979) carries this quotation from Bellow:

> We are well supplied with interesting writers, but Owen Barfield is not content to be merely interesting. His ambition is to set us free. Free from what? From the prison we have made for ourselves by our ways of knowing, our limited and false habits of thought, our 'common sense'. These, he convincingly argues, have produced a 'world of outsides with no insides to them,' a brittle surface world, an object world in which we ourselves are mere objects. It is not only what we perceive that determines the quality of the world we live in, and what we have collectively chosen not to perceive is the full reality of consciousness, the 'inside' of everything that exists.

Are Barfield's caveats and warnings still valid or have they become outdated with the advent of the internet and the Human Genome Project? Bellow's evaluation contains some of the elements which assure Barfield's continued relevance even in the 21st century, this age of genetics, neurology and information technology.

The last decade or so has seen major breakthroughs in science and technology, and it seems that new links between mind and nature have been discovered and forged. Or have they? At least on the surface, it seems that scientists in their search for the principles of life and consciousness are looking at the 'inside' of things. In a recent Berlin exhibition entitled *Seven Hills*, one of the panels in a room dedicated to genetics read: "Old forms of biology examined bodies from the outside in. In [the] future, biology will follow the opposite path, from the inside out." The exhibition contained a section on what was called the 'nucleus' featuring a magnified model of the double helix and film sequences portraying various levels of cellular activity. It is clear now that such simulations as well as the near-complete decoding of human DNA have only become possible through the use of computers, for decoding is largely a mathematical task only manageable by the most powerful calculators. The book of nature seems to be on the verge of disclosing its last secrets. So it seems that the combination of information technology and molecular biology may result in a significant step forward as far as understanding ourselves is concerned. Viewed from a more critical perspective, however, nature has become readable, but in a peculiar way – it has become machine-readable. Yet machines have been coded by humans and will therefore produce results conditioned by the thoughts preceding them. In this sense, all results are coloured by prior assumptions and often simply reflect contemporary fixations and beliefs. When we break down nature into its components, we may gain rather insight into our own methods and theories which make up our world-picture than into nature. Owen Barfield once labelled this kind of insight "dashboard knowledge" – the sort of knowledge necessary to manipulate nature successfully. Or, as a poet once put it when he tried to make sense of an earlier scientific revolution, the Copernican paradigm shift:

> Man hat weav'd out a net, and this net throwne
> Upon the Heavens, and now they are his owne.
> [John Donne, "An Anatomie of the World", 1612]

In other words, though new insights may create new ownership, such insights do not necessarily mean an access to truth. When truth finally makes its appearance, it turns out to have a human face, our face. Barfield wanted to take human participation into account when looking at the phenomenal world. This is why he speaks of the 'inside' of evolution. What he has in mind is a revolution from inside the human – and this means learning about the inside of things through the imagination. When we see films transporting us through the inside of a cell, what we see is still the outside. As a matter of fact, this kind of micro- or macrophotography has simply extended the outside of things. More and more 'outside' has become available through what Barfield refers to as the "camera eye" in his essay on "The Harp and the Camera" (reprinted in *The Rediscovery of Meaning*). In opposing the camera to the romantic concept of the Aeolian harp in which humans experience themselves as the inside of creation, he comes to this conclusion:

> The camera up to date has won the war. We live in a camera civilization. Our entertainment is camera entertainment. Our holidays are camera holidays. [...] Our science is almost entirely a camera science.

The camera is the tool of separation, a function that Barfield does not disapprove of as such. On the contrary, he finds separation necessary for the development of the modern individual. Separation or analysis has been the primary method of modern science for the last three or four centuries. It seems that the analytical method has been necessary for our consciousness to become conscious of its very nature. It is also inextricably linked to our concept of individuality. Implicitly, such statements about the 'necessity' point to an aim of the historical process. Barfield, however, is very cautious not to be too explicit about teleological patterns.

Another case in point where the 'inside' seems to have surfaced is neurology. Again, we are reaching the watershed and ask ourselves: where does consciousness begin, where does it become a biological fact and how do its mental and physical aspects interconnect? Work by contemporary researchers such as Damasio, Eccles, Roth, Varela and others focuses on these questions. With Barfield one can assume that inside and outside are ultimately and of necessity a unit. But before we recognize this we still have a long way to go.

This age has also been called the information age. If we consider the importance granted software, networks and cyberspace today, it seems that the immaterial has won over the material. Matter – geography, physical shape, location – has been superseded or replaced by informational values. Space is shrunk, while time is sped up almost limitlessly. Simultaneously, our electronic environment exerts a constant pull that dissociates the bodily and mental realms. We have to create fitness centres and event parks in order to complement and counteract our increasing dependence on monitors. This is bound to happen because information as a principle is based on separation: a dualism that can be found at its core and which we call digitalism. Information is machine-readable or readable by those parts of the brain that work mechanically. All of computer culture may very well be a projection or externalisation of this level of neural functioning. The mind is more complex though, as neurologists such as Antonio Damasio have shown: the brain is inherently capable of operating on a level that comprises and cognizes wholes, but imagination and emotion are required for it to function at this level. In *Feeling of What Happens* (1998) Damasio demonstrates compellingly to what extent the body, emotion, consciousness and reason must interact in order to permit us to make decisions quite different from the simple optimising analyses produced by computers. Disembodied thought, in other words, leads us into an autistic universe, or nowhere. Original participation, which Barfield supposes conditioned human interaction with the world at the beginning of history, disappeared in the modern age but was remembered by the poets and artists who were constantly forging invisible, metaphorical links between the subjective and objective sides of reality. Poetry was the living memory of a drowned continent. It located these memories in parts of the body, hence 'remembering' was often seen as a re-membering. Now that we are on the verge of leaving this planet in both a literal and a metaphorical sense, poetic intuition may help us to re-embody our cerebral success, or at least part of it. For poetry alone will not suffice, according to Barfield. His view of a 'final participation' centers around a type of imagination that is trained by the will, a kind of future imagination. In Rudolf Steiner's anthroposophy Barfield found resonances this kind of imagination, one that may have to be supplemented with other techniques that the West is re-discovering by taking detours through Asian and other cultures. The marriage of spirit and matter, it seems, is inextricably bound up with a marriage of East and West, or those states of consciousness we associate with them and which are not necessarily part of geography. It is no coincidence, then, that late in life Barfield discovered the Oriental philosophy of Ibn Arabi in the scholarly work of Henry Corbin. Another Eastern philosopher, Sri Aurobindo, who attempted a fusion of Western and Indian thought, could be seen as further step in the Barfieldian dialogue between evolutionary thought and individual consciousness. And one could study Ken Wilber's impressive panorama of Eastern und Western thought in which Barfield's ideas assume their place and meaning.

Barfield, it seems, is a gateway to new syntheses of which we are in dire need. Why does his philosophy lead to so many new and fruitful venues, why does it open up so much new territory? I believe it is due to the fact that Barfield does not present so much thought as thinking, not so much product but production. In his works we witness the dynamics of philosophical enquiry. Hence it is no coincidence that in his later works such as *Worlds Apart* or *Unancestral Voice* he resorted to the dialogue or even to narrative in order to make the reader experience these processes and the excitement they generate. Another important reason for Barfield's relevance today is the openness which characterizes his idea about the human being who is seen as work in progress, as it were. There is no finality in his philosophy, and particularly in later life, he abhorred the implications of closed and even teleological systems, though, on the other hand, there is always *direction* in his thought. In *Unancestral Voice*, the mystical voice of the Meggid defines "brain-thinking" as something particularly concerned with the regular and the finished product. It then goes on to say:

> Your brain and your nerves, which are all that this kind uses, are themselves the finished part of your physique – a legacy of the past. It is to other parts that you look, whether you know it or not, for the promise of the future. It is this kind of thinking that seeks and finds regularity; it can do no other; and if it finds, or seems to find, anything else, it is at a loss. The irregular is the unfinished part – on which the possibility of change and transformation depends.

Even if Barfield was not an enthusiastic reader of Nietzsche – at least there is no evidence of such enthusiasm – I think he would have subscribed to Zarathustra's words: "What is great in man is that he is a bridge and not a goal." Whatever may come next, Barfield helps us to prepare for it.

Elmar Schenkel, Leipzig University

Appendix:
An Interview with Owen Barfield

(Forest Row, East Sussex, 25 March 1994)

1. Introduction

In the interview printed below I had the opportunity of asking Mr Barfield about the beginnings of *Poetic Diction*. I asked him about the various influences that helped him to put his thoughts into shape: specifically about the first reactions to his new ideas, about the general intellectual climate of the time and his own reactions to it, and more generally about the role of Anthroposophy in the development of his thought.

Owen Barfield is a contemporary of C.S. Lewis and T.S. Eliot – in some ways two very contrasting literary figures in twentieth century English literature. While C.S. Lewis was, since his undergraduate days, a close friend of Barfield's, T.S. Eliot became the publisher of *Poetic Diction* and other works of his. Among the questions I posed were, finally, those concerning his relation to Lewis and Eliot. He once remarked (in relation to C.S. Lewis, but it applies equally to himself): "A good deal could be said about the absolute necessity of humour, as an available ingredient to any really deep thinker, as distinct from either a merely rapid or a merely solemn one". I am most grateful for the humour and the patience he displayed in answering, with great generosity, all those many questions of mine.

A note on the edition of the interview: First, where corrections in speech occur, both in my questions and in Mr Barfield's replies, I have chosen the variant that most plausibly preserves the general flow of the speech. Secondly, several of my questions and comments are introduced by sometimes quite lengthy explorations. For the sake of readability I have, in such cases, summarized and given them in their essence, without altering them in content or meaning. Wherever this occurs it is indicated by italics. Italics are also used for indicating emphasis in speech where prominent, and for marking foreign words as well as publications. Pauses in speech are represented by three dots.

2. The Interview

After a few introductory remarks I ask the following question:

Astrid Diener: You stress very much that your ideas, with your turning towards Romanticism, were so much against the stream that, in a way it seems, if one thinks of you at this time, that you were rather an 'isolated' figure in the way you were thinking. It would therefore be interesting to learn from you about the reaction of your friends and surroundings when you communicated your new ideas about poetry to them.

Owen Barfield: I communicated most of them to C.S. Lewis. And he was – I wouldn't call him quite a Romanticist, but he had this love of literature, and certainly of the Romantic poets, as much as I did. And he had a very powerful imagination. But I wasn't really in touch with the contemporary literary people much. I just felt the impulse to put down what poetry meant to me, and therefore what it could mean to other people, I suppose.

Diener: Your ideas about poetry seem so strikingly new at the time that I wonder how easy or difficult it actually was for you to put them into shape, and to communicate them.

Barfield: I tried to put down what I was thinking. And, as I say, what I thought about poetry, particularly lyric poetry of the recent past, even more particularly Romantic poetry, was not what was being said by the literary circles of the time particularly. So, I just wasn't interested in them ... I didn't care for T.S. Eliot's poetry at all. I think that is really all I can say ... My family – they weren't by any means philistines, but they weren't specially interested in poetry. So, I had no particular audience or literary companionship there ... It just happened, really [laughs].

Diener: You say you were discussing your ideas with C.S. Lewis. I take it that one of the things you were dicussing was the importance of imagination and whether it could be a vehicle for truth, or whether it was simply a desirable pleasure of the human soul[97] ...

Barfield: Yes. Sorry for interrupting you, but there I could go a little further in answering your previous question ... Imagination as a vehicle for truth: I was very much struck, as I began to get fond of poetry, with the fact that it wasn't just enjoying the poetry at the time, but, also, it did enlarge or deepen my experience of the world around me, especially the natural world, of course. And that aspect of poetry reading didn't seem to be attracting any attention, particularly, from anyone else.

Diener: And it seems that it also didn't quite attract C.S. Lewis's attention in the same way as it attracted yours.

Barfield: I think that's not quite true; he had a great love of nature. There was very much poetry he knew by heart, far more than I did [laughs]. And he would certainly very often come up with appropriate quotations if we went out for a walk or anything; and if he was struck by anything he would be more likely to cap it with a quotation from English poetry, or even both Latin and Greek poetry, than I would. He didn't theorize about it. That's the difference. He didn't want to theorize about imagination – he loved it.

Diener: And this theory about poetry as a means of cognition seems to be something on which you and Lewis actually disagreed.

Barfield: Very much so. Yes. He didn't like the idea of having any concrete relation between imagination and knowledge: Knowledge was a job for science. He was, philosophically, really a materialist – in the kind of deepened form where it was called Subjective Idealism. When it came to actual detailed knowledge of any sort, that was a job for scientists. He accepted the materialist assumption of nineteenth and twentieth century science. I think somebody put it (it was a man, who wrote about history) who said all history was history of thought; he said that couldn't be applied to nature because nature has no inside. And Lewis would certainly have agreed with it – that nature had "no

---

[97] This, and most of my other remarks about C.S. Lewis refer to the book *Owen Barfield on C.S. Lewis*. It contains texts by Owen Barfield adapted from their original form as lectures or portions of books, and three interviews.

inside". But I think that's something where I convinced him a bit (or he said so in things he wrote) – that it *had* an inside in a similar sense to what individual human beings have: they have their inside of the body and their inside of the mind.

Diener: Once asked about C.S. Lewis's relationship to imagination you said "he was in love with it ... But I wanted to marry it"[98] ...

Barfield: Yes [laughs].

Diener: This remark tells something about two different concepts of life, and about two different ways of wanting to lead one's own life.

Barfield: Oh yes, quite.

Diener: And recently, when I reread your book on Lewis, your idea of 'wanting to marry imagination', of bringing it into everyday life, as it were (which differs so much from Lewis's approach), struck me as having a parallel with a little book by Virginia Woolf called *A Room of One's Own*, published only a year after your book *Poetic Diction*.[99]

Barfield: I'm not very sure I've read that. It was very much talked about at the time, I remember. She didn't theorize about imagination exactly, did she?

I refer to his remark where he compares Lewis's attempt to keep imagination apart from everyday life with the Victorians' attitude towards women,[100] *and point out to him that this is exactly what Virginia Woolf reacted against (though not in a very theoretical way): the insulation of women, as well as of imagination. And I ask him how closely related he feels to any such thoughts as those of Virginia Woolf.*

Barfield: I never read much of Virginia Woolf. I read *To the Lighthouse*, and one or two other things. I think I thought she was a bit of a dilettante, but I did her quite wrong. I didn't really read enough of her to justify or form any opinion, I think. I associated her with the

---

[98] Cf. interview of 1984 with George Tennyson, rpt. in Barfield 1989a, 137.

[99] *A Room of One's Own* is based on two lectures Virginia Woolf delivered in 1928 to two women colleges in Cambridge, and was published in 1929.

[100] Cf. Barfield 1989a, 98.

Bloomsbury Group. Also, I tended rather to shun books just because they were very popular then [laughs]. And I knew that the people whose books were popular had quite different ideas about life than I had [laughs].

Diener: It's only when comparing what Virginia Woolf says with what you say (I'm not very sure how close the relation is) – it seems there was 'something in the air', which was picked up by different people independently, by Virginia Woolf, or by yourself, or having been long developed by Rudolf Steiner in Germany, for instance.

Barfield: Also by the German *Naturphilosophen*. And they were brought to England by Coleridge, of course. Coleridge meant a lot to me.

Diener: When were you actually acquainted with Steiner's writings? – One finds oneself confronted with lots of conflicting dates: Some people say in 1922 ...

Barfield: Have you got the book *Romanticism Comes of Age*? Didn't I tell there in the introduction? – 1922, some time around there.

Diener: Yes, you say there: "a year or two" before you published *History in English Words*.[101]

Barfield: Yes, while I was composing it. It took me a long time, not just the writing, but the collecting of material, all the different words and so forth. I spent a lot of time in the library of the British Museum, just looking at the *Oxford English Dictionary* to see how words had changed their meaning. I think I mentioned Steiner in the introduction to *Poetic Diction*, didn't I? I had come across him while I was writing it.[102]

---

[101] Cf. Barfield 1986e, 12. *History in English Words* was first published in 1926 by Methuen and Co., London.

[102] This suggests that Barfield developed an interest in Anthroposophy some time between 1922 and 1924. First signs of his growing interest can be detected in an entry in Lewis's journal dated 7 July 1923 where Lewis says: "I was very much disappointed to hear that both Harwood [i.e. a common friend of Barfield's and Lewis's] and Barfield were impressed by him [sc. Steiner]." Lewis 1993a, 254. Cf. above, 92 ff.

Diener: Well, I remember you saying in the introduction that, at the time, you were not acquainted with Steiner's writings on the same subject, and that you'd find it quite improper to 'father upon him' many of the views on poetry you held.[103]

Barfield: Oh yes.

Diener: So, at one point your own ideas ran into those of Steiner. But when *exactly* did Steiner come in?

Barfield: I gave a lecture on myself once in the Anthroposophical Society, which was reprinted as *Owen Barfield And the Origin of Language*.[104] What I mentioned there was rather curious, really. The essence of Steiner's teachings, as you will know (you've read a fair amount of Steiner?), is the evolution of human consciousness, the kind of pictorial consciousness in earlier times. I, in a way, came to the same conclusion on my own before I heard of Steiner, but in terms of language rather, of human beings' experience of language and of nature. In effect, you could say that I came to the conclusion that human beings in earlier stages of evolution had, what you might call, a pictorial consciousness. Steiner, of course, taught that too. He called it sometimes "atavistic clairvoyance". It was rather curious that I was taken by his whole metaphysic, but for a long time they were more or less parallel – his thought of "atavistic clairvoyance" and mine of "original participation", as I called it later. And I didn't connect them. I remember, quite late, after I'd been reading Steiner off and on for a year or two, suddenly saying to myself, this "atavistic clairvoyance" he is talking about *is* what I am talking about. For a time they went on side by side.

---

[103] "[...] yet it would, it seems, be impossible in a Preface to convey half *my own* sense of indebtedness without appearing, quite improperly, to father upon him many of the views on poetry which I have expressed – whereas I can scarcely recollect anything he has said or written on that subject at all, nor am I yet acquainted with his lectures on Language." The 1927 preface of the first edition, rpt. in Barfield 1987, 12.

[104] The lecture was given in June 1976 at Rudolf Steiner House, London, and printed in *Towards*, 1,2 (June 1978) and *Towards* 1,3 (December 1978), and is available separately in George Publications, New York, no date.

Diener: That would mean your thoughts were already fully developed before you actually came across Steiner. Would you say then that Steiner was confirming your own views?

Barfield: Confirming them and also strengthening and setting them in a true context, somehow. And also his whole teaching, the detailed account of the evolution of consciousness, the spiritual hierarchies and so forth ... I think I put it once that he began where I left off. All I had done was to establish, in a hostile intellectual atmosphere, that there *was* such a thing as the evolution of consciousness from a more pictorial, more living, if you like, form or quality to our own. He assumes that, to start with, and builds on that this terrific edifice. But, of course, I got a lot from Coleridge. Coleridge was very enlightening for me, with his concept of polarity.

Diener: Well, once you put it that Rudolf Steiner's thought is really Romanticism come of age.[105]

Barfield: Yes, I put it in that way. That, I should have thought, you ought to be able to appreciate because, in a sense, the German *Naturphilosophen* were predecessors of Anthroposophy, weren't they?

Diener: Yes, and considering the fact that I as a German will be able to appreciate this root of Anthroposophy in German philosophy, I would like to ask you, as a witness of the time, and as one of the first Anthroposophists in England, what impact it made, and what it meant to you, as an Englishman, when it first came to England.

Barfield: Reading Steiner and reading the translations,[106] or the writings of the very few English Anthroposophists were two very different things, because there were very few English Anthroposophists, and they weren't, for the most part, particularly philosophically educated people. And in those days there was rather a strong flavour of the old Theosophical Society among a good many members. I didn't have a lot of contact with the English Anthroposophists. But there something personal comes in because my wife, whom I married just about the same time when I discovered Rudolf Steiner, disliked Anthroposophy intensely.

---

[105] Cf. introduction to Barfield 1986e, 14.

[106] Barfield did not learn German until 1929.

Diener: What, if you allow me to ask, were her main reasons for disliking Anthroposophy?

Barfield: Well, she was a member of the High Anglican Church. And it just wasn't her line, that whole business of self-knowledge and so forth. She was particularly horrified by the teachings of the two Jesus boys.[107] She felt it was a kind of sacrilege ..., or nonsense or something. But I don't want to go into all that, it was a tragedy. It really spoilt our married life, although we had a happy one, in many ways.

Diener: Your own initial reactions to Anthroposophy seem a little ambiguous – you once said that, when you first attended talks about Anthroposophy, you were impressed and full of doubts.[108] What was it in particular that made you feel doubtful about Anthroposophy?

Barfield: The doubts were the fact that it started with assumptions totally contrary to the assumptions we had arrived at in the intellectual and social atmosphere we had been brought up in. The doubts were the kind of doubts of any ordinary scientist, or any person who accepts materialistic science as the only true account of the nature of the world. We took for granted the kind of thing that the sciences were saying about the origin of the world and so forth, just as all the people around us did. And here was Steiner, quietly saying exactly the opposite to a great deal of it. Naturally we felt doubtful. But it became

---

[107] Steiner was not so much interested in Jesus as an 'ordinary' human being (as it was the case in nineteenth-century historical research), but in his 'extraordinariness'. In his explorations he came to the conclusion that there must have been two Jesus boys, the one being the incarnation of Zarathustra, the other having had no previous incarnation, but having a special relation to Buddha; at the age of twelve the former died, and his spirit entered the body of the latter who by his baptism at the age of thirty took on his 'Christ nature', living on earth, as an embodiment of the divine, until his crucifixion. Cf. e.g. Steiner's 1909 lecture *Das Lukas-Evangelium*, and his 1910 lecture *Das Matthäus-Evangelium*. And for Barfield's own comment on this teaching and its evolutionary significance cf. his book *Unancestral Voice*.

[108] Cf. Elmar Schenkel, "Interview mit Owen Barfield" [Schenkel 1993, 25]. Barfield relates here his first aquaintance with Anthroposophy through his friend A.C. Harwood, and says they attended these talks, which were organized by George Kaufmann in London, in "1922 or 1923".

more and more convincing. It was a far more rational explanation of the nature of the world than the kind you get from the sort of *Weltanschauung* that is either assumed or specifically taught nowadays in schools.

Diener: The specific stress on the examination of self-consciousness, the examination of thought and the turning *inward* to imagination for a better understanding of reality – would this have been one of the things that would have aroused doubts initially?

Barfield: Yes, in a sense, because that lay at the beginning of the divergence from contemporary assumptions, that you take thinking seriously – not only thought, but the *activity* of thinking. I was tremendously impressed, of course, by his [sc. Steiner's] philosophical books: *The Philosophy of Freedom*, or, as it was then called in English translation, *The Philosophy of Spiritual Activity*, and *Truth and Science*. They really convinced me finally, I think, that in spite of its being contrary to everything that was being taught around me, it was the truth.

Diener: The impulse of examining self-consciousness, seems, at that very time, to have been considered as something coming specifically from Germany.

Barfield: Oh yes, I agree.

Diener: And sometimes one finds in England some kind of an aversion to it. Let me, for instance, read to you a remark by Harold Nicolson (where he quotes the German diplomat Albrecht Bernstorff's manual for German students going up to Oxford): 'The egocentric German habit of constantly relating the universe to themselves and themselves to the universe is a morbid habit "which may lead us to disaster". It does not produce individualism, it produces only self-consciousness; and in so doing it diminishes the sense of personal responsibility and tempts the young German to surrender in despair to something outside himself – "to the State or to a Party."'[109]

---

[109] Cf. Nicolson, "Albrecht Bernstorff" [Nicholson, 110]. This particular passage comprises two perspectives on self-consciousness: the German and the English, the pre-First World War view of Bernstorff's manual (1912) and the post-Second World War view in Nicolson's commentary on Bernstorff.

Barfield: Yes, of course, that is a valid criticism of one of the effects of the emphasis on self-consciousness. Well, it comes down to Hegel, doesn't it, really? – Hegel's "deification of the state". That is the dark side of it, as I see it. But that doesn't mean that one should ignore the bright side. I'm not putting it very skilfully, I'm afraid

Diener: C.S. Lewis, as you say in your book about him, had a fear of drifting into the dark side, the irrational, and refused the idea of examining his own consciousness. Was his criticism fruitful to you in the sense that it would sharpen your awareness of this dark side ...

Barfield: It was only fruitful in the sense that, in order to fight with him, I had to go into the best way of expressing, defending, what I thought. His reaction to Anthroposophy was a tragedy, in a way. It was very much affected by the fact that in an earlier period of his life he had a time when he was rather attracted to occultism in the bad sense, which some Theosophists went in for, I think. And he had this rather phoney attraction for it. And he reacted very strongly against it. He mixed up all this in his mind. For he thought it was all trying to come back again in Anthroposophy.

Next, I hark back to what he said earlier about the beginnings of his dispute with C.S. Lewis, and then I go on to ask him specifically about how it led to the so-called "Great War" controversy between Lewis and himself, and he asks:

Barfield: Have you read the book about the "Great War"?[110]

Diener: By Lionel Adey? – Yes. Adey says that the "Great War" began with Lewis's disappointment by your interest in Rudolf Steiner and that he began to try to dissuade you from Anthroposophy.[111]

Barfield: Yes.

Diener: But what you said about the development of your thought before your acquaintance with Anthroposophy makes me think that the "Great War" controversy was perhaps not really *only* about

---

[110] The book Barfield refers to is Lionel Adey, *C.S. Lewis's "Great War" with Owen Barfield* [Adey 1978].

[111] ibid., 13.

Anthroposophy but about the thoughts you had been arguing about before that. Would that be true?

Barfield: I'm not quite sure what you said – that the difference between us didn't arise out of the fact that I was interested in Anthroposophy, but it was there before that altogether? I think that's true. On the other hand ... have you read his book *The Allegory of Love*? – in the introduction there he recommends my method not only in theory but in practice.[112] He didn't quite carry out that. It was a muddle in a way, of course, but the efforts to clear up the muddle were what produced the "Great War".

Diener: So, your "Great War" was, in a way, about Anthroposophy as well as finding your individual positions ...

Barfield: It is so, yes ...

Diener: ... which had developed beforehand ...

Barfield: And also one learnt a lot from him. I owe quite a lot to Lewis. He forced me to think my position out responsibly and fully, to defend it against his. And he was certainly a more strenuous thinker than I was in the sphere of abstract thought, equipped with the quick mind he had. I owe a tremendous lot to him. I think he says in *Surprised by Joy* that he thought that I influenced him more than he influenced me.[113] It may be true that I influenced him more, but I think I learnt more from him than he learnt from me, really [laughs].

---

[112] *The Allegory of Love* is dedicated "To Owen Barfield, wisest and best of my unofficial teachers", and in the introduction, which Barfield quotes, Lewis writes: "Above all, the friend to whom I have dedicated the book, has taught me not to patronize the past, and has trained me to see the present itself as a 'period'. I desire for myself no higher function than to be one of the instruments whereby his theory and practice in such matters may become more widely effective." Lewis 1935, viii.

[113] In *Surprised by Joy* Lewis describes their friendship and how it began during their undergraduate days, and he characterizes Barfield as a kind of "anti-self", "the man who disagrees with you about everything": "Actually (though it never seems so at the time) you modify one another's thought. [...] But I think that he changed me a good deal more than I him." Lewis 1977a, 161.

Diener: Would this very strenuous way of arguing with Lewis have been something that couldn't be found so easily within the Anthroposophical movement?

Barfield: Yes, I think there are books by Steiner, and books by his followers, and so forth. It's certainly all there, but it's one thing to have it in a book, and another thing to have someone you're constantly arguing with. It forces the pace a bit, you might say.

Diener: Something else again, also connected with Lewis. He reacted very strongly against the poetry of T.S. Eliot. In almost every single book he has some attack on Eliot, whereas Eliot didn't seem to pay much attention to Lewis at all ...

Barfield: Later on they were all right. They collaborated in a translation of the Psalms.[114] What happened to it, and whether it was published, I don't know.

Diener: But in those early days they seem to begin on almost opposite ends.

Barfield: Yes. Well, of course Lewis had a big change, on what he called, his conversion. And he was in sympathy with the later Eliot of the *Four Quartets*, and so forth. In a way he couldn't be when he himself was not a Christian, or even a Theist. And Eliot, of course, had his own view.

We talk a little about Eliot, and I return to the differences between the early Eliot and the early Lewis, and his particular relation with Eliot.

Diener: In contrast to Lewis, Eliot approached his own way of looking at things by examining self-consciousness. Now, in *Poetic Diction* you say that Eliot's poetry, in a way, mirrors the twentieth

---

[114] This was in the mid or late 1950s, as Humphrey Carpenter records it, who also mentions that in 1959 they met privately, "an event which the pre-war Lewis would have declared to be in every respect impossible" [Carpenter, 246]. The translation of the Psalms was first published in 1961; the complete edition appeared in 1963 and is still used in its amended version as *The Revised Psalter, The amended text as approved by the Convocations of Canterbury and York in October 1963 with a view to legislation for its permissive use* (London: S.P.C.K., 1964).

century despair of the isolated individual, the "patient etherized upon the table"[115] ...

Barfield: Oh, do I? ... In the introduction to one of the later editions – yes.

Diener: It's very interesting, though, that, in his poetry he is very much concerned with examining the self, and with self-consciousness.

Barfield: Yes, indeed.

Diener: That correlates a little with some of your own interests in the exploration of self-consciousness, in a way. – What was your exact relation to Eliot? Of course, he was your publisher of *Poetic Diction* at Faber and Faber's, wasn't he?

Barfield: Yes. Well, you already pointed out that I wrote some disparaging remarks about his poetry in *Poetic Diction*, didn't I? But he published one of the earliest – not articles – sketches, that I wrote, in the *Criterion*. It's in there[116] ... My literary connection with T.S. Eliot is described quite fully in the introduction there, and also the things he published in the *Criterion* ... He was impressed by my book *Saving the Appearances* very much.[117] It was through him that I was introduced to the American publishers, the Wesleyan University Press, who published most of my books. And it is only in America where they have had any real impact. Practically all my publicity is American. No-one cares twopence about my writings in England, or hardly anybody does, a very very small circle. But in restricted circles, in different parts of America they're read and discussed, and even

---

[115] Cf. the 1951 preface to the second edition, rpt. Middletown, Connecticut: Wesleyan University Press, 1973, 36: "they [sc. the modern poets] have presented us with the human spirit as bewildered observer, or as agonized patient, compassionate in Hardy, humbled or repentant in Eliot, but always the observer, always the patient, helpless to alter anything but his own pin-pointed subjective emotion".

[116] Here he points out a book to me: *A Barfield Sampler, Poetry and Fiction by Owen Barfield*, Barfield 1993.

[117] *Saving the Appearances: A Study in Idolatry,* was first published by Faber and Faber in 1957.

movements are started, and so forth. This is partly through Eliot, I think.

Diener: Unfortunately, I haven't read the *Barfield Sampler* yet. But would you perhaps be prepared now to say a little more about how you got to know T.S. Eliot, and what it was, at the time, that interested him in your *Poetic Diction*?

Barfield: I don't know whether he *was* interested ... He must have been fairly interested in *Poetic Diction*. But it was later on, after I had had some contact with him, in contributions he published in his periodical *Criterion*. One he accepted, one he refused. He wanted something more like the one I had written before, that was very pessimistic.[118] The introduction to the *Barfield Sampler* quotes a letter of mine where I said that I was rather tired of the kind of literature that does nothing but point out ironically all the disintegration and decay that was going on.[119] We had a kind of correspondential, as it were, relation – between editor and contributor, in a small way. I suppose he read *Poetic Diction*. I don't remember him ever commenting on that, but he certainly did comment frequently on *Saving the Appearances*. I think there's some quotation on one of the editions: He talks about "strange highways of thought", or something like that.

Diener: So would you say it was a literary exchange, or friendship between you and Eliot?

Barfield: No, I wouldn't go as far as that, no. There was a time when he and a few other young or youngish literary aspirants used to meet for lunch somewhere in the West End. That was much later, after I had gone into law, and was practising as a solicitor. And I did attend one or two of those luncheons. I can't remember the names of the other people, young poets – except that Richard Aldington was one of them; but it was too difficult, and long, a journey, and I had to go back

---

[118] The piece accepted by Eliot is the short story 'Dope', published in *The Criterion* 1.

[119] The letter is dated 30 April 1924, and is kept at the Bodleian Library in: Owen Barfield, Letters to and from T.S. Eliot, 1924–48, Bodleian Library, Oxford, Ms. Eng. Lett. c. 782, fols. 25–32, fol. 25. The date of the letter given by Hunter and Kranidas (*Barfield Sampler*, 6) is wrong.

to my office then. I never really was in touch with the literary cliques at all, or with Eliot personally.

Here the interview ends and is followed by a more general conversation not related to the subject matter of the preceding interview, and therefore not printed here.

Notes

Note 1, 62: "Ich sagte mir: die Gegenstände und Vorgänge, welche die Sinne wahrnehmen, sind im Raume. Aber ebenso wie dieser Raum außer dem Menschen ist, so befindet sich im Innern eine Art Seelenraum, der der Schauplatz geistiger Wesenheiten und Vorgänge ist. In den Gedanken konnte ich nicht etwas sehen wie Bilder, die sich der Mensch von den Dingen macht, sondern Offenbarungen einer geistigen Welt auf diesem Seelen-Schauplatz. Als ein Wissen, das scheinbar von dem Menschen selbst erzeugt wird, das aber trotzdem eine von ihm ganz unabhängige Bedeutung hat, erschien mir die Geometrie. Ich sagte mir als Kind natürlich nicht deutlich, aber ich fühlte, so wie Geometrie muß man das Wissen von der geistigen Welt in sich tragen.

Denn die Wirklichkeit der geistigen Welt war mir so gewiß wie die der sinnlichen. [...] Bei der Geometrie sagte ich mir, hier *darf* man etwas wissen, was nur die Seele durch ihre eigene Kraft erlebt; in diesem Gefühle fand ich die Rechtfertigung, von der geistigen Welt, die ich erlebte, ebenso zu sprechen wie von der sinnlichen." Steiner 1990, 18–9.

Note 2, 64: "[...] [Es] beschäftigte mich unaufhörlich die Tragweite der menschlichen Gedankenfähigkeit. Ich empfand, daß das Denken zu einer Kraft ausgebildet werden könne, die die Dinge der Welt wirklich in sich faßt. Ein 'Stoff', der außerhalb des Denkens liegen bleibt, über den bloß 'nachgedacht' wird, war mir ein unerträglicher Gedanke. Was in den Dingen ist, das muß in die Gedanken des Menschen herein, das sagte ich mir immer wieder." Steiner 1990, 31.

Note 3, 65: "Gedacht hat sie (die Natur) und *sinnt* beständig; aber nicht als ein Mensch, sondern als Natur ... Sie hat keine Sprache noch Rede, aber *sie schafft Zungen und Herzen, durch die sie fühlt und spricht* ... Ich sprach nicht von ihr. Nein, was wahr ist und was falsch ist, alles hat sie gesprochen." Steiner 1985a, 51

Note 4, 65: "Das naive Bewußtsein behandelt [...] das Denken wie etwas, das mit den Dingen nichts zu tun hat, sondern ganz abseits von denselben steht und seine Betrachtungen über die Welt anstellt. Das

Bild, das der Denker von den Erscheinungen der Welt entwirft, gilt nicht als etwas, was zu den Dingen gehört, sondern als ein nur im Kopfe des Menschen existierendes; die Welt ist auch fertig ohne dieses Bild. Die Welt ist fix und fertig in allen ihren Substanzen und Kräften; und von dieser fertigen Welt entwirft der Mensch ein Bild. Die so denken, muß man nur fragen: mit welchem Rechte erklärt ihr die Welt für fertig, ohne das Denken? Bringt nicht mit der gleichen Notwendigkeit die Welt das Denken im Kopfe des Menschen hervor, wie die Blüte an der Pflanze? Pflanzet ein Samenkorn in den Boden. Es treibt Wurzel und Stengel. Es entfaltet sich zu Blättern und Blüten. Stellet die Pflanze euch selbst gegenüber. Sie verbindet sich in eurer Seele mit einem bestimmten Begriffe. Warum gehört dieser Begriff weniger zur ganzen Pflanze als Blatt und Blüte?" Steiner 1992, 86.

Note 5, 66: "Wir geben uns aber der Hoffnung hin, daß wir zu einer Überwindung des Subjektivismus, der den von Kant ausgehenden Erkenntnistheorien anhaftet, den Grund gelegt haben. Und zwar glauben wir dies durch unseren Nachweis getan zu haben, daß die subjektive Form, in welcher das Weltbild vor der Bearbeitung desselben durch die Wissenschaft für den Erkenntnisakt auftritt, nur eine notwendige Durchgangsstufe ist, die aber im Erkenntnisprozesse selbst überwunden wird. [...] Und indem wir dieses zeigen, begründen wir den *objektiven Idealismus* als notwendige Folge einer sich selbst verstehenden Erkenntnistheorie." Steiner 1989, 15–6.

Note 6, 66: "Die einzelnen Tatsachen treten in ihrer Bedeutung in sich und für die übrigen Teile der Welt erst hervor, wenn das Denken seine Fäden zieht von Wesen zu Wesen. Diese Tätigkeit des Denkens ist eine *inhaltvolle*. [...] Diesen Inhalt bringt das Denken der Wahrnehmung aus der Begriffs- und Ideenwelt entgegen. Im Gegensatz zum Wahrnehmungsinhalte, der uns von außen gegeben ist, erscheint der Gedankeninhalt im Innern. Die Form, in der er zunächst auftritt, wollen wir als *Intuition* bezeichnen. Sie ist für das Denken, was die *Beobachtung* für die Wahrnehmung ist. Intuition und Beobachtung sind die Quellen unserer Erkenntnis. Wir stehen einem beobachteten Dinge der Welt so lange fremd gegenüber, so lange wir in unserem Innern nicht die entsprechende Intuition haben, die uns das in der Wahrnehmung fehlende Stück der Wirklichkeit ergänzt. Wer nicht die Fähigkeit hat, die den Dingen entsprechenden Intuitionen zu finden, dem bleibt die volle Wirklichkeit verschlossen. Wie der Farbenblinde nur Helligkeitsunterschiede ohne Farbenqualitäten sieht, so kann der Intuitionslose nur unzusammenhängende Wahrnehmungsfragmente beobachten." Steiner 1992, 95.

Note 7, 67: "Das menschliche Bewußtsein ist der Schauplatz, wo Begriff und Beobachtung einander begegnen und wo sie miteinander verknüpft werden. Dadurch ist aber dieses (menschliche Bewußtsein zugleich charakterisiert. Es ist der Vermittler zwischen Denken und Beobachtung. [...] Er [der Mensch] betrachtet den Gegenstand als *Objekt*, sich selbst als das denkende *Subjekt*. Weil er sein Denken auf die Beobachtung richtet, hat er Bewußtsein von den Objekten; weil er sein Denken auf sich richtet, hat er Bewußtsein seiner selbst oder *Selbstbewußtsein*. Das menschliche Bewußtsein muß notwendig zugleich Selbstbewußtsein sein, weil es *denkendes Bewußtsein ist*. [...] Darauf beruht die Doppelnatur das Menschen: er denkt und umschließt damit sich selbst und die übrige Welt; aber er muß sich mittels des Denkens zugleich als ein den Dingen gegenüberstehendes Individuum bestimmen." Steiner 1992, 59–61.

Note 8, 68: "Für die Denkgewohnheiten unserer Zeit scheint es annehmbar, sich vorzustellen: in der Vorzeit haben die Menschen Naturvorgänge, Wind, Wetter, das Keimen des Samens, den Gang der Sterne beobachtet und sich zu diesen Vorgängen geistige Wesenheiten, als die tätigen Bewirker, *hinzugedichtet*; dagegen liegt es dem gegenwärtigen Bewußtsein ferne, anzuerkennen, daß der Mensch der Vorzeit die Bilder so erlebt hat, wie der spätere Mensch die Gedanken erlebte – als seelische Wirklichkeit.

Man wird allmählich erkennen, daß im Laufe der Menschheitsentwickelung eine Umwandlung der menschlichen Organisation sattgefunden hat. Es gab eine Zeit, in der die feinen Organe der menschlichen Natur noch nicht ausgebildete waren, welche ermöglichen, ein inneres abgesondertes Gedankenleben zu entwickeln; in dieser Zeit hatte der Mensch die Organe, die ihm sein Mit-Erleben mit der Welt in Bildern vorstellte.

Wenn man dies erkennen wird, wird ein neues Licht fallen auf die Bedeutung des Mythus einerseits und auch auf diejenige von Dichtung und Gedankenleben andererseits. Als das innerlich selbständige

Gedanken-Erleben auftrat, brachte es das frühere Bild-Erleben zum Erlöschen. Es trat der Gedanke auf als das Werkzeug der Wahrheit. In ihm lebte aber nur ein Ast des alten Bild-Erlebens fort, das sich im Mythus seinen Ausdruck geschaffen hatte. In einem anderen Aste lebte das erloschene Bild-Erleben weiter, allerdings in abgeblaßter Gestalt, in den Schöpfungen der Phantasie, der Dichtung. – Dichterische Phantasie und gedankliche Weltanschauung sind die beiden Kinder der einen Mutter, des alten Bild-Erlebens, das man nicht mit dem dichterischen Erleben verwechseln darf." Steiner 1985, 38–9.

Note 9, 69: "In Griechenland wird das Streben geboren, die Weltzusammenhänge durch dasjenige zu erkennen, was man gegenwärtig *Gedanken* nennen kann. – Solange die Menschenseele durch das Bild die Welterscheinungen vorstellt, fühlt sie sich mit diesen noch innig verbunden. Sie empfindet sich als ein Glied des Weltorganismus; sie denkt sich nicht als selbständige Wesenheit von diesem Organismus losgetrennt. Da der Gedanke in seiner Bildlosigkeit in ihr erwacht, fühlt sie die Trennung von Welt und Seele. Der Gedanke wird ihr Erzieher zur Selbständigkeit." Steiner 1985, 27.

Note 10, 70: "Nun aber erlebt der Grieche den Gedanken in einer anderen Art als der gegenwärtige Mensch. Dies ist eine Tatsache, die leicht außer acht gelassen werden kann. Doch ergibt sie sich für eine echte Einsicht in das griechische Denken. Der Grieche empfindet den Gedanken, wie man gegenwärtig eine Wahrnehmung empfindet, wie man "rot" oder "gelb" empfindet. Wie man jetzt eine Farben- oder eine Tonwahrnehmung einem "Dinge" zuschreibt, so schaut der Grieche den Gedanken *in und an* der Welt der Dinge. Deshalb bleibt der Gedanke in dieser Zeit noch das Band, das die Seele mit der Welt verbindet. Die Loslösung der Seele von der Welt beginnt erst; sie ist noch nicht vollzogen. Die Seele erlebt zwar den Gedanken in sich; sie muß aber der Ansicht sein, daß sie ihn aus der Welt empfangen hat, daher kann sie von dem Gedankenerleben die Enthüllung der Welträtsel erwarten." Steiner 1985, 27–8.

Note 11, 71: "Die führenden Philosophen fühlen die Kraft des Gedankenlebens wieder erwachen. Die Menschenseele hat die durch

Jahrhunderte durchlebte Selbständigkeit innerlich befestigt. Sie beginnt zu suchen: was denn eigentlich ihr ureigenster Besitz ist. Sie findet, daß dies das Gedankenleben ist. Alles andere wird ihr von außen gegeben; den Gedanken erzeugt sie aus den Urgründen ihrer eigenen Wesenheit heraus, so daß sie bei diesem Erzeugen mit vollem Bewußtsein dabei ist. Der Trieb entsteht in ihr, in den Gedanken eine Erkenntnis zu gewinnen, durch die sie sich über ihr Verhältnis zur Welt aufklären kann. Wie kann in dem Gedankenleben sich etwas aussprechen, was nicht bloß von der Seele erdacht ist? Das wird die Frage der Philosophen dieses Zeitalters. [...] Die Menschenseele versucht, das Gedankenleben auf seinen Wirklichkeitscharakter hin zu prüfen." Steiner 1985, 30.

Note 12, 72: "In der vierten Epoche tritt ein Naturbild auf, das sich seinerseits von dem seelischen Eigenleben losgelöst hat. Es entsteht ein Bestreben, die Natur so vorzustellen, daß in die Vorstellungen von ihr sich nichts einmischt, was die Seele aus sich und nicht aus der Natur selbst schöpft. So findet sich in dieser Epoche die Seele mit ihrem inneren Erleben auf sich selbst zurückgewiesen. Es droht ihr, sich eingestehen zu müssen, daß alles, was sie von sich erkennen kann, auch nur für sie selbst eine Bedeutung habe und keinen Hinweis erhielte auf eine Welt, in der sie mit ihrem wahren Wesen wurzelt. Denn in dem Naturbild kann sie von sich selbst nichts finden." Steiner 1985, 32.

Note 13, 72: "Spencer und Mill haben auf die Weltanschauungsentwickelung der letzten Jahrhunderthälfte einen großen Einfluß geübt. Das strenge Betonen der Beobachtung und die einseitige Bearbeitung der Methoden des beobachtenden Erkennens durch Mill; die Anwendung naturwissenschaftlicher Vorstellungen auf den ganzen Umfang des menschlichen Wissens: sie mußten den Empfindungen eines Zeitalters entsprechen, das in den idealistischen Weltanschauungen Fichtes, Schellings, Hegels nur Entartungen des menschlichen Denkens sah und dem die Erfolge der naturwissenschaftlichen alleinige Schätzung abgewannen [...]." Steiner 1985, 465–6.

Note 14, : "Den Materialismus bekämpfen oder zum Zerrbild machen, kann nicht Aufgabe einer geschichtlichen Darstellung sein. Denn er hat seine eingeschränkte Berechtigung. Man ist nicht auf falscher Fährte, wenn man die materiell bedingten Vorgänge der Welt materialistisch darstellt; man gelangt erst dahin, wenn man nicht zur Einsicht gelangt, daß die Verfolgung der materiellen Zusammenhänge zuletzt zur Anschauung des Geistes führt." Steiner 1985, 11.

Note 15, 75: "Friedrich Eckstein vertrat nun energisch die Meinung, man dürfe die esoterische Geist-Erkenntnis nicht wie das gewöhnliche Wissen öffentlich verbreiten. Er stand mit dieser Meinung nicht allein; sie war und ist die fast aller Kenner der 'alten Weisheit'. [...] [Er] wollte, daß man als 'Eingeweihter in altes Wissen' das, was man öffentlich vertritt, einkleidet mit der Kraft, die aus der 'Einweihung' kommt, daß man aber dieses Exoterische streng scheide von dem Esoterischen, das im engsten Kreise bleiben solle, der es voll zu würdigen versteht." Steiner 1990, 290.

Note 16, 75: "Die Aufgabe einer Geist-Erkenntnis ist nun, in Besonnenheit durch den Erkenntniswillen Ideen-Erleben an die geistige Welt heranzubringen. Der Erkennende hat dann einen Seeleninhalt, der so erlebt wird wie der mathematische. Man denkt wie ein Mathematiker. Aber man denkt nicht in Zahlen oder geometrischen Figuren. Man denkt in Bildern der Geistwelt. Es ist, *im Gegensatz* zu dem wachträumenden alten Geist-Erkennen, das vollbewußte Drinnenstehen in der geistigen Welt. [...] Zu diesem neueren Geisterkennen konnte man innerhalb der Theosophischen Gesellschaft kein rechtes Verhältnis gewinnen. Man war mißtrauisch, sobald das Vollbewußtsein an die geistige Welt heranwollte. Man kannte eben nur ein Vollbewußtsein für die Sinnenwelt. Man hatte keinen rechten Sinn dafür, diese bis in das Geist-Erleben fortzuentwickeln. Man ging eigentlich doch darauf hinaus, mit Unterdrückung des Vollbewußtseins, zu dem alten Traumbewußtsein zurückzukehren." Steiner 1990, 320–1.

Note 17, 78: "Der Verfasser sagt es unumwunden: er möchte vor allem Leser, die nicht gewillt sind, auf blinden Glauben hin die vorgebrachten Dinge anzunehmen, sondern welche sich bemühen, das Mitgeteilte an den Erkenntnissen der eigenen Seele und an den Erfahrungen des eigenen Lebens zu prüfen. [...] Der blinde Glaube kann so leicht das Törichte und Abergläubische mit dem Wahren verwechseln." Steiner 1987, 14–5.

Note 18, 81: "(22) Überall *Symptome eines Absterbens* der Bildung, einer völligen Ausrottung. Hast, abflutende Gewässer des Religiösen, die nationalen Kämpfe, die zersplitternde und auflösende Wissenschaft, die verächtliche Geld- und Genußwirtschaft der gebildeten Stände, ihr Mangel an Liebe und Großartigkeit. Daß die gelehrten Stände durchaus in dieser Bewegung darin sind, ist mir immer klarer. Sie werden täglich gedanken- und liebloser. Alles dient der kommenden Barbarei, die Kunst sowie die Wissenschaft – wohin sollen wir blicken? Die Große Sündflut der Barbarei ist vor der Tür.

(23) Ein Zeitalter der Barbarei beginnt, die Wissenschaften werden ihm dienen! –

(24) Nachweis der *barbarisierenden* Wirkungen der Wissenschaften. Sie verlieren sich leicht in den Dienst der 'praktischen Interessen'.". Nietzsche, Band I, 895.

Note 19, 82: "(26) *Die Förderung einer Wissenschaft auf Unkosten der Menschen* ist die schädlichste Sache von der Welt. Der verkümmerte Mensch ist ein Rückschritt der Menschheit, er wirft in alle Zeit hinaus seine Schatten. Er entehrt die Gesinnung, die natürliche Absicht der einzelnen Wissenschaft: sie selber geht daran endlich zugrunde; sie steht gefördert da, wirkt aber nicht oder unmoralisch auf das Leben." Nietzsche, Band I, 895.

Note 20, 82: "Verglichen mit dem *Künstler*, ist das Erscheinen des *wissenschaftlichen* Menschen in der Tat ein Zeichen einer gewissen Eindämmung und Niveauerniedrigung des Lebens [...]." Nietzsche, Band I, 881–2.

Note 21, 83: "Die Bewußtheit ist die letzte und späteste Entwickelung des Organischen und folglich auch das Unfertigste und Unkräftigste daran. Aus der Bewußtheit stammen unzählige Fehlgriffe, welche machen, daß ein Tier, ein Mensch zugrunde geht, früher als es notwendig wäre [...]." cited in Steiner 1983, 92.

Note 22, 83 : "Ich denke, wahrhafte Bildung nimmt das Große einer Persönlichkeit auf und verbessert kleine Irrtümer oder denkt halbfertige Gedanken zu Ende." Steiner 1983, 94.

Note 23, 84: "Aus meiner weitgehenden Beschäftigung mit Nietzsche verblieb mir die Anschauung von seiner Persönlichkeit, deren Schicksal war, das naturwissenschaftliche Zeitalter der letzten Hälfte des neunzehnten Jahrhunderts in Tragik mitzuerleben, und an der Berührung mit ihm zu zerbrechen. Er *suchte* in diesem Zeitalter, konnte aber in ihm nichts *finden*." Steiner 1983, 190.

Note 24, 84: "Jeder philosophische Gedanke, der nicht von diesem Leben selbst gefordert wird, ist zur Unfruchtbarkeit verurteilt [...]. [...] Ein Zeitalter, das solchem Denken abgeneigt ist, zeigt dadurch nur, daß es kein Bedürfnis empfindet, das Menschenleben so zu gestalten, daß dieses wirklich nach allen Seiten seinen Aufgaben gemäß zur Erscheinung kommt. Aber diese Abneigung rächt sich im Laufe der menschlichen Entwickelung. Das Leben bleibt verkümmert in solchen Zeitaltern. Und die Menschen bemerken die Verkümmerung nicht, weil sie von den Forderungen nichts wissen wollen, die in den Tiefen des Menschenwesens doch vorhanden bleiben und die sie nur nicht erfüllen. Ein folgendes Zeitalter bringt die Nichterfüllung zum Vorschein. Die Enkel finden in der Gestaltung des verkümmerten Lebens etwas vor, das ihnen die Unterlassung der Großväter angerichtet hat. Die Unterlassung der vorhergehenden Zeit ist zum unvollkommenen Leben der Folgezeit geworden, in das sich diese Enkel hineingestellt finden. Im Lebens*ganzen* muß Philosophie walten; man kann gegen die Forderung sündigen; aber die Sünde muß ihre Wirkung hervorbringen." Steiner 1985c, 12–3.

Note 25, 85: "Die Geschichtsphilosophen betrachten das Vergangene als Gegensatz und Vorstufe zu uns Entwickelten: – wir betrachten das *sich Wiederholende, Konstante, Typische* als ein in uns Anklingendes und Verständliches." Burckhardt, 6.

Note 26, 86: "[...] Rückwärts gewandt zur Rettung der Bildung früherer Zeiten, vorwärts gewandt zu heiterer und unverdrossener

Vertretung des Geistes in einer Zeit, die sonst gänzlich dem Stoff anheimfallen könnte." Marx in Burckhardt, 286.

Note 27, 86: "Hier hatte jeder etwas geahnt, aber keiner von seinem engen Standpunkte aus die einzige und umfassende Lösung gefunden, die seit den Tagen Nietzsches in der Luft lag, der alle entscheidenden Probleme bereits in Händen hielt, ohne daß er als Romantiker es gewagt hätte, der strengen Wirklichkeit ins Gesicht zu sehen [...] Darin liegt aber auch die tiefe Notwendigkeit der abschließenden Lehre, die kommen mußte und nur zu dieser Zeit kommen konnte." Spengler, 37.

Note 28, 86: "Der allgemeine philosophische Untergrund der Spenglerschen Weltanschauung ist ein brutaler Biologismus. Das Leben, das die geschichtlichen Prozesse hervortreibt, ist nicht mehr wie bei Hegel die Idee oder bei Bergson ein 'élan vital', sondern eine Vitalität im Sinne von Brutalität." Hirschberger, Band II, 589.

Note 29, 87: "Dann aber folgt zugleich mit dem Rationalismus die Erfindung der Dampfmaschine, die alles umstürzt und das Wirtschaftsbild total verwandelt. Bis dahin hatte die Natur Dienste geleistet, jetzt wird sie als Sklavin ins Joch gespannt. [...] Aber gerade damit ist der faustische Mensch zum *Sklaven seiner Schöpfung* geworden. Seine Zahl und die Anlage seiner Lebenshaltung werden durch die Maschine auf eine Bahn gedrängt, auf der es keinen Stillstand und keinen Schritt rückwärts gibt." Spengler, 396–7.

Note 30, 87: "Es handelt sich in der Geschichte immer nur um das Leben und immer nur um das Leben, die Rasse, den Triumph des Willens zur Macht, und nicht um den Sieg von Wahrheiten, Empfindungen oder Geld. Die Weltgeschichte ist Weltgericht: sie hat immer dem stärkeren, volleren, seiner selbst gewisseren Leben Recht gegeben, Recht auf das Dasein, gleichviel ob es vor dem Wachsein recht war, und sie hat immer die Wahrheit und die Gerechtigkeit der Macht, der Rasse geopfert und die Menschen und Völker zum Tode verurteilt, denen die Wahrheit wichtiger war als Taten und Gerechtigkeit wesentlicher als Macht." Cited in Hirschberger, Band II, 589.

Note 31, 111: *"Wir Modernen sind darauf angewiesen, den Geist wieder zu erleben, das heißt Urerfahrung zu machen.* Dies ist die einzige Möglichkeit, den Zauberkreis des biologischen Geschehens zu durchbrechen. [...] Wer diesen Aspekt der menschlichen Seele nicht sieht, ist blind, und wer ihn wegerklären oder gar aufklären will, hat keinen Tatsachensinn." Jung 1991, 56

Note 32, 112: "Vor allem schien mir Freuds Einstellung zum Geist in hohem Maß fragwürdig. Wo immer bei einem Menschen oder einem Kunstwerk der Ausdruck einer Geistigkeit zutage trat, verdächtigte er sie und ließ 'verdrängte Sexualität' durchblicken. Was sich nicht unmittelbar als Sexualität deuten ließ, bezeichnete er als 'Psychosexualität'. Ich wandte ein, daß seine Hypothese, logisch zu Ende gedacht, zu einem vernichtenden Urteil über die Kultur führe. Kultur erschiene als bloße Farce, als morbides Ergebnis verdrängter Sexualität. 'Ja', bestätigte er, 'so ist es. Das ist ein Schicksalsfluch, gegen den wir machtlos sind.'" Jung 1985, 154.

Bibliography

Abrams, M. H. 1971. *Natural Supernaturalism: Tradition and Revolution in Romantic Literature*, New York: Norton.

——— . 1993. ed. *The Norton Anthology of English Literature*, 2 vols. New York, London: W.W. Norton.

Adams, George. n.d. "Rudolf Steiner in England", in *Rudolf Steiner, Recollections by Some of His Pupils*, ed. Arnold Freeman, and Charles Waterman, London: n.p., 1–21.

Adey, Lionel. 1975. "The Barfield-Lewis 'Great War'", *Bulletin of the New York C.S. Lewis Society* 6, 10 (1975), 10–4.

——— . 1978. *C. S. Lewis's "Great War" with Owen Barfield*, British Columbia: University of Victoria Press.

——— . 1984. "The 'Great War' Revisited", *Bulletin of the New York C.S. Lewis Society* 15, 5 (1984), 6–11.

Altick, Richard T. 1973. *Victorian People and Ideas*, London: J. M. Dent.

Anon. 1925. "Anthroposophical Society in Great Britain: Report of Executive for the Year 1924, Read and Adopted at the General Meeting, 31st January, 1925", *Anthroposophical Movement: Weekly News for English-speaking Members of the Anthroposophical Society* 2, (8 February 1925), 6.

Anon. 1964. *The Revised Psalter, The amended text as approved by the Convocations of Canterbury and York in October 1963 with a view to legislation for its permissive use*, London: S.P.C.K..

Anon. 1916-22. *The Wadham College Gazette* 5 (1916–22).

Arnold, Matthew. 1932. *The Letters of Matthew Arnold to Arthur J. Clough*, ed. H. F. Lowry, London, New York: OUP, and Humphrey Milford.

——— . 1950. *The Poetical Works of Matthew Arnold*, ed. C. B. Tinker, and H. F. Lowry, London, New York, Toronto: OUP.

——— . 1970a (1861). "On Translating Homer", in *Matthew Arnold, Selected Prose*, ed. P. J. Keating, Harmondsworth: Penguin, 76–84.

——— . 1970b (1862): "On Translating Homer", in *Matthew Arnold, Selected Prose*, ed. P. J. Keating, Harmondsworth: Penguin, 85–98.

——— . 1972. "A French Critic on Milton", in *Matthew Arnold, Essays Religious and Mixed*, ed. R. H. Super, Ann Arbor: University of Michigan UP, 165–87.

———. 1995a (1864). "The Function of Criticism at the Present Time", in *Culture and Anarchy and Other Writings*, ed. Stefan Collini, Cambridge: CUP.

———. 1995b (1867–9). *Culture and Anarchy: An Essay in Political and Social Criticism*, in *Culture and Anarchy and Other Writings*, ed. Stefan Collini, Cambridge: CUP.

Avens, Robert. 1980. *Imagination is Reality: Western Nirwana in Jung, Hillman, Barfield and Cassirer*, Dallas, Texas: Spring Publications.

Babbel, Ulrich, and Craig Giddens. 1977. *Bibliographical Reference List of Published Works of Rudolf Steiner in English Translation*, 2 vols., London Rudolf Steiner Press.

Badewien, Jan. 1990: *Anthroposophie: Eine Kritische Darstellung*, mit einem Vorwort von Kirchenrat Klaus-Martin Bender, Konstanz: Friedrich Bahn Verlag.

Barfield, [Arthur] Owen. 1921a. "Wilfred Owen", Rev. of *Poems* by Wilfred Owen, *New Statesman* 16 (15 January 1921), 454.

———. 1921b. "George Santayana", Rev. of *Character and Opinion in the United States*, by George Santayana, and *Little Essays, Drawn from the Writings of George Santayana*, by Logan Pearsall Smith, *New Statesman* 16 (26 March 1921), 729–30.

———. 1921c. "Some Elements of Decadence", *New Statesman* 18 (24 December 1921), 344–5.

———. 1922. "Seven Letters", *The Weekly Westminster Gazette* (4 March 1922), 16.

———. 1923a. "Idiom", Rev. of *English Idioms* by Logan Pearsall Smith, *New Statesman* 21 (30 June 1923), 368, 370.

———. 1923b. "Milton and Metaphysics", Rev. of *Milton Agonistes*, by E. H. Visiak, *New Statesman* 21 (11 August 1923), 524–5.

———. 1923c (1922). "Ruin", *London Mercury* 7 (1922), 164–70; rpt. as "'Ruin': A Word and a History", *Living Age* 316 (1923), 164–70.

———. 1924. Letter to the editor, *New Age* 36 (30 October 1924), 9.

———. (1924-48). Unpublished Letters to and from T.S. Eliot, 1924-48, Bodleian Library, Oxford, Ms. Eng. Lett. c. 782, fols. 25–32.

———. 1925a. Letter to the editor, *G. K.'s Weekly* 1 (20 June 1925), 306.

———. 1925b. *The Silver Trumpet*, illustrated by Gilbert James, London: Faber and Gwyer.

———. c. 1925 (?). *Danger, Ugliness and Waste*, London: n.p., n.d..

———. 1926a. "Metaphor", *New Statesman* 26 (20 March 1926), 708–10.

———. 1926b. "Romanticism and Anthroposophy", Anthroposophy 1 (Easter 1926), 111–24.

———. 1928. "Rudolf Steiner", Rev. of *The Story of My Life* by Rudolf Steiner, *New Age* (8 March 1928), 226.

———. 1929a. "The Lesson of South Wales", *The Nineteenth Century* 105 (February 1929), 215–22.

———. 1929b. "The Problem of Financing Consumption", *The Nineteenth Century* 105 (June 1929), 792–801.

———. 1929c. "Financial Inquiry", *Nineteenth Century* 106 (December 1929), 774–84.

———. 1930a. Rev. of *Rudolf Steiner Enters My Life* by Dr. Friedrich Rittelmeyer, *Anthroposophy* 5 (Easter 1930), 121–2.

———. 1930b. "Psychology and Reason", *The Criterion* 9 (July 1930), 606–17.

———. 1931. Rev. of *Coleridge as Philosopher* by J. H. Muirhead, *Criterion* 10 (April 1931), 543–8.

———. 1933a. "The Relation between the Economics of C. H. Douglas and those of Rudolf Steiner", *Anthroposophy* 8 (Michaelmas 1933), 77–9.

———. 1933b. With C.S. Lewis, "Abecedarium Philosophicum" *The Oxford Magazine* 52 (30 November 1933), 298.

———. 1965 (1965). *Unancestral Voice*, London: Faber and Faber; rpt. Middletown, Connecticut: Wesleyan UP.

———. 1976. "Youth", in "Cecil Harwood: 5 January 1898 – 22 December 1975", *Anthroposophical Society in Great Britain, Supplememt to Members' News Sheet* (February 1976).

———. (1976). n.d. *Owen Barfield and the Origin of Language*, [lecture delivered to the Anthroposophical Society at Rudolf Steiner House, London, in 1976], Spring Valley, New York: St. George Publications.

———. 1983 (1972). *What Coleridge Thought*, London: OUP; rpt. Middletown, Connecticut: Wesleyan UP.

———. 1985 (1926). *History in English Words*, London: Methuen and Co.; rpt. Edinburgh: Floris Classics.

———. 1986a (1927). "Thinking and Thought", *Anthroposophy* 2 (Easter 1927), 48–67, rpt. in *Romanticism Comes of Age*, Middletown, Connecticut: Wesleyan UP, 47–66.

———. 1986b (1927). "Speech, Reason and Consciousness Soul", *Anthroposophy* 2 (Christmas 1927), 537–54, rpt. as "Speech, Reason and Imagination", in *Romanticism Comes of Age*, Middletown, Connecticut: Wesleyan UP, 67–83.

———. 1986c (1930). "An Introduction to Anthroposophy", *Anthroposophy* 5 (Easter 1930), 58–80, rpt. as "From East to West", in *Romanticism Comes of Age*, Middletown, Connecticut: Wesleyan UP, 25–46.

———. 1986d (1944). "The Philosophy of Samuel Taylor Coleridge" (From a lecture given at the Goetheanum, Dornach, Switzerland, during the Goethe Centenary Festival, August, 1932, and slightly revised), in *Romanticism Comes of Age*, London: Anthroposophical Publishing Co.; rpt. Middletown, Connecticut: Wesleyan UP, 144–63.

———. 1986e (1944). *Romanticism Comes of Age*, London: Anthroposophical Publishing Co.; rpt. Middletown, Connecticut: Wesleyan UP.

———. 1987 (1928). *Poetic Diction: A Study in Meaning*, London: Faber and Gwyer; rpt. Middletown, Connecticut: Wesleyan UP.

———. 1988 (1957). *Saving the Appearances: A Study in Idolatry*, London: Faber and Faber; rpt. Middletown, Connecticut: Wesleyan UP.

———. 1989a. *Owen Barfield on C.S. Lewis*, ed. G.B. Tennyson, Middletown, Connecticut: Wesleyan UP.

———. 1989b. "Either: Or: Coleridge, Lewis, and Romantic Theology", in *Owen Barfield on C.S. Lewis*, ed. G.B. Tennyson, Middletown, Connecticut: Wesleyan UP. 42-51.

———. 1993. *A Barfield Sampler: Poetry and Fiction by Owen Barfield*, ed. Jeanne Clayton Hunter and Thomas Kranidas, New York: State University of New York Press.

———. 1993a (1923). "Dope", *Criterion* 1 (1923), 322–8; rpt. in *A Barfield Sampler: Poetry and Fiction by Owen Barfield*, ed. Jeanne Clayton Hunter and Thomas Kranidas, New York: State University of New York Press, 71–6.

———. 1993b (1924). "The Devastated Area", *New Age* (3 July 1924), 116–8, rpt. in *A Barfield Sampler: Poetry and Fiction by Owen*

Barfield, ed. Jeanne Clayton Hunter and Thomas Kranidas, New York: State University of New York Press, 77–84.

———. 1994. Unpublished Letter to Astrid Diener, 15 July 1994.

Barguirdjian, Maria. [1994]. Letter to Astrid Diener, 13 May 1994.

Baumann, Adolf. 1991. *Wörterbuch der Anthroposophie: Grundlagen, Begriffe, Einblicke*, München: mvg Verlag.

Bell, David. 1972. "Philosophy", in *The Twentieth Century Mind: History, Ideas and Literature in Britain*, ed. C.B. Cox and A.C. Dyson, 3 vols., Oxford: OUP, vol. i, 174–224.

Bock, Emil. 1986. *Urgeschichte: Beiträge zur Geistesgeschichte der Menschheit*, Frankfurt/Main: Fischer.

Bowra, C. M. 1961. *The Romantic Imagination*, Oxford: OUP.

Brooker, Peter. 1992. ed.. *Modernism / Postmodernism*, London, and New York: Longman.

Burckhardt, Jacob. 1949. *Weltgeschichtliche Betrachtungen*, mit einem Nachwort herausgegeben von Rudolf Marx, Stuttgart: Alfred Kröner Verlag.

Burtt, E. A. 1959. *The Metaphysical Foundation of Modern Physical Science: A Historical and Critical Essay*, London: Routledge and Kegan Paul.

Butler, Marilyn. 1981. *Romantics, Rebels and Reactionaries: English Literature and its Background 1760–1830*, Oxford, New York: OUP.

Carpenter, Humphrey. 1982. *The Inklings: C.S. Lewis, J.R.R. Tolkien, Charles Williams and Their Friends*, London: Allan & Unwin.

Carr, Edward Hallet. 1981. *Was ist Geschichte?* Stuttgart, Berlin, Köln, Mainz: Verlag W. Kohlhammer.

Carter, G. S. 1958. *A Hundred Years of Evolution*, London: Sidgwick and Jackson.

Christ, Carol T. 1981. "T. S. Eliot, and the Victorians", Modern Philology 79 (November 1981), 157–65.

Clark, David. 1987. "Douglas, Clifford Hugh (1879–1952)", *The New Palgrave Dictionary of Economics*, ed. John Eatwell, Murray Milgate and John Newman, London, New York, Tokyo: Macmillan, vol. i, 920.

Colbert, James G., Jr. 1975. "The Common Ground of Lewis and Barfield", *Bulletin of the New York C.S. Lewis Society* 6, 10 (1975), 15–8.

Coleridge, Samuel Taylor. 1848. *Hints Towards the Formation of a More Comprehensive Theory of Life*, ed. Seth B. Watson, M.D., London: John Churchill.

——— . 1912. *The Complete Poetical Works of Samuel Taylor Coleridge, Including Poems and Versions of Poems Now Published For the First Time*, ed. Ernest Hartley Coleridge, 2 vols., Oxford: Clarendon Press.

——— . 1956–71. *Collected Letters of Samuel Taylor Coleridge*, ed. Earl Leslie Griggs, 6 vols., Oxford: The Clarendon Press.

——— . 1957 ff. *The Notebooks of Samuel Taylor Coleridge*, ed. Kathleen Coburn, 4 vols. to date, London: Routledge & Kegan Paul; Princeton: Princeton UP.

——— . 1969a. *Coleridge: Poetical Works*, ed. Ernest Hartley Coleridge, London, New York, Toronto: OUP.

——— . 1969b. *The Friend*, ed. Barbara E. Rooke, 2 vols., London: Routledge & Kegan Paul; Princeton: Princeton UP.

——— . 1972. *The Statemen's Manual* in *Lay Sermons*, ed. R.J. White, London: Routledge & Kegan Paul; Princeton: Princeton UP.

——— . 1983. *Biographia Literaria: Or Biographical Sketches of My Literary Life and Opinions*, ed. James Engell, and W. Jackson Bate, 2 vols., London: Routledge & Kegan Paul; Princeton: Princeton UP.

Copleston, Frederick. 1966. *A History of Philosophy, Volume VII: Bentham to Russell*, London: Burns and Oates.

Crook, Paul. 1994. *Darwinism, War and History: The Debate over the Biology of War From the 'Origin of Species' to the First World War*, Cambridge: CUP.

Darwin, Charles. 1985. *The Origin of Species by Means of Natural Selection, or The Preservation of Favoured Races in the Struggle for Life*, Harmondsworth: Penguin.

Davidson, Graham. 1990. *Coleridge's Career*, London: Macmillan.

Davis, Robert Con, and Ronald Schleifer. 1991. *Criticism and Culture: The Role of Critique in Modern Literary Theory*, Harlow: Longman.

Dawkins, Richard. 1989. *The Selfish Gene*, Oxford, New York: OUP.

Denzinger, Heinrich. 1991. *Kompendium der Glaubensbekenntnisse und kirchlichen Lehrentscheidungen*, Freiburg, Basel, Rom, Wien: Herder Verlag.

Dickstein, Morris. 1992. *The Double Agent: The Critic and Society*, New York, Oxford: OUP.

Diener, Astrid. 1995. "An Interview with Owen Barfield: *Poetic Diction* – Between Conception and Publication", (conducted 25 March 1994), *Mythlore: A Journal of J.R.R. Tolkien, C.S. Lewis Charles Williams, and the Genres of Myth and Fantasy* 20, 4 (Winter 1995), 14–9.

――――. "'Opposition is true friendship': The differences between Owen Barfield and C. S. Lewis", *Inklings: Jahrbuch für Literatur und Ästhetik* 16 (1998), 62–80.

Douglas, C. H. 1920. *Credit-Power and Democracy*, London: Cecil Palmer.

Easton, Stewart C. 1980. *Rudolf Steiner: Herald of a New Epoch*, New York: Anthroposophic Press.

Edmunds, Francis. 1990. *From Thinking to Living: The Work of Rudolf Steiner*, Longmead: Element Books.

Eliot, T. S. (1924). Unpublished Letter to Owen Barfield, dated 14 May 1924, (Bodleian Library, Oxford, MS.Eng.Lett. c.782), fol. 26.

―――― (1933). *After Strange Gods: A Primer of Modern Heresy (The Page Barbour Lectures at the University of Virginia 1933)*, London: Faber and Faber.

―――― 1948. *Notes Towards the Definition of Culture*, London: Faber and Faber.

――――. 1975. "Ulysses, Order and Myth", in *Selected Essays*, ed. Frank Kermode, London: Faber and Faber, 177–8.

――――. 1986a. "Arnold and Pater", in *Selected Essays*, London, and Boston: Faber and Faber, 431–43.

――――. 1986b. "The Metaphysical Poets", in *Selected Essays*, London, Boston: Faber and Faber, 281–91.

――――. 1986c (1927). "Francis Herbert Bradley", in *Selected Essays*, London, Boston: Faber and Faber, 452-63.

――――. 1987a. "*The Hollow Men*", in *Collected Poems*, London, Boston: Faber and Faber, 81–6.

――――. 1987b. *The Waste Land*, in *Collected Poems*, London, Boston: Faber and Faber, 61–80.

Ellmann, Richard, and Charles Feidelson, Jr. 1965. ed. *The Modern Tradition: Backgrounds of Modern Literature*, New York: OUP.

Feuer, L. 1962. "What is alienation? The career of a concept", *New Politics* 1 (Spring 1962), 116–34.

Finlay, John L. 1972. *Social Credit: The English Origin*, Montreal, London: McGill – Queen's UP.

Flieger, Verilyn. 1981. "Barfield's *Poetic Diction* and Splintered Light", *Studies in the Literary Imagination* 14, 2 (1981), 47–66.

Frank, Armin Paul. 1973. *Die Sehnsucht nach dem unteilbaren Sein: Motive und Motivation in der Literaturkritik T. S. Eliot's*. München: Wilhelm Fink Verlag.

Fridell, Eugen. n.d. *Kulturgeschichte der Neuzeit: Die Krisis der europäischen Seele von der schwarzen Pest bis zum Ersten Weltkrieg*, Berlin, Darmstadt, Wien: C.A. Koch's Verlag Nachf.

Fromm, Erich. 1955. *The Sane Society*, New York: Fawcett.

Frye, Northrop. 1963. *T.S. Eliot*, Edinburgh, London: Oliver and Boyd.

Fulweiler, Howard W. 1984. "'Here a Captive Heart Busted': From Victorian Sentimentality to Modern Sexuality", in *Sexuality in Victorian Literature*, Knoxville: University of Tennessee, 234–50.

─────. 1993. "The Other Missing Link: Owen Barfield and the Scientific Imagination", *Renacence: Essays on Value in Literature* 46, 1 (Fall 1993), 39–54.

Fussell, Paul. 1975. *The Great War and Modern Memory*, New York, London: OUP.

Gebser, Jean. 1986. *Ursprung und Gegenwart*, 3 vols., München: Deutscher Taschenbuch Verlag.

Gillispie, Charles Coulston. 1951. *Genesis and Geology: A Study in the Relations of Scientific Thought, Natural Theology, and Social Opinion in Great Britain 1790–1850*, Cambridge, Mass. Havard UP.

Glass, S. T. 1966. *The Responsible Society: The Ideas of the English Guild Socialists*, London: Longman's.

Gordan, Lyndall. 1977. *Eliot's Early Years*, Oxford: OUP.

─────. 1989. *Eliot's New Life*, Oxford: OUP.

Grant, Patrick. 1979. *Six Modern Authors and Problems of Belief*, London: Macmillan.

———— . 1982. "The Quality of Thinking: Owen Barfield as Literary Man and Anthroposophist", *Seven: An Anglo-American Literary Review* 3 (1982), 113–25.

Grom, Bernhard. 1993. "Anthroposophie", *Lexikon für Theologie und Kirche*, ed. Joseph Höf and Karl Rahner, Freiburg, Basel, Rom, Wien: Herder Verlag, vol. i, 737–41.

Hamilton, Paul. 1983. *Coleridge's Poetics*, Oxford: Blackwell.

Hayes, Paul. 1973. *Fascism*, London: George Allen & Unwin.

Hill, John, Spencer. 1978. *Imagination in Coleridge*, London, Basingstoke: Macmillan.

———— . 1983. *A Coleridge Companion: An Introduction to the Major Poems and the 'Biographia Literaria'*, London: Macmillan.

Hipolito, T. A. 1993. "Owen Barfield's *Poetic Diction*", Renacence: Essays on Value in Literature 46, 1 (Fall 1993), 3–38.

Hirschberger, Johannes. 1991. *Geschichte der Philosophie, Band II: Neuzeit und Gegenwart*, Freiburg, Basel, Wien: Herder Verlag.

Hocks, Rick. 1995. "*'Phantoms Dim of Past and Future Wrought': Coleridge, Barfield, Derrida, and Contemporary Epistemology*", Diss. University of Missouri-Columbia.

Hoffmann, David Marc. 1991. *Zur Geschichte des Nietzsche-Archivs (Supplementa Nietzscheana)*, Berlin, New York: De Gruyter Verlag.

Hooper, Walter. 1996. *C.S. Lewis: A Companion and Guide*, London: Harper Collins Publishers,

Hough, Graham. 1949. *The Last Romantics*: London: Methuen.

Hunter, Jeanne. 1984a. "Owen Barfield: Christian Apologist", *Renascence: Essays on Value and Literature* 36, 5 (1984), 171–9.

———— . 1984b. "Owen Barfield: A Change of Consciousness", *The Nassau Review: The Journal of Nassau Community College Devoted to Arts, Letters and Sciences*, 4, 5 (1984), 93–101.

Hynes, Samuel. 1991. *The Edwardian Turn of Mind*, London: Pimlico.

Jaffe, A.J. 1968. "Ogburn, William Fielding", *International Encyclopedia of the Social Sciences*, ed. David L. Sillis, 18 vols., London: Macmillan, vol. xi, 279.

Julius, Anthony. 1995. *T. S. Eliot, Anti-Semitism, And Literary Form*, Cambridge: CUP.

Jung, C[arl] G[ustav]. 1977. *Memories, Dreams, Reflections*, rec. and ed. Aniela Jaffe, trans. Richard and Clara Winston, Collins: Fountain Books.

─────── . 1985. *Erinnerungen, Träume, Gedanken*, aufgez. und hg. von Aniela Jaffe, Olten, Freiburg: Walter-Verlag.

─────── . 1990 (1932). "Sigmund Freud als kulturhistorische Erscheinung", *Charakter* 1 (January 1932), 65–70, rpt. in *Wirklichkeit der Seele*, München: Deutscher Taschenbuch Verlag, 59–66.

Jung, C[arl] G[ustav]. 1991 (1929). "Der Gegensatz Freud und Jung", in *Seelenprobleme der Gegenwart*, München: Deutscher Taschenbuch Verlag, 51–8

Kadrmas, Karla Smart. 1987. "Owen Barfield Reads Margaret Atwood: The Concepts of Participatory and Nonparticipatory Consciousness as Present in *Surfacing*, in *Margaret Atwood": Reflection and Reality*, (Living Author Ser. 6), ed. Beatrice Mendez-Egle, and James M. Haule (gen. ed.), Edinburgh: Pan American University, 71–88.

Keach, William. 1993. "Romanticism and Language", in *The Cambridge Companion to British Romanticism*, Cambridge, CUP.

Kegler, Karl R. 1998. "Travels, Towers, Space & Time: Lewis's *The Dark Tower* and its Correspondences", *Inklings: Jahrbuch für Literatur und Ästhetik* 16 (1998), 119–37.

Kermode, Frank. 1957. *Romantic Image*, London: Routledge and Kegan Paul.

Knight, Gareth. 1990. *The Magical World of the Inklings: J.R.R. Tolkien, C.S. Lewis, Charles Williams, Owen Barfield*, Longmead: Element Books,

Kojecky, Roger. 1971. *T. S. Eliot's Social Criticism*, London: Faber and Faber.

Kranidas, Thomas. 1980. "C.S. Lewis and the Poetry of Owen Barfield", *Bulletin of the New York C.S. Lewis Society* 12, 2 (1980), 1–2.

─────── . 1985. "The Defiant Lyricism of Owen Barfield", *Seven: An Anglo-American Literary Review* 6 (1985), 23–33.

Leask, Nigel. 1988. *The Politics of the Imagination in Coleridge's Critical Thought*, London: Macmillan.

Levy, Oscar. 1924. "The Spiritual Basis of Fascism", *New Age* 36 (23 October 1924), 305–7.

Lewis, C. S. 1935. *Allegory of Love: A Study in Medieval Tradition*, London: OUP.

———. 1977a. *Surprised by Joy: The Shape of my Early Life*, London: Fount.

———. 1977b. *The Dark Tower and Other Stories*, ed. Walter Hooper, London: Collins.

———. 1987 (1943). *The Abolition of Man*, Oxford: OUP; rpt. Glasgow: Collins/Fount.

———. 1988. *Prayer: Letters to Malcolm*, Glasgow: Collins, Fount.

———. 1989. *Perelandra*, in *The Cosmic Trilogy*, London: Pan Books.

———. 1993a. *All My Road Before Me: The Diary of C.S. Lewis, 1922–1927*, ed. Walter Hooper, London: Fount.

———. 1993b. *The Silver Chair*, London: Lions.

———. n.d. Letters to Owen Barfield, 'The Great War', c. 1927–30s, with (fols. 14–25, 29–35) two letters from Barfield to Lewis, 1927, n.d., Bodleian Library, Oxford, Ms. Facs. c. 54, 156 leaves [photocopies acquired by the Bodleian Library from Wheaton College, Illinois, U.S.A.]. © C.S. Lewis Pte. Ltd. UK. / Marion E. Wade Center, Wheaton College, USA.

Lindenberg, Christoph. 1988. *Rudolf Steiner: Eine Chronik 1861–1925*, Stuttgart: Verlag Freies Geistesleben.

———. 1993. *Rudolf Steiner, mit Selbstzeugnissen und Bilddokumenten*, Reinbek bei Hamburg: Rowohlt Taschenbuch Verlag.

Lissau, Rudi. 1987. *Rudolf Steiner: Life, Work, Inner Path and Social Initiatives*, Wallbridge: Hawthorn Press.

Mairet, Philip. 1934. ed. *The Douglas Manual: Being a Recension of Passages from the Works of Major C. H. Douglas Outlining Social Credit*, London: Stanley Nott.

Marx, Karl. 1962. *Ausgewählte Schriften*, ed. Boris Goldenberg, München: Kindler Verlag.

———. 1964. "Estranged Labour", in *Economic and Philosophic Manuscripts of 1844*, New York: International Publishers.

McConnell, W.K. 1932. *The Douglas Credit Scheme: A Simple Explanation and Criticism*, Sydney: Angus & Robertson.

McFarland, Thomas. 1981. *Romanticism and the Forms of Ruin: Wordsworth, Coleridge and the Modalities of Fragmentation*, Princeton: Princeton UP.

Medcalf, Stephen. 1991. "Language and Self-consciousness: The Making and Breaking of C.S. Lewis's Personae", *Word and Story in C.S. Lewis*, ed. Peter J. Shakel and Charles Huttar, Columbia and London: University of Missouri Press, 109–44.

Mood, John, J. 1965. "Poetic Language and Primal Thinking: A Study of Barfield, Wittgenstein and Heidegger", *Encounter* 26 (1965), 417–33.

Morris, Francis J. and Ronald C. Wendling. 1989. "Coleridge and 'the Great Divide' between C.S. Lewis and Owen Barfield", *Studies in the Literary Imagination* 22,2 (1989), 149–59.

Myers, Doris. 1996. "Breaking Free: The Closed Universe Theme in E. M. Forster, Owen Barfield, and C. S. Lewis", *Mythlore: A Journal of J.R.R. Tolkien, C.S. Lewis Charles Williams, and the Genres of Myth and Fantasy* 21, 3 (Summer 1996), 7–11.

Näher, Jürgen. 1994. *Oswald Spengler, mit Selbstzeugnissen und Bilddokumenten*, Hamburg: Rowohlt.

Nemerov, Howard. 1972. "Owen Barfield, *Poetic Diction: A Study in Meaning*", in *Reflections on Poetry and Poetics*, New Brunswick: Rutgers UP, 60–5.

Neumann, Erich. 1984. *Ursprungsgeschichte des Bewußtseins*, Frankfurt/Main: Fischer.

Nicolson, Harold. 1948 (1945). "Albrecht Bernstorff" (10 August 1945), in *Comments 1944–1948*. London: Constable & Co., 110.

Nietzsche, Friedrich. 1952. *Nietzsches Werke in zwei Bänden*, Salzburg: Verlag "Das Bergland Buch".

Nuttall, A. D. 1974. *A Common Sky: Philosophy and the Literary Imagination*, London: Chatto & Windus.

―――. 1985. "Is there a Legitimate Reductionism?", in *Reductionism in Academic Disciplines*, ed. Arthur Peacocke, Guildford: The Society for Research into Higher Education & NFER-NELSON, 1113–24.

―――. 1987. "Personality and Poetry", in *Persons and Personality: A Contemporary Inquiry*, ed. Arthur Peacocke and Grant Gilett, Oxford, Blackwell, 164–71.

―――. 1989. "Jack the Giant Killer", in *The Stoic in Love: Selected Essays on Literature and Ideas*, New York, London: Harvester Wheatsheaf, 153–70.

Ott, Ulrich. 1987. ed. *Literatur im Industriezeitalter: Eine Ausstellung des Deutschen Literaturarchivs im Schiller-Nationalmuseum Marbach am Neckar*, 2 vols., Marbach: Deutsche Schillergesellschaft.

Pappenheim, F. 1959. *The Alienation of Modern Man*, New York: Monthly Review Press.

Patrick, James. 1985. *The Magdalen Metaphysicals: Idealism and Orthodoxy at Oxford 1901-1945*, Mercer: Mercer UP.

Penty, Arthur J. 1925. "The Line of Least Resistance", *G. K.'s Weekly* 1 (25 May 1925), 200-1.

Peters, Jason Randall. 1994. "Owen Barfield and the Heritage of Coleridge", Diss. Michigan State University.

Potts, Donna L. 1994. *Howard Nemerov and Objective Idealism: The Influence of Owen Barfield*, Columbia, London: University of Missouri Press.

Price, Geoffrey. 1985. "Reductionism and the Differentiations of Consciousness", in *Reductionism in Academic Disciplines*, ed. Arthur Peacocke, Guildford: The Society for Research into Higher Education & NFER-NELSON, 125-41.

Prickett, Stephen. 1970. *Coleridge and Wordsworth: The Poetry of Growth*, Cambridge: CUP.

——— . 1981. *The Romantics, (The Context of English Literature)*, ed. Stephen Prickett, London: Methuen.

Quinton, A.M. 1972. "Social Thought in Britain", in *The Twentieth Century Mind: History, Ideas and Literature in Britain*, 2 vols., ed. C.B. Cox and A.E. Dyson, London, Oxford, New York: OUP, vol. i, 113-35.

Reilly, Robert J. 1971. *Romantic Religion*, Athens, Georgia: University of Georgia Press.

Rittelmeyer, Friedrich. 1982. *Rudolf Steiner Enters My Life*, Edinburgh: Floris Books.

Russell, Bertrand. 1989. "A Free Man's Worship", in *Mysticism and Logic: Including A Free Man's Worship*, London: Allen & Unwin.

Sallust. 1947. *Bellum Catilinae*, l.ii,22, in *Sallust*, with an English translation by J. C. Rolfe, Loeb Classical Library, London: Heinemann.

Samuels, Andrew et al. 1991. *Wörterbuch Jungscher Psychologie*, München: Deutscher Taschenbuch Verlag.

Schäfer, Christian. 1986. "Die Philosophie der Freiheit: Grundzüge einer modernen Weltanschauung", *Kindlers Literaturlexikon im dtv, Band 9*, München: Deutscher Taschenbuch Verlag, 7469–70.

Schenkel, Elmar. 1991. "Phantasie und Bewußtseinsgeschichte: Zur Philosophie von Owen Barfield", *Inklings: Jahrbuch für Literatur und Ästhetik* 9 (1991), 111–25.

―――. 1993. "Interview mit Owen Barfield" (September 1991, Forest Row, Sussex), *Inklings: Jahrbuch für Literatur und Ästhetik* 11 (1993), 23–38.

―――. 1998. "Sprache im Sinn: Owen Barfield und die Geschichte des Bewußtseins", *Novalis* 10 (1998), 22–5.

Schwanitz, Dietrich. 1996. *Englische Kulturgeschichte von 1500 bis 1914*, Franfurt/Main: Eichborn Verlag.

Scott, Peter Dale. 1994. "The social critic and his discontents", in *The Cambridge Companion to T. S. Eliot*, ed. David Moody, Cambridge: CUP, 60–76.

Segeberg, Harro. 1887a. "Technikbilder in der Literatur des zwanzigsten Jahrhunderts", in *Technik in der Literatur: Ein Forschungsüberblick und zwölf Aufsätze*, ed. Harro Segeberg, Frankfurt, Main: Suhrkamp, 411–35.

―――. 1887b. "Literaturwissenschaft und interdisziplinäre Technikforschung", in *Technik in der Literatur: Ein Forschungsüberblick und zwölf Aufsätze*, ed. Harro Segeberg, Frankfurt, Main: Suhrkamp, 9–32.

Shakel, Peter J. 1984. *Reason and Imagination in C. S. Lewis: A Study of Till We Have Faces*, Grand Rapids, Michigan: Eerdmans.

Shepherd, A. P. 1991. *A Scientist of the Invisible*, Edinburgh: Floris Books.

Simmel, O. 1957. "Anthroposophie", *Lexikon für Theologie und Kirche*, ed. Joseph Höf and Karl Rahner, Freiburg: Herder Verlag, vol. i, 630–2.

Smidt, Kristian. 1961. *Poetry and Belief in the Work of T. S. Eliot*, London: Routledge & Kegan Paul.

―――. 1994. "Eliot and the Victorians", in *T. S. Eliot and the Turn of the Century*, ed. Marianne Thormählen, Lund: Lund UP, 188–97.

Spengler, Oswald. 1959. *Der Untergang des Abendlandes: Umrisse einer Morphologie der Weltgeschichte*, München: Verlag C.H. Beck.

Stallworthy, Jon. 1974. *Wilfred Owen*, London: OUP and Chatto and Windus.

Stead, C. K. 1977. "Eliot, Arnold, and the English Poetic Tradition", in: David Newton-De Molina, *The Literary Criticism of T. S. Eliot: New Essays*, University of London: Athlone Press, 185–206.

Steiner, Rudolf. 1928. *Goethe's Conception of the World*, trans. H. Collison, London: Anthroposophical Publishing Company, New York: Anthroposophic Press.

———. 1951. *The Course of My Life: An Autobiography*, trans. Olin D. Wannamaker, New York: Anthroposophic Press.

———. 1959. *Das Matthäus-Evangelium*, Dornach: Rudolf Steiner Verlag.

———. 1961a. *Aufsätze über die Dreigliederung des sozialen Organismus und zur Zeitlage 1915–1921*, Dornach: Verlag der Rudolf Steiner-Nachlaßverwaltung.

———. 1961b. *Die Kernpunkte der sozialen Frage in den Lebensnotwendigkeiten der Gegenwart und Zukunft*, Dornach: Verlag der Rudolf Steiner-Nachlaßverwaltung.

———. 1962–3. *Occult Science: An Outline*, trans. George and Mary Adams, London: Rudolf Steiner Press.

———. 1964. *The Philosophy of Freedom (The Philosophy of Spiritual Activity): The Basis for a Modern World Conception, Some Results of Introspective Observation Following the Methods of Natural Science*, translated from the German, and with an introduction by Michael Wilson, London: Rudolf Steiner Press.

———. 1968. *Das Lukas-Evangelium*, Dornach: Rudolf Steiner Verlag.

———. 1973. *The Riddles of Philosophy*, trans. Fritz Koelln, Spring Valley, New York: The Antroposophic Press.

———. 1979. *Die geistig-seelischen Grundkräfte der Erziehungskunst: Spirituelle Werte in Erziehung und sozialem Leben, Zwölf Vorträge, gehalten in Oxford vom 16. bis 29. August 1922, mit einem Sondervortrag, Oxford 20. August 1922, zwei Einleitungen zu Eurythmieaufführungen und einem Schlußwort*, Dornach: Rudolf Steiner Verlag.

———. 1981. *Geisteswissenschaftliche Spachbetrachtungen: Eine Anregung für Erzieher, Sechs Vorträge, gehalten in Stuttgart vom 26. Dezember 1919 bis 3. Januar 1920 für die Lehrer der Freien Waldorfschule*, Dornach: Rudolf Steiner Verlag.

———. 1983. *Friedrich Nietzsche: Ein Kämpfer gegen seine Zeit*, Dornach: Rudolf Steiner Verlag.

---. 1985c. *Die Rätsel der Philosophie in ihrer Geschichte als Umriß dargestellt*, Dornach: Rudolf Steiner Verlag.

---. 1985a. *Goethes Weltanschauung*, Dornach: Rudolf Steiner Verlag.

---. 1985b. *Theosophie: Einführung in die übersinnliche Welterkenntnis und Menschenbestimmung*, Dornach: Rudolf Steiner Verlag.

---. 1987. *Die Geheimwissenschaft im Umriß*, Dornach: Rudolf Steiner Verlag.

---. 1988. *Grundlinien einer Erkenntnistheorie der Goetheschen Weltanschauung, mit besonderer Rücksicht auf Schiller, zugleich eine Zugabe zu "Goethes Naturwissenschaftlichen Schriften" in Kürschners "Deutsche National-Literatur"*, Dornach: Rudolf Steiner Verlag.

---. 1989. *Wahrheit und Wissenschaft: Vorspiel einer "Philosophie der Freiheit"*, Dornach: Rudolf Steiner Verlag.

---. 1990. *Mein Lebensgang: Eine nicht vollendete Biographie, mit einem Nachwort*, hg. Marie Steiner 1925, Dornach: Rudolf Steiner Verlag.

---. 1992. *Die Philosophie der Freiheit: Grundzüge einer modernen Weltanschauung, Seelische Beobachtungsresultate nach naturwissenschaftlicher Methode*, Dornach: Rudolf Steiner Verlag.

---. 1993. *Truth and Science: Prelude to a "Philosophy of Spiritual Activity"*, trans. William Lindeman, Spring Valley, New York: Mercury Press.

Stern, Fritz. 1986. *Kulturpessimismus als politische Gefahr: Eine Analyse nationaler Ideologie in Deutschland*, München: Deutscher Taschenbuch Verlag.

Sternhell, Zeev. 1979. "Fascist Ideology", in *Fascism: A Readers Guide; Analyses, Interpretations, Bibliography*, ed. Walter Laqueur, Harmondsworth: Penguin, 325–408.

Sternhell, Zeev, Mario Snajder, and Maia Asheri. 1994. *The Birth of Fascist Ideology: From Cultural Rebellion to Political Revolution*, Princeton: Princeton UP.

Stevenson, John. 1984. *British Society 1914–1945, The Penguin Social History of Britain*, Harmondsworth: Penguin.

Sugerman, Shirley. 1976. "A Conversation with Owen Barfield", in *Evolution of Consciousness: Studies in Polarity*, ed. Shirley Sugerman, Middletown, Connecticut: Wesleyan UP, 3–30.

Tennyson, George. 1969. "Owen Barfield and the Rebirth of Meaning", *Southern Review* 5 (January 1969), 42–54.

———. 1976. "A bibliography of the works of Owen Barfield", in *Evolution of Consciousness: Studies in Polarity*, ed. Shirley Sugerman, Middletown, Connecticut: Wesleyan UP, 227–39.

Thesig, William B. 1987. *The London Muse: Victorian Poetic Responses to the City*, Athens: University of Georgia Press.

Thorson, Stephen. 1983. "Knowing and Being in C.S. Lewis's 'Great War' with Owen Barfield", *Bulletin of the New York C.S. Lewis Society* 15, 1 (1983), 1–9.

———. 1990. "Lewis and Barfield on Imagination", *Mythlore* 17,64 (1990), 12–8, 32.

———. 1991. "Lewis and Barfield on Imagination, Part II", *Mythlore* 17, 65 (1991), 16–21.

Tillyard, E. M. W., and C. S. Lewis. 1965. *The Personal Heresy: A Controversy*, London, New York, Toronto: OUP.

Topitsch, E. 1969. "Fortschritt", *Wörterbuch der Soziologie*, ed. Wilhelm Bernsdorf, Stuttgart: Ferdinand Enke Verlag, 299–301.

Van der Meulen, Jelle. 1997. *Mittendrin: Anthroposophie hier und jetzt*, Stuttgart: Urachhaus.

Warnock, Mary. 1976. *Imagination*, London, Boston: Faber and Faber.

Wehr, Gerhard. 1990. *C. G. Jung und Rudolf Steiner: Konfrontation und Synopse*, Zürich: Diogenes Verlag.

———. 1993. *Rudolf Steiner: Leben, Erkenntnis, Kulturimpuls*, Zürich: Diogenes Verlag.

Wende, Peter. 1985. *Geschichte Englands*, Stuttgart, Berlin, Köln, Mainz: Kohlhammer.

Whicher, Olive. 1977. *George Adams, Interpreter of Rudolf Steiner: His Life and a Selection of his Essays*, East Grinstead: Henry Goalden.

Williams, Raymond. 1987. *Culture and Society: Coleridge to Orwell*, London: Hogarth Press.

Wilson, A. N. 1991. *C.S. Lewis: A Biography*, London: Flamingo.

Woodcock, George. 1980. "Romanticism: Studies and Speculations", *The Sewanee* 88 (April to June 1980), 298–307.

The Lewis Letters to Owen Barfield

(typed from the scripts printed on pages 56-58)

Plate 1

The clouds behind me are το`όν [Greek for "everything that exists"]. The post to which I am tied so that I can't turn round is finite personality. In front of me is a mirror, representing as much of the reality (and such disguise of it) as can be seen from my position. It includes, of course, "myself" as an empirical object. It is surrounded by a steel frame which represents the finitude and deadness of every mere object. I am studying the mirror with my eyes (equals explicit cognition) but reach back with my hands so as to get some touch (implicit "truth" or "faith") of the real.

Plate 2

Here we see a gentleman (not identified) engaged on seeing whether a departure from dry academical methods and a newer, freer theory of knowledge may not get some new images out of the mirror. The mirror seems to be playing up well so far. Meanwhile the clouds have ebbed to his ankles. Something like despairing hands stretches to reach from behind but he doesn't notice them. Overhead I detect a curious figuration of cloud that fancy may interpret as a gigantic face in laughter. The hammer and chisel are occult science, yoga, "meditation" (in technical sense) etc.

Plate 3

An awful example. Study of a gentleman reaching vainly for the inner reality he has scorned, while he shrinks in horror from the phantom he has created on the black wall from which he was succeeding in chipping off <u>all</u> the looking glass. (Only those who are not poets cld [could]) get as far as this, of course [.] On a second mirror invisible to him but visible to his neighbours, ambulance, asylum, cemetery appear successively.

www.ingramcontent.com/pod-product-compliance
Lightning Source LLC
Chambersburg PA
CBHW070313240426
43663CB00038BA/2117